MW01000114

HOW WE GIVE NOW

A Philanthropic Guide for the Rest of Us

LUCY BERNHOLZ

The MIT Press
Cambridge, Massachusetts
London, England

This book was set in Adobe Garamond Pro by New Best-set Typesetters Ltd. Printed and bound in the United States of America.

Library of Congress Cataloging-in-Publication Data

Names: Bernholz, Lucy, author.
Title: How we give now : a philanthropic guide for the rest of us / Lucy Bernholz.
Description: Cambridge : The MIT Press, 2021. | Includes bibliographical references and index.
Identifiers: LCCN 2020048458 | ISBN 9780262046176 (hardcover)
Subjects: LCSH: Endowments—United States. | Charities—United States. | Generosity. | Nonprofit organizations—United States—History.
Classification: LCC HV91 .B396 2021 | DDC 361.7—dc23
LC record available at https://lccn.loc.gov/2020048458

10   9   8   7   6   5   4   3   2   1

This book is dedicated to Paula and Harry, who give me everything.

Contents

INTRODUCTION

"No, thank you," I told the oddly solicitous cashier. I didn't want to help cure cancer. "Not today."

I took my change and hurried to my doctor's appointment on Market Street. The spasms in my neck flared with every step, as had been happening for a week. I handed the receptionist my insurance card, and she handed me a blue-and-yellow-encased iPad that looked like it had been designed for deep-sea divers. Unlike a clipboard stacked with paper forms, the iPad offered no hint of how many pages of questions would follow. I tapped in my name, address, and social security number. Relief and a bit of wonder hit me when the device asked if I wanted to autofill the rest. I clicked Yes, thinking of all the previous appointments when I'd spent forever filling out the same forms. I stretched my aching neck and scrolled through decades of my medical history. Finally, the last question: Did I understand that the clinic was part of a teaching hospital and that tissue samples or blood tests taken during my visit might be used for research? As always, I paused at this question. Would they cancel my appointment if I wasn't OK with this? My neck spasmed again. I clicked Yes.

Thirty minutes later, I'd seen a doctor, received a referral for physical therapy, and was out the door. Even with digital help, I'd spent more time scrolling through my own health information than getting treated.

I stared straight ahead as I walked to the bus stop. The pain in my neck made it hard to avoid eye contact with the red-vested, binder-bearing young man standing directly in my path. "Spare a minute to save the planet?" "Sorry, not today." I kept walking. "Oh, c'mon," he called, his cheery voice catching the attention of his similarly vested buddy. "You can make time for the polar bears, can't you?"

"No, I wish I could help, but I can't. I guess you hear 'no' a lot?" I asked. He ignored this. "How about your email address? Can we stay in touch to keep you up to date on the bears?"

I scribbled an email address and excused myself. "That's my bus," I said, walking away. I found a seat, dropped my bag, and pulled out my phone. The email I'd given him was the one I use just for subscriptions, donations, and purchase receipts. I half-expected to find a note from the polar bear organization already waiting for me.

I scrolled through and deleted dozens of emails, including three requests for money. One was from the development department of my undergraduate college. One was from someone who "knows me" on LinkedIn and was raising money to help a family who'd lost their house in a wildfire. The third was from a nonprofit I'd never heard of. It was in the same account I had just scribbled on the red-vested man's clipboard, the one I only use for transactions, meaning a nonprofit I'd given to in the past had sold my email. Annoyed, I put away my phone and angled my way off the bus. I grabbed a handful of solicitation envelopes and bills out of my mailbox and went inside. In the time since I'd left home, I'd been asked for money at the cash register, in my email, and by snail mail. I'd been asked for my time, money, and data on the sidewalk. The doctor's office hadn't really "asked" for my data; it felt more like I'd been told it was being taken. I still wondered what would have happened had I said no. I put away my coat, collapsed on the couch, and felt like Scrooge.

This is a book about how we use our time, money, and digitized data to make change happen. The focus of this book is on the *how* of doing this. The how is important for a number of reasons. For more than a century, US law and the media have concentrated their attention on financial donations to charitable nonprofits as the crux of giving. Books, magazines, movies, and radio shows celebrate and criticize wealthy philanthropists, encourage people to become "social entrepreneurs," and profile well-intentioned software coders using "civic technology" to improve government services. These are interesting stories, but they ignore the sort of everyday situation chronicled at the start of this introduction. They also ignore century-old traditions of mutual aid, cooperation, and reciprocity, especially those that thrive in African American, Indigenous, and diasporic communities. They center nonprofits and charitable donations, even though people give much more than money. And, for the most part, the media overhype and the laws ignore our dependence on digital technologies like mobile phones and the internet.

I'm aiming for something different with this book. I want to bring people from many races, abilities, ages, and traditions into the center of the conversation to show how we give now: people making daily decisions about how to help others; using all of their resources to lift up their communities; using time, money, and data to advance causes; and people facing a dizzying array of giving choices with no guidance, only sales pitches. It's these people who power change in the world. But it's also these people whose choices about giving are ignored and devalued in current legal frameworks and incentive structures. Some of the choices being made by the majority of givers reflect their commitment to help and support others without questioning the broader political context. Others anchor their choices in commitments to collective well-being, or a vision of solidarity and abundance, or approaches that have sustained their communities and cultures for millennia. These visions and practices are legitimate in their own right, even as they are ignored or dismissed by laws, professional practices, and incentives of formal, financialized philanthropy. Recrafting the legal definitions and institutions to reflect and embrace this range of approaches would benefit all who participate. It might even mark a true effort to expand, dare I say democratize, philanthropy.

As in so many other areas of life in the United States, the very wealthy, their advisors, and the industries that serve them have stacked the rules in their favor. This has led to inequitable schools, inadequate public transit, inaccessible health care, unbearable student loan debt, and a lack of the most basic resources—housing, water, and food—across the country. The rules about giving are currently written in ways that benefit only the wealthy, even as the vast majority of giving comes from everyday people. Our national laws and stories about philanthropy focus on individuals in ways that are out of sync with the ways we really act, as well as the ways that are most likely to lead to real change. The breadth and diversity of strategies we use to "make the world a better place" include much more than money, and they depend on connection and reciprocity, whereas the policies, privileges, and products that regulate and shape giving are focused on individual intent, rooted in the financial industry, and ignorant of digital systems. My hope for this book is to expand our understanding of how we give so that we can collectively make more powerful choices, change the laws, and craft a more just and equitable future.

WHY DOES IT MATTER?

There are two levels at which the changes in philanthropy matter. The first is for individual people. We have more choices, get asked more often, and see needs everywhere, but we have so little visibility into what happens behind the scenes when we buy certain products, respond to social media solicitations, or try to choose how to spend our time. It's hard to make choices about money and time, but it's even harder to understand how we might donate digital data, if doing so is worth it, and how to differentiate between donating data to a cause and just having it taken from you.

The second level at which these changes matter is at the point where they intersect with public policy. What is the role of giving and voluntary action, what counts in these categories, and what should be done by governments? This is an enormous question. It sits at the root of political theory, political parties, and government power in democracies. It may seem a stretch that your giving has political implications, but it does. Philanthropy can be a source of power. If it is concentrated among a few people making big financial contributions, then it becomes one more way for the extremely wealthy to wield outsized influence on schools, health care, art and culture, scientific research, the environment, and the justice system. In a time of extreme inequality, like now, big giving can become a substitute for government funding. This became very visible in the United States in the area of pandemic preparedness, but it can also be seen over time in issues like school reform. Such philanthropic power is inherently undemocratic as it puts a handful of donors in positions to sway systems meant to serve—and be governed by—all of the people.

The power of giving by the rest of us, however, is in our numbers. While your financial donations, time, or data may not amount to much on their own, they can be very influential when combined with others. Just as our votes are intended to aggregate into statements of what the majority wants, when we come together to make gifts of money, time, or data, we also send strong signals about the world we want. There is power in the collection of our individual choices.

Finally, the power of our giving matters in terms of that enormous political question: What is the role of government? As a society, we build systems that are intended to serve, protect, and enable all of us to thrive, individually and collectively. We often refer to these systems as *infrastructure*. There's physical infrastructure, like roads, bridges, electrical grids, and internet transmission systems, and civic or social infrastructure, like schools, hospitals, libraries, and parks.[1] If these systems are to work for anyone, everyone needs be able to use them.

In the United States, more and more of these services and systems have been underfunded publicly (by taxes), and so philanthropy has stepped in. These are two sides of the American historical coin: we underinvest in our shared public systems while we celebrate individual generosity. This places a burden on voluntary acts and giving that is both too big and inappropriate to their purpose in democracies. Philanthropy and nonprofits are supposed to provide either an alternative to or a bolster for public programs and investments. But we've been placing the weight of collective care on this alternative space for too long. Philanthropy can't, and shouldn't, carry the burden of public responsibilities. Philanthropy and our democracy will both fail if the burden of public services is placed on voluntary actions. Conversely, philanthropic support for complements, alternatives, and long-term visions can only succeed when public systems are strong enough to meet the needs of the moment.

WHY FOCUS ON HOW?

A good place to start is to explain what I mean by *how*. There are three important parts of how. The first part is how we divide our giving among politics, charity, shopping, saving, and investing. These categories are distinct in the eyes of the law and the tax code. They are monitored by different regulatory bodies. But these categories are not as distinct to everyday givers as they are to the legal system. The historical bounds around these domains make it difficult to see actions that cut across them. Throughout this book, you'll meet people who give in all kinds of ways, mixing and matching across the categories of politics, charity, consumption, and culture. This is especially true among people and communities pushed to the margins by White systems, whether those be government programs or private businesses. Barred from access to banks, churches, jobs, stores, and housing Black people, immigrants, and other communities of color have created alternative economies, within which their traditions of giving can thrive. Here we see people living their values and using every opportunity they have to advance their concerns and try to change the world around them. They do everything they can, from patronizing certain businesses and avoiding others to canvassing for candidates, donating money, and making certain choices with their retirement funds. People may disagree on the *what* or *to whom*, but we pick from the same menu of options for *how*. The menu of how to give has also grown much longer than the few privileged options—mostly tax-deductible gifts to tax-exempt nonprofits—that our legal and tax systems have counted as giving.

The second part of how has to do with collectivity. Giving is inherently a social act—we give when we're asked, we give to see ourselves as part of something, we give to be part of something bigger than ourselves, we give because we depend on the group, and we give to belong. I hope I do a good enough job introducing other people's stories that you can feel these connections. I also hope that seeing the vibrancy and power of practices that aren't currently privileged or counted in US philanthropy will inspire those doing research, writing public policy, managing nonprofit organizations, and working toward justice to imagine more inclusive paths forward. Giving is one way we find ourselves and act in relation to others.

Each of the book's upcoming stories highlights relationships between the person(s) profiled and their communities. Most of our formally sanctioned and legally privileged forms of giving draw distinctions between givers and recipients. In chapter 2, I outline the commodification of giving and the growth of giving products, most of which assume this distinction and focus on making transactions more efficient. I call this the *givingscape*. In the last thirty years, there's been an explosion in the products and tools we use to give, from the rise of donor-advised funds to crowdfunding platforms; from products affiliated with certain causes to the creation of new types of organizations for bundling political donations. Collectively, these products constitute the givingscape. Some of the products are sold by financial companies, like banks and mutual fund managers. Others, such as crowdfunding platforms, enable people to give money directly to other people, replacing old intermediaries such as churches with new intermediaries. Some products are hybrids of other trends, such as a commercial firm's donor-advised funds that can be invested in an impact investing pool. Nonprofit, investment, and philanthropy professionals tend to be familiar with these products and the industries behind them. For others, the very notion of industries and sales and products as part of giving will be new, surprising, and perhaps even a bit distasteful. Either way, it's important to understand that there are businesses selling giving products and that not all products are the same.

By focusing on products, I mean to highlight the commodification of giving and to refute claims that what is going on is somehow democratizing. The former is about selling things to more people; the latter is about sharing power. In the last decades, we've heard lots of talk about democratizing giving. But what's really going on is a commodification process—making products out of relationships. The marketing of products like donor-advised funds, crowdfunding platforms, and retail items that donate money (red iPhones, branded T-shirts, search engines and credit cards that make donations) has atomized and financialized acts of caring, compassion, protest, and resistance. These products might still be useful, and they're definitely being marketed at more and more people—but they are means, not ends, and commodities, not democracy.

Transactional relationships between giver and recipient abound, but the people that I present in the book are all seeking something more than a transaction. The racial, religious, ethnic, and linguistic diversity of the United States is rich with giving traditions built around reciprocity, mutual aid, interdependence, and obligation. Seeing these values in action is important as they are what the *commodification of giving* threatens. The legal systems for giving in the United States privilege products over community, value hierarchies over more cooperative or consensus-based models, and incentivize individual intentions over collective action. As in so many other domains, top-down, White practices are treated as "normal," and all others are marginalized and seen as alternative. These are reasons enough for us to reimagine the legal and institutional frameworks for how we give now.

The stories to come provide examples of people adapting these products to their own more inclusive purposes. Giving circles (a type of community), for example, may use donor-advised funds (a product) to manage their money. In these cases, the donor-advised fund is just a simple tool. If there is anything democratic in the story, it is the collective decision-making process of the people in the circle. This is important because we are in a period when many of our most persistent traditions of collective giving, such as mutual aid networks and cooperatives, are adapting these products and morphing them in positive ways. These adaptations show the power of collective decision-making, positive applications of the existing product mix, and they are early signals of the hybridization that is at the heart of innovation. These hybridizing acts are producing new organizational forms, some of which may last and come to define the givingscape of the future.

The third part of how comes from our growing dependence on digital technologies. Part of understanding the givingscape is realizing that each of us also has a new resource to consider when we think about our giving. In addition to time and money, we now have digitized data to think about. We've had the first two—time and money—for millennia and have built most of our behaviors and institutions around them. The third one—digitized data—is new, and it's a very different thing than time or money.

People are beginning to deliberately collect and use digitized data—from photographs to DNA—to create change in the world. How they do this is new. How we think about this and what rules and institutions we create to facilitate it (or prevent it) will soon matter to everyone with a cell phone or an email address. It's also possible that thinking hard about whether or not we should be able to donate our data, to use it as a philanthropic resource, will encourage more people to care about the ways companies and governments currently take our data and use it.

How will you think about using your newfound wealth—the digital data you generate with every tap on your cell phone, swipe of your loyalty card, or trip to the doctor? You probably know that companies profit from the data we generate by using their products. It's time to also consider how this information, in aggregate, might be used to address the causes to which you donate time and money and whether and how you get to make that choice. We also need to consider the costs to our communities of using data in this way, and the costs of ceding control of the decisions. The opportunity to influence how those rules are written, to ensure that they are equitable, just, and protect your rights to decide what you do or don't give, is before us now. Each of us as a giver—and as a member of a family and a community—has a stake in the outcome of those rules and decisions. They also provide an opportunity to think about full sets of laws and incentives for giving, and perhaps engage in creating laws that would benefit more of us.

Some of these ideas might be uncomfortable or unpopular. It's strange to think of giving as part of a marketplace of products and to focus on how our legal system discriminates. But this is why it's worth taking a closer look at how we give, the choices all around us, and the rules that are at work. My hope is that by doing so you will make the most of what you give.

The focus on how also allows us to skip over the questions of who, to what, and how much. Skipping over those questions—which are the ones we're usually asked, if we ever talk about our giving—allows us to skip over some of the more polarizing and individualizing elements of giving. Who you give to and how much are very personal questions. The people we'll meet in the next chapters mix and match from a wide range of activities to accomplish their goals, and they use different giving products to do so. These products are available across a wide spectrum of income or wealth, but not to everyone (which is one reason the marketing language of *democratization* is misleading). They don't discriminate by cause, faith, or ideology. They are used by people of every race, ethnicity, gender identity, ability, citizenship status, and age. That is not to say they are marketed equitably or to all, nor that their benefits don't accrue unfairly to the wealthy. They are products; their widespread availability is a result of the commodification of giving. Focusing on the how allows for better and deeper questions about how the system works and who benefits.

1 PHILANTHROPY BY THE REST OF US

I've worked in and around philanthropy for thirty years, but I got involved with foundation philanthropy by accident. I was in graduate school and was (and still am) interested in a single question: What's public, what's private, and who decides? It's a good question for political scientists, but I'm a historian. So I looked at the question through the lens of philanthropic money—mostly grants from companies and foundations—to public schools in the 1960s and 1970s. That led to working in foundations, consulting for them, and writing and researching about them. I learned there were a lot of books written for philanthropists and foundations. A lot of books written about big money, big giving, and big philanthropy for the people doing it.

I also learned that most of what is counted as philanthropic in the United States—that is, charitable gifts to tax-exempt nonprofits—comes from small gifts that are made by not-rich people. For decades, most of this philanthropy—70 percent or more—has come from everyday people in small increments. All of our four-dollar or twenty-five-dollar contributions add up to the majority of the $420-plus billion in charitable donations to tax-exempt nonprofits every year. These are big numbers, yet they reveal a massive undercount of what we do. It doesn't include the significant giving that occurs outside of donations to nonprofits, such as mutual aid and collective care, political activism, and funds or care given directly from one person to another. I learned there were few books written that told stories of people doing the things I did or that I saw other people doing.

My educational and professional experiences, along with my demographic identities as middle-aged, White, gay, Jewish, mother, influence what I see and how I understand the world around me. They're certainly part of how I understand nonprofits, philanthropy, legal systems, and industry perspectives. I set out to learn how we give now precisely because my experiences in professional philanthropy and review of the research weren't answering my questions. That mismatch is why I went looking for people and ways of giving other than those that are privileged in the world of formal, institutional philanthropy. What I found is why I argue that the marketing rhetoric of democratization is (at best) misleading. I hope that my contribution here is to help everyday White givers—and the White majority that dominates professional philanthropy—to see that our current laws and practices are narrow and exclusionary, built on racist structures and stolen wealth, and in need of change.

The people you'll meet in the coming chapters come from across the United States, although there is a heavy emphasis on California. They range in age; are Black, White, Indigenous, Latinx, Asian American, and of mixed race; come from many ethnic and religious backgrounds; and have different physical abilities. Some are indigenous to North America, some are descended from immigrants, some are descended from enslaved people, and some are immigrants themselves. They speak many languages. I try not to speak for them, but to listen and learn. Their stories are illustrative of the richness and diversity that is the *us* in the book's subtitle. Each of their stories and practices is worthy of intense focus and research, but this book doesn't do that. As a White interviewer, I tried to be honest about my position as an outsider and checked my questions, assumptions, and purpose throughout my interviews. I lack the deep insider knowledge and expertise to do justice to certain giving practices. I take responsibility for any mistakes I make in portraying them. I relied on those who told me their stories, research sources they pointed me to, and scholarly literature. Black people, Indigenous people, and people of color are asked to spend too much time educating White people about their communities and practices.

In addition to the people interviewed and highlighted, I draw insights from conversations with several hundred people who are neither named nor identified by the usual demographic categories. These people (338 in all) participated in more than thirty *mapping conversations* held in 2019. These mapping conversations are described in detail in appendix A. These conversations were designed and facilitated to encourage people to reflect on how they give. We met and heard from church groups, beer drinkers, coffee klatches, library-based book groups, and groups of people who didn't know each other.[1] Conversations were held in community centers, libraries, conference rooms, coffee houses, bars, and basements and conducted in Spanish and English.

One group not included is that of individuals deemed *wealthy* or *high net worth* by US standards, as there already exists a large body of literature about their giving behaviors. The people in this book range in income from low income to working class, with some who earn high professional incomes. Few—if any—identify themselves as philanthropists, and many of them have been beneficiaries of philanthropy or mutual aid support. These are the people who make up the majority of people in the United States, yet very little is written about how they are giving. This book doesn't provide detailed looks at age-delineated, race-delineated, religious, or gendered giving practices, although I hope it will draw attention to—and inform—some of that research. In looking for the *how*, I don't dig into the *to whom*. Whether certain groups of people gravitate to or away from certain ways of giving is research for another time. The focus on how is about the choices we have or don't have, the rules that guide those choices, and the use of digital data as a giving choice. I hope the book helps readers see the options they have so they might make more informed choices to achieve their goals. It may also help community organizations, nonprofits, political groups, and corporate marketers see themselves from the outside. Wealthy philanthropists and foundations may find that this book challenges many of their assumptions about how others give.

HOW ARE WE GIVING?

The thirty-three mapping conversations we held in 2019 produced 2,277 individual responses to the question, How do you give? Every respondent mentioned donating money and giving time. These two choices each accounted for about 16 percent of the total responses, with no distinctions being made about the recipient of the monetary or time donation (meaning these categories include formal, informal, religious, political, and charitable donations and volunteering).[2] We clustered the full set of responses into a total of twenty-two categories.[3] The breakdown of responses per category is shown in figure 1.1. This breadth of options and the ways people mix and match between them reveals a much more dynamic and inclusive picture of giving than the typically separate counts of charitable donations, political contributions, investment choices, or consumer behavior.

These mapping conversations build on earlier research done by the Urban Institute, a nonprofit organization in Washington, DC, that conducts a variety of research on charitable giving and hosts the National Center for Charitable Statistics. In 2018, the Urban Institute released an infographic that it called "On Track to Greater Giving." It is reproduced in figure 1.2.[4]

There are a few different types of data in the Urban Institute graphic. In general, the circles to the right of center focus on the kind of *how*

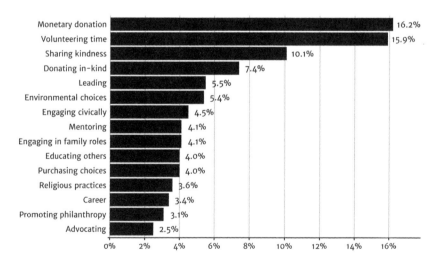

Figure 1.1

Frequency of individual responses in *How We Give Now* mapping conversations. *Source:* Data from *How We Give Now* mapping conversations. Graph by Noah Friedlander.

Figure 1.2

Infographic. *Source:* Data from The Urban Institute, "On Track to Greater Giving."

answers that our mapping conversations surfaced—from charitable donations to political gifts, consumer and investor choices, workplace giving,
and remittances (which were captured in the mapping conversations under
family obligations). Both the Urban Institute graphic and the mapping conversations reveal the range of ways people are using their time and money
to represent their values, to better their communities, or to create change.
On the website for the Urban Institute project, you can find the extensive
list of data sources that informed their research. The range of sources is why
the graphic includes both hard numbers and percentages: we don't have
common, consolidated tracking for these different behaviors that would
give us a complete, comparable picture of what we do over time. Creating
such measures and tracking these data at the national level would be a positive step for both research and public policy.

WHAT COUNTS AS GIVING

Philanthropy, as it is usually talked about in the United States, focuses on
financial donations to certain kinds of organizations. But the word itself
means *love of humankind*. The distinctions that have been drawn about
giving money or time to certain kinds of organizations are choices we've
encoded into law over time, not distinctions born of some natural difference. By definition, these laws privilege some actions over others. Most of
the laws and the institutions they created (like foundations or nonprofits)
in the United States reflect the White, Eurocentric traditions and worldviews of those who wrote them. This is visible in the ways today's charitable laws reveal shadows of the English Poor Relief Act of 1601 and in
the nonprofit itself, a corporate form derived from enterprises built for
colonization. We've written laws about, developed oversight bodies for, and
conducted research on some activities more than others.

Nationally, we collect data on different giving activities in lots of different places. What we count is a reflection of what we value. Thus we have
a lot of data on some kinds of giving activities (namely, tax-deductible
gifts to tax-exempt nonprofits), less data on other kinds of giving, and big
debates about whether some activities should count at all. That we have

better data on those activities is not a reflection of the worthiness of the "uncounted" activities but merely a signal of what we've been counting over the years. The mapping conversations and interviews reveal that we do a lot of things that aren't included in official counts of philanthropy. The next few paragraphs introduce the kinds of data we do have, and who collects it, on the different activities people actually perform.

TAX-DEDUCTIBLE DONATIONS

We've been counting and studying the data on charitable donations to tax-exempt nonprofits since the late 1940s. Organizations such as Candid, formed from a merger of the Foundation Center and GuideStar, along with nonprofit research organizations such as the Urban Institute and the Giving Institute, and university programs such as the Lilly Family School of Philanthropy at Indiana University collect and analyze lots of this information. Annual tallies of "philanthropy" in the United States are usually citing statistics on these kinds of donations. The top-line figure for charitable giving in the United States in 2020 topped $449 billion according to Giving USA, an annual report that has been tracking tax-deductible donations to tax-exempt nonprofits since 1956.[5]

VOLUNTEERING TIME

The data we collect on volunteering is less robust than that on charitable donations. Independent Sector, a national association of nonprofits, annually calculates how much time is donated by volunteers to charities, as does the Corporation for National and Community Service (CNCS). Scholars have noticed the same trend in volunteering since 2000 that we saw in charitable giving: fewer people are participating.[6] This only captures volunteering for nonprofit organizations, however. It leaves out time a person might dedicate to a neighborhood council, helping with outreach about candidates or ballot issues, or driving elderly neighbors to appointments. In 2018, CNCS reported that about 30 percent of Americans volunteered for nonprofit organizations, an estimate almost four percentage points higher than a team of scholars from the University of Maryland reported.[7] The University of Maryland study also quantified some of the giving categories from our mapping conversations, noting that 43 percent of respondents reported helping out family members and 51 percent reported helping their neighbors.[8] These data predate the pandemic, which may well have reset how many of us spent time helping others near and far.

POLITICAL GIVING

Giving to political campaigns, political parties, PACs, and super PACs is reported to the Federal Election Commission. Several nonprofits, including the Sunlight Foundation, MapLight, Capital Research Center, and Center for Responsive Politics, collate this data and make it available via their websites. These groups do a remarkable job, but the laws that regulate reporting of these contributions, and the machinations of people and organizations that use the money, make for a constant game of cat and mouse. The money can be counted, but the most accurate tallies are only possible after elections. In 2016, more than $6.8 billion was spent on all federal elections; in 2020 that number reached almost $14 billion.[9]

INVESTING

In the last decade, attention has shifted from taking certain types of investments out of an investment portfolio to creating investment opportunities that actively improve social or environmental conditions. The term *impact investing* was coined in the mid-aughts. The Global Impact Investing Network, which tracks the industry, sized the global market at $714 billion focused on positive social and environmental impact.[10]

SHOPPING AND ETHICAL CONSUMPTION

Data on ethical consumption—which includes shopping for products that give back or that are more environmentally or socially friendly—is scattered, inconsistent, and often proprietary. Companies that have a vested interest in products that raise money for charity—often called *cause marketing*—report that this is a big and growing behavior. Many marketing firms study and report information on consumer interest in branded partnerships between companies and causes. These firms use this research to build their own businesses and rarely release auditable figures about the size of this phenomenon. It's not that anyone is cheating; it's just that there aren't (yet) standard, reliable, independent auditors or even reporters of these kinds of behaviors.

CHANGES IN CHARITABLE GIVING

Many of the activities people told us about in our mapping conversations and some of the activities discussed in this book are not captured in the conventional definition of *philanthropy* or *giving*. That's a key point of this book: what we're counting is out of sync with what we're doing. In the United States, we have a tax system that provides benefits for donating money and time to charitable nonprofits that don't apply to other kinds of financial activities. People who choose to do so can deduct the money they donate to charitable nonprofits from the income they report to the IRS, lowering the amount on which they must pay taxes. The rules for doing this changed dramatically in 2017 with the passage of the Tax Cuts and Jobs Act. The law raised the income levels at which it makes sense to claim tax deductions for charitable giving, making the benefit beneficial to wealthier people only. Economists quickly started making predictions about the effect of this legal change on charitable giving. The predictions ranged from drops of $16 to $50 billion per year, on a baseline of about $400 billion.[11] By mid-2019, the percentage of taxpayers taking the charitable deduction had declined from 25 percent to 8.5 percent. The vast majority of those who benefit from these laws are wealthy and White.[12] As it happened, total giving in 2019 and 2020 continued to rise, contrary to predictions about tax effects and through the great uncertainty of the first year of the COVID-19 pandemic.

That all the predictions were for decreases reveals the extent to which economists link giving behavior to tax incentives. But only one kind of giving behavior—financial donations to charitable nonprofits—intersects with these laws. It's logical to assume that pushing on the lever of tax reform will change the one kind of giving that is linked to tax rates. It is myopic to equate this one kind of behavior with all of giving, given the many other activities people consider part of their giving. It's important to study the rate at which we give money to nonprofits, but it's a mistake to think that's the whole story of how we give now.

As it turns out, the story of charitable giving and tax cuts is more complicated than an across the board decrease. In 2019, the Lilly Family School of Philanthropy dug into the trend data from Giving USA to better understand changing patterns of behavior. In its report, *Changes to the Giving Landscape*, it finds that the wealthy make up more and more of that total. Figure 1.3 shows these findings since 2000.[13]

The data in figure 1.3 stop in 2016 (tax data takes a long time to collect). The graph reflects a growing gap between the overall amount of charitable giving (dotted line), which includes individuals, foundations, bequests, and corporations, and the amount that comes from us as individuals (solid line). The researchers conclude that a growing percentage of

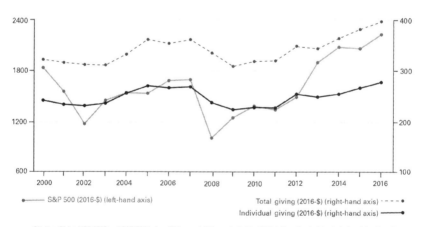

Citation: Giving USA 2019 and S&P 500 Index. All figures inflation adjusted to 2016 dollars. Total giving includes giving from four sources: (1) individuals, (2) foundations, (3) bequests, and (4) corporations.

Figure 1.3

Aggregate total and individual giving compared with the S&P 500 Index (amounts in billions). *Source:* Data from *Changes to the Giving Landscape*.

charitable giving is coming from the other three categories—corporations, foundations, and bequests. Wealthier individuals use foundations and bequests, therefore revealing a growing influence of the wealthy on charitable giving.

One question that these data cannot answer is, What are the rest of us doing, if we're not giving (or giving less) to charity? This is where the breadth of activities people count as giving comes into play. The people who participated in our mapping conversations count a lot of activities as giving, but the official counts ignore these actions.

Looking through the list of ways people give (figure 1.1), many are shaped not by taxes but by family traditions, faith, and political or social views of how we should act (visiting the sick, caring for young children, or protesting against almost anything). We also see choices motivated by ease of the action or a desire to show a certain affinity or memorialize a certain event (rounding up your lunch bill, carrying a museum-branded tote bag, or buying bumper stickers to support candidates). People give for many reasons. Certain incentives, such as tax rules, may influence some of our behaviors, but not others. By better understanding how we give, we can look at the whole of our giving—how our different choices influence each other. This will help each of us think about our overall contributions. Its critical for fundraisers and philanthropists to understand the range of actions we're taking. It also can inform policy makers as they change old rules and consider new ones.

IS ALL GIVING EQUAL?

We've already seen that the tax system doesn't treat all ways of giving the same. For people above a certain income level, there is a clear incentive to make financial donations to charitable nonprofits as a way to reduce their tax bills. But what about all the other giving products? Is buying a charity-branded T-shirt as good as donating your time? Is donating to a political cause as powerful as investing in companies whose methods and products align with your values? You can't answer these questions without first choosing how you're going to measure quality or outcomes or effectiveness. That debate rages within nonprofits and among big foundations.

But there is no universal answer to such a question; we want different things from our individual giving and community traditions and political frames position giving differently. Some of us care about seeing an immediate difference in another person's life, while others have committed themselves to causes they know won't change in their own lifetime. For many communities, cultures of care, mutual support, or solidarity-focused economic practices position giving differently than its place in White traditions. In a givingscape filled with options, our individual circumstances matter. My focus in answering the question doesn't get into the metrics of any specific act or donation; I can't possibly address all the permutations you might face. Remember that I said there are two levels to thinking about the changes in giving options—individual and societal. I'm interested in how the different ways of giving help us connect to each other, to the causes we care about, and to the bigger systems and avenues for change, our political structures. In looking at each type of giving, I'll be focused on how they enable long-term and collective involvement.

We don't have equal resources or equal access to different products. The people in the coming chapters make many different choices and mix different ways of giving together. Each of the following chapters looks at the trade-offs we make in choosing some giving products over others. Success is not a result of the individual product that is chosen; it depends more on how and with whom these choices are applied. All giving is not equal.

MORE DOESN'T MEAN BETTER

Nor is more giving always better. White culture in the United States venerates giving and celebrates philanthropists. But many of the current rules that guide philanthropy privilege the interests of a few over the needs of the many. This is most often discussed in the realm of funding political issues or politicians—but it's also true in the realm of charities that become beholden to a few donors.

The praise for individual actions over collective commitment is a constant theme in US history. It's at the core of every decision we make about what to fund collectively, through taxes and public investment. Over time, public policy decisions consistently cut budgets for public education, health care, social services, housing, public transportation, or digital infrastructure. The shift is usually toward private commercial or nonprofit options. This shifts power from the collective public to private actors—often corporations and, increasingly, philanthropists. The effects of this—nominally public systems that are ever more dependent on the largesse of wealthy individuals—are found across the United States. Low-income communities, as well as Black communities, Indigenous communities, and communities of color are all too familiar with the effects of this steady public disinvestment. Even the most basic underpinnings of modern society, such as clean and affordable water or electricity, are not available across the United States. Relying on philanthropy to provide basic public services—from school supplies to pandemic preparedness—is a recipe for disaster.

For people with smaller wallets, those who aren't rich enough to singlehandedly influence an organization or a cause, the question of whether more giving is always good is partly a question of what's public and what's private. Should public schools rely on private donors, or should we tax ourselves appropriately to pay for equitable schooling? What about health care? Americans have spent billions of dollars on crowdfunding platforms to help families, friends, and strangers with medical bills, while at the same time we've handcuffed national politics to a seemingly endless debate over providing access to health insurance. Economists and psychologists have long known that some decisions "crowd out" others. These are questions of public policy versus private action. These are political questions. Underinvesting in public systems or turning them over to private companies or philanthropists is a political decision.

The current US tax system enables the development of massive private fortunes at the expense of revenue that would support public services. We then turn around and ask individual or corporate donors to pay for art classes in our schools, water for our city residents, and Wi-Fi hotspots for students. There are ways to encourage giving without sacrificing core public support and oversight—but those are not the choices our elected representatives have been making. More giving at the expense of equitably resourced and publicly governed public systems is neither democratic nor sustainable. Good giving requires us to see the relationships between our public and private choices; it requires us to remove the false cover of political neutrality.

Traditions that center mutual aid, community self-sufficiency, interdependence, and cooperation make the political assumptions of US giving even more visible. As Caroline Shenaz Hossein notes, mutual aid among Black and Caribbean populations is a long-standing tradition, built in part from Black women's "lived experience of how to organize in inclusive ways to help an array of people."[14] These practices are political acts, providing safety, trust, and necessary financial resources to communities continually oppressed by White supremacy. They are deliberate alternatives to racist and exclusionary financial and philanthropic systems. They emphasize a commitment to sharing resources and building collective power. They operate within a different set of economic and political frames than those that incentive large private endowments and competition between nonprofits. One sign of the political values at work is the frequency with which mutual aid networks and community bail funds pay "extra" contributions forward to other networks or funds. Although it's not unheard of for a nonprofit or a community foundation to forward donations on to other organizations (especially in disasters), it's not common. The difference is whether there is a focus on serving community, expanding access to resources, and ensuring everyone has enough (mutual aid, for example), or whether the norms and laws emphasize institution-building and growth (organizational capacity and endowment-building efforts, for example). Since 2015 a growing network called Community-Centric Fundraising has been organizing, advocating for, and teaching an approach to giving that centers principles of shared abundance and economic and racial justice. This movement is exciting, but its current marginality only further reveals its distance from the norm.

If our legal systems and national conversations about giving are to be more inclusive and just, we need to open them up to the values and practices that power mutual aid networks and other traditions. However, it is not sufficient for participants in existing White systems just to engage with these practices without examining and changing their assumptions and expectations. Megan Ming Francis and Erika Kohl-Arenas have documented the long history of how this kind of White "discovery" often leads to co-optation and capture.[15] The first six months of the COVID-19 pandemic in 2020 saw a rush of people joining and creating mutual aid networks and calls for nonprofits and foundations to support them. Only if the newcomers adapt their ways to respect the political intentions of the Black, Indigenous, or diasporic traditions will we be able to take the next step and institute a more inclusive set of norms and laws. However, hope comes from what Shenaz Hossein points out: "Any general trends towards mutual aid in the U.S. should be understood, not simply or principally as a return to earlier giving habits, but also as an echo of ongoing giving practices among the Global majority around the world." Demographic changes—along with our clearly interdependent challenges of climate catastrophe, wealth inequality, and structural racism—provide motivation and inspiration for improving majority practices.[16]

Giving is political in that it is a statement of values, something to build community around, and something that powers communities. Giving is also political because we write laws that privilege certain behaviors. Our current tax laws about charity clearly prioritize a small number of wealthy people, and the nonprofit organizational form privileges hierarchy over reciprocity. Recently, more White people have gotten involved with community efforts such as bail funds and mutual networks, and there are efforts to encourage "institutional" philanthropy to support these efforts as well. Doing so respectfully takes more than money; it takes recognizing and working within a different set of values and practices.

A NEW PHILANTHROPIC CHOICE

So far, I have discussed time and money. But we have a new resource—digital data—to consider as part of our giving as well. Throughout this book, you will meet people donating photographs, audio recordings, medical information, exercise data, and their DNA, all in digital form. Being able to donate digital data opens up a host of new possibilities and concerns. What does it mean to donate a digital photograph when you'll still have a copy of it? Who gets to decide what happens with the digital data on your phone? You? Facebook? Verizon? How does donating data fit into broader public policy questions about how companies and governments use digital data? Is donating digital data a good idea?

One of the most significant changes influencing how we give is our ability to communicate and connect instantly using tools such as cell phones and the internet. These tools change *what* we give (digital data), as well as *how* we give. Answering these questions about data is a new challenge for us as individual givers. Setting the rules for how it will work is a new challenge for us as a society. We definitely need to address these questions about digital data. We also have the opportunity to revisit related questions about time and money—because the existing policies, regulations, and institutions may no longer be doing what we need them to do.

A QUICK SCAN OF CURRENT STRUCTURES

The nonprofit corporation was created as a solution to a nineteenth-century problem. One hundred and thirty years ago, states and the federal government in the United States began writing the laws that would eventually lead to the modern-day nonprofit organization. This history unfolded over decades and was motivated by railroad barons seeking to maximize their profits, efforts to protect religious freedom, elite concerns about status, political candidates seeking to shut out opponents, and tax policy.[17] Much has changed since the 1880s, and it's time to revisit the questions that are part of that history.

More than a century later, we've come to see nonprofits as a standard part of the giving landscape and of civil society in the United States. Today, as we experiment with ways to donate digital data for public purposes, we face a similar kind of problem—one which may well be solved through the creation of a new form of institution. Recognizing this may motivate you not only to think about today's challenges but also to realize that we have changed and can change the conventions of philanthropy as the times demand. The next few pages are provided to orient you to some of the current conventions—not because they're perfect and immutable, but precisely because they're not.

NONPROFITS AND GIVING

If you've been asked to give money to a cause, there's a pretty good chance the person doing the asking has emphasized that the organization is a *501(c) (3)*. You may have nodded your head, acknowledging this as important, without really knowing what you were nodding about. Not to worry, most of us don't walk around with various subsections of the Internal Revenue Code memorized—and that's exactly what 501(c)(3) refers to, a subsection of the tax code. It happens to be the most common category of nonprofit corporations in the United States.

There are about 1.5 million 501(c)(3)s in the country, providing everything from social services to education, health care, environmental work, scientific research, animal welfare, cultural programs, and religious worship and services. This distinction is often misunderstood to be more important than it really is. Given how frequently fundraisers in particular talk about 501(c)(3)s, you'd be forgiven for thinking this is what distinguishes nonprofit organizations from for-profit corporations. But it isn't.

There are two different sets of laws, piled on top of each other. One is the corporate code, which distinguishes nonprofits from profit-making ventures; this legal distinction is tied to the nineteenth-century robber barons. The 501(c) subsections are part of the tax code, a different set of laws. The corporate code works at the state level; the tax code operates nationally. Corporate regulations state that if a nonprofit corporation takes in more money than it uses to pay its expenses, it must put the remaining funds back into the corporation. Nonprofit corporations have no shareholders, and no one is allowed to profit by "owning" them. There are also regulations about conflicts of interest and self-dealing, all of which are designed to create a corporate form that uses all its money for its mission.

Section 501 of the tax code, on the other hand, lays out rules about how these organizations and the funds they raise are or are not taxed. The fact that it is subsection (c)(3) under discussion is a good hint that there are many kinds of organizations in the code. There are twenty-nine such subsections, covering a wide range of associations, including cemeteries, certain insurance schemes, and professional associations. And the tax rules vary across subsections. In general, 501(c)(3) nonprofits don't pay federal tax on donations made to them. In addition, people who give money to 501(c)(3) nonprofits can, if they choose, deduct the amount of their gift from their income, thereby owing income tax on a lower amount than they would have otherwise. All of this is what gets shorthanded into talking about tax-exempt nonprofits and charitable giving. It's much more complicated than that last paragraph and, mostly more boring, so we'll leave it at that.

There is another category within Section 501(c) that matters, however, and that is subsection (4). It applies to organizations that are called *social welfare nonprofits*. These groups can involve themselves in public policy on behalf of their members, although via what kinds of activities and how deeply are both limited by law. Right away, you can start to see that there are no clear lines between charity and politics.

POLITICAL GIVING

The blurriness between political and charitable issues may help explain why it's increasingly common for organizations to have both (c)(3) and (c)(4) arms.[18] These two-part organizations can be found on every side of almost every issue. For example, access to guns motivates both the (c)(3) National Rifle Association and the (c)(4) National Rifle Association Institute for Legislative Action, and their frequent opponents, the (c)(4) Brady Campaign and (c)(3) Brady Center. Protecting and providing reproductive rights and women's health care is the work of (c)(3) Planned Parenthood and the (c)(4) Planned Parenthood Action Fund; opposition to these services motivates their opponents, including (c)(3) Concerned Women for America and the (c)(4) Concerned Women for America Legislative Action Fund (C4).

All of these organizations are nonprofits, governed by nonprofit corporate law and overseen by state governments and the Internal Revenue Service. The lines that divide the (c)(3)s from the (c)(4)s are hard to see when you look at either the issues or the activities. The only places the lines are clearly drawn are in the laws that apply to these groups regarding taxes and transparency. Rather than get more lost in the weeds of these laws, let's consider why we'd want to treat political and charitable activities differently in the first place.

ANONYMITY AND TRANSPARENCY

Democratic participation includes participating directly in our systems of government, by voting, running for office, or working with politicians to change laws and regulations. It also includes all the ways we participate in communities and in voluntary associations outside of politics. In politics, the need to know who's paying for what is part of both building trust and trying to reduce corruption. So transparency rules. On the other hand, anonymity is an important option for voluntary associations outside of politics.[19] Simply put, disclosing contributions is intended to build trust in politics. Allowing anonymous contributions is intended to build trust in the associational sector. It's tough to draw lines between political and charitable activity, and the laws are not perfect. But this imperfect system is motivated by good intentions—building trust in our institutions. Any efforts to improve these systems should begin from the same intention—broad public trust.

One key issue that is meant to differentiate politics from charity is the question of anonymity. Specifically, can you contribute money without being identified as the giver? There are good reasons that we might want some kinds of giving to be anonymous and some to be identifiable. For example, one core assumption of democratic governance is that people should know who is making the decisions on their behalf. Political activity should be visible to the public, including details about who is funding politicians, political parties, and political campaigns. Your vote is private, but the people and money that make up the electoral system should be visible.

These rules are intended to prevent (or at least reveal) corruption. For the most part, then, there is an assumption that money in politics should be identifiable and transparent.

But we bring a different assumption to promoting participation in associational life. For participation to be a meaningful choice, you need to be able to make it free from interference, based on your own preferences. Privacy is a prerequisite for this: if everyone knows who's in and who's not, then there are many kinds of pressure that can be brought to bear. If you want to make your giving public, if you want your name to be known, that's fine. But many people want to participate in a cause, including by making donations, without drawing attention to themselves. The rules about private participation and contributions to associations and community groups also reflect the influence of Judeo-Christian religious traditions on American law. Both religions (and others) venerate anonymous charitable giving. So our laws allow charitable nonprofits to accept anonymous gifts, while political organizations have to disclose their donors.

Becoming familiar with the values that underpin rules and regulations makes it possible to see why we have a system that allows anonymity when it comes to charitable gifts but not political donations. As givers, we need to understand which giving tools/options/resources provide the degree of anonymity or visibility we value. Sometimes anonymous giving can be effective and necessary. And sometimes it can open the floodgates to undue influence and other forms of corruption.

PRIVILEGING GIVING TO NONPROFITS

These are the principles behind anonymity and transparency in giving, but where do taxes fit in? The US tax code encourages some financial giving by linking it to tax breaks. The history of this goes back to the creation of the income tax in the early twentieth century and a desire to keep wealthy people giving even as they were subject to new taxes.[20] Although discussions of the role of these tax breaks has changed over time, their beneficiaries have not. The US tax code has, since 1917, privileged giving by the wealthy through tax incentives. Changes to the tax code in 2017 targeted charitable tax breaks even more specifically for the wealthy. Because tax breaks for donations are linked to income, they are generally less useful to (and thus less meaningful for) the majority of US taxpayers.[21] A review by two economists in 2019 found that the 2017 law reduced the percentage of taxpayers claiming the charitable deduction from about 25 percent to 8.5 percent. In the economists' words, low- and middle-income households were "effectively eliminated from any tax benefits."[22]

If the tax breaks themselves don't matter to the giving that the rest of us do, are there other reasons to care about the tax laws? Yes. Linked to the tax laws are regulations about reporting on sources of funding. While the financial benefits of the tax law focus on the wealthy, the ability to remain anonymous in your giving depends on whether you give to a (c)(3), to a (c)(4), or to any of the myriad types of organizations specific to campaign politics, such as PACs, super PACs, 527s, political parties, or specific campaigns.[23] Gifts to (c)(3)s can be anonymous; after the IRS changed rules about donor disclosure, several states responded by requiring that donations to (c)(4)s be disclosed. There are lots of details, and lawyers make a lot of money hashing through these requirements. It's also true that the rules for 501(c)(4)s are murky enough to make manipulation of the rules relatively easy. This is what has led to the rise in so-called dark money in political campaigns. Clever donors can find lots of ways to contribute money to political activities and not be identified. One of the most widespread is to make a donation to a (c)(4) that describes its activities in ways that allow it to pass through the regulatory loopholes on donor disclosure, pretending these funds are indistinguishable by donor. Another is for the (c)(4) to contribute its operating budget money to a political candidate or campaign. In the process of moving the money from the (c)(4) to the campaign, the names of donors to the (c)(4) get "washed off," enabling anonymity to reside where disclosure is the rule.

All of these rules were written in the days before the internet made donor disclosure a primarily digital activity. Filing information digitally makes it easier to abide by some of the laws and easier to evade, or potentially violate, others. The digital nature of these reports makes it easier for third-party reviewers and accountability organizations, as well as journalists, to keep track of who is funding what.

It has also complicated things. For example, both major political parties in the United States have their preferred online fundraising platforms. The Republicans promote the use of Revv and WinRed, whereas many Democrats use ActBlue. These tech companies in turn process payments to groups like Americans for Prosperity or Supermajority. To comply with rules on donor disclosure, the software companies report donations to the Federal Election Commission. Although the disclosure rules apply only to gifts larger than a certain size and for specific activities of (c)(4)s, the easiest choice for the tech companies is to report all gifts to make sure they are in compliance with the law. So small-dollar contributions to (c)(4)s for nonpolitical activity get reported alongside larger, decidedly political contributions. This is a case of our technology systems getting ahead of our laws and potentially disclosing activities that aren't legally required to be made public.[24] This kind of reporting infringes on people's privacy and ability to associate with whom they choose. The opposite action—the nondisclosure or obfuscation of big contributions to politics—is arguably the more common and more corrupting problem. The rules are arcane, but they reveal how policy makers use public budgets, tax law, and reporting requirements as a means of rewarding or preventing certain behaviors. They also reveal an entire infrastructure—albeit a broken one—for collecting and reporting data on giving to the public. This is important as we think about reporting requirements for other types of giving, such as crowdfunding or data donations.

THE EFFECTS OF DIGITAL SYSTEMS ON GIVING

Digital systems like mobile phones and networked computers make it ever easier to ask for money and to give it—possibly even too easy, as the Scrooge-like feeling I recounted having at the opening of this book reveals. It should make it easier to track donations, as every online transaction is recorded, whereas we lose track of the coins and bills that we drop in a basket or hand to someone on the street. Ironically, because so many of our online donations are made on proprietary systems such as GoFundMe, the public doesn't have access to this data.

Online giving has also helped blur the lines between giving to nonprofits, for-profits, individuals, or politics as each of these options looks basically the same on a crowdfunding platform. This may be another reason that the tax code, which has played such a big role for nonprofits, seems to be less and less important to givers.

From donating online to donating cryptocurrencies like Bitcoin, the last decade has seen an ever-expanding dependency on digital tools for giving time and money. One mapping conversation participant noted, "I do give money to people on the streets sometimes. But I rarely carry cash anymore." This point was brought home to me on a subway ride not long ago. As happens on subways everywhere, a person came pushing through the doors between cars as the train was moving. As he walked through the crowded car asking for money, he repeated himself, "Need a dollar, please. Help me out. I've got Venmo. Need a dollar, please. I take cash and Venmo."[25]

For some people, the digital underpinnings of giving are just assumed. It's stranger for them to use cash (for anything) than to be impressed with the ability to give via text message or inside of a gaming platform such as Twitch. For others, online tools are the exception, not the rule. But anytime—and every time—there is a digital technology involved, we face the question of what happens with the digital data.

This assumption of digital facilitation—and dependence on it—is important. Among other things that digital transactions enable is (some) visibility into actions that are harder to see when they happen offline. People put dollar bills into collection boxes every week, but tracking those dollars is hard—either from the perspective of the giver or the recipient. Making a donation online (or via phone, via messaging app, or on a crowdfunding or gaming platform) leaves a trail. The giving isn't necessarily new, but the act is more visible to researchers, to outsiders, and, of course, to the organizations (usually companies) that own the digital platform on which the action occurred.

The ways we give online, especially the growth in crowdfunding, raises questions about how much the tax code and (c)(3)s and (c)(4)s matter to people. Some significant portion (again, we can't get the data) of crowdfunding ignores these structures all together. Five years ago, 75 percent of American taxpayers didn't benefit from charitable tax deductions. The 2017 changes to the law made charitable exemptions irrelevant to more than 90 percent of all tax filers.[26] Tax privileges associated with certain behaviors are not a meaningful criterion for how most of us decide to give.

While tax benefits may not actually matter to people's pocketbooks, the categorizations of *nonprofit* and *tax-deductible* still have a strong grip on our collective idea of where good gets done. The value of the tax status of certain nonprofits is not in the financial benefit it provides to most of us as givers but in the signal it theoretically sends regarding purpose and trust. There is an aura of trust associated with nonprofits; we tend to equate them with using money for good and not for profit. But long-term measures of trust in nonprofits show it to be declining, a result of both scandals among nonprofits and a concerted effort by commercial businesses to associate themselves with good causes.[27]

PHILANTHROPY AS A POLITICAL ARTIFACT

Helping other people is basic human behavior. The laws that shape philanthropy result from political decisions. In her 2020 book, *Civic Gifts*, sociologist Elisabeth Clemens analyzes the relationship between nonprofit organizations and American government, and in the process she forces us to set aside a powerful myth about the philanthropic world: the myth of independence.[28] Focusing on nonprofits and philanthropy without talking about the public systems that surround them and the public policy choices that shape them is the equivalent of a young farmer polishing the apples she submits to judges at a county fair while ignoring the health of the soil in which those apples were grown.

Specifically, it's irresponsible to ignore the broader tax code in the United States and its role in privileging philanthropic giving while also preventing us from being a more equitable society. Current tax laws are very much part of what's driving unprecedented income inequality. The laws allow individuals to become trillionaires and corporations to pay nothing in taxes. These laws enable the amassing of philanthropic fortunes so large that people turn to them when government efforts fail. One particularly egregious example of this form of "philanthropic privatization" came in the 2020 U.S. presidential election when the federal government refused to provide adequate funding for election safety, and so wealthy individuals donated hundreds of millions of dollars to the states to run elections.[29]

Philanthropic fortunes, created at the expense of shared investment in government programs, will not and cannot remedy issues such as structural racism, inequitable health care, housing, education and employment opportunities, or climate change. Those failures are ours collectively. Only together can we solve them. It isn't simply that the funding doesn't add up—it's that relying on philanthropy and nonprofits to do the public's work is a form of lower-cost outsourcing with less accountability. It's not democratic. And it's not working.

In addition to the choices we each make as individuals, we face some big questions as a society. The convoluted nature of (c)(3)s and (c)(4)s, the rise of dark money and ways in which people skirt the laws on anonymity and transparency, the blurriness of politics and charity, and the rise of crowdfunding are all reasons to question whether our existing rules about donating time and money are working for or against justice.

Because digital data is a new potential philanthropic resource, it's easy to understand that we need to create new rules and regulations for if and how to use it. In the nineteenth century we morphed the corporation (first created in the Netherlands to colonize southeast Asia: the Dutch East India Company) to create nonprofit corporations that would facilitate donations of time and money for public benefit. So it stands that we can ask what kinds of institutions we can create now to facilitate donations of digital data for public benefit. Digital data is collected on us everywhere we go, from our laptops to our public spaces, at school, home, and work. What kinds of protections do we want for this data, our identities, and our intentions?

If we build something new, how will we ensure equitable access and control or consider questions of human dignity and justice? How will we determine who—you or companies—will be making this decision about data from and about you? These questions tie into—and may be useful additions to—ongoing public policy debates about the unbounded commercial control of data on elections, trust, and identity.

Our data represent us, but until now we have had very little say over how the data are used. Now's a chance to change that.

It's important to note that most of the research for this book was completed in 2019, and writing was finished in the summer of 2020. The pandemic, protests against police brutality, economic collapse, a rise in White nationalism, and 2020 US elections happened after most of the writing was done. These events highlighted two things of great importance to this book: first, our public systems are broken; second, people come together to help each other in every crisis and from every walk of life. Some of the ideas in this book—the focus on working together and using every resource you have—took on the urgency of life and death for millions of people during this time. The months of 2020 changed, for at least a period of time, the national conversation about racism, structural inequality, the abandonment or direct sabotage of public systems (like the US Postal Service), and an underinvestment in physical and social infrastructure that was failing children, elders, parents, and workers.

As I am writing, I don't know where the country will be in the fall of 2021, when you will be reading this. I do know that there's no single change that could have fixed all these problems in the time between now and then (although many things that might have made them even deadlier). The practices described in the stories to come—of collective action, activating political and civic power, listening to community experts, repairing the harms of our racist and colonizing systems and assumptions, mobilizing against corporate power and politicians beholden to wealthy donors, and building alliances for justice that are led by those most harmed—will still be necessary. My concern about these issues shapes the stories presented in the chapters ahead. The giving products described in the next chapter are available across the political spectrum; the stories that follow center people addressing economic, racial, and environmental injustices.

This is the beginning of the story of how we give. In the coming pages, you'll meet people writing the outlines of this future, people who refuse to feel like Scrooge. I hope their stories inspire you to look closely at your practices, find ways for your giving to connect you to others, and help shape a better future for all.

2 THE GIVINGSCAPE: OLD AND NEW COME TOGETHER

Graduate students and artists aren't known for having a lot of disposable income. When Christine Liu, a PhD candidate in neuroscience, and her friend, Tera Johnson, decided to take action to protect public funding of science, they had to find a way to raise some money. They decided to make art—specifically, small enamel pins that celebrated science. Neither knew how to do this, but they were undaunted. "If someone else can do something, we can do it too," Christine tells me. "We learned how to make the pins on YouTube. We were happy with a high failure rate, because it meant we were learning. We experimented with how to design them and then found a factory that would manufacture the pins."[1] Christine and Tera wanted pins that would give people a cheeky way to show their support for women and people of color in science. "This was at the time Americans were holding marches for science," Christine says. "Science isn't partisan, but it is political. Science is for everyone, and when politicians and others stand in the way, then its political." Their first year, the pair, now operating as Two Photon Art, sold the pins and donated what they earned to three organizations that support women of color in science. "These are our people," Christine laughs. "I'm Chinese American and Tera is Black and Filipino. And we're both scientists."

Since that beginning, Two Photon Art has expanded its offerings from pins to T-shirts, turned an Instagram group into a fourteen-thousand-member online community called STEM Squad, and created its own grants program to provide emerging scientists with a few hundred dollars to advance their research. "That was really hard, picking twelve people when we had so many applications." Christine and Tera both work full time, so their approach to reaching out and partnering is focused on both getting the word out and involving people in doing the work. They now work with Massive Science, an online publication focused on helping scientists communicate with the public, to give other people a chance to make selections for the grants program.[2] Christine works on Two Photon every night, every minute she's not doing her own research. "It's the right way for me to get involved. I'm shy. I don't like public speaking. This way I can be part of a growing community and make a difference for other scientists and women of color, but I don't have to give speeches or be out in front."

In three years, Christine and Tera have connected thousands of people and given away more than $11,000. Their motivations are both political and community oriented. The contributions include unquantifiable hours and an impressive amount of money, and they have data on lots of people. They use the data to fulfill sales orders, to develop new products, and to help expand their online communities. The online stores for Two Photon and STEM Squad are hosted by Shopify, and STEM Squad got its start on Instagram, so both Shopify and Facebook (which owns Instagram) have access to all the digital data generated by sales and the community. If you were to try to categorize Christine and Tera's efforts, you'd have to mark them as volunteering time, donating money, providing charitable support, taking political action, and using digital systems that make all of this easy and low cost for both of these hard working scientists and their community.

The idea of making something to sell to give away the earnings (or do something socially positive with the profits) is not new or unique. It's a retail practice that we'll look at more closely in chapter 7 and that (institutionally) dates back at least 120 years to the founding of Goodwill. Blurring the lines between commerce and charity is familiar and is often described as *social innovation* or *corporate social responsibility*. Two Photon Art exemplifies the hybridization of the giving we do now. Doing good is no longer just about contributing time or money to a charitable organization (if it ever was). We give in many ways, to many types of activities, and we use money, time, and digital systems to do it.

The mixing and matching that Christine and Tera do is even more interesting when you zoom in on the possibilities of digitized data. While Two Photon Art relies on digital systems (social media, community blogs, and online shopping platforms) to do what it does, Christine and Tera are not using the data from their activities as an actual giving resource. To see an example of giving data, let's turn to another kind of scientific support.

Cat Chang started using iNaturalist because mushroom guidebooks are heavy. A Native Hawaiian, Cat carries two distinct universes of knowledge in her head. She remembers walking with her grandmother on the community land her family inhabited for generations, talking to and petting each plant. "That's how she kept in touch with them, knew if they were healthy or not, if they were ready to be picked for food or medicine." Her father moved the family to Northern California when Cat was in high school. She focused on math and science and grew apart from the natural world. In college, she turned to botany and horticulture—once again learning about plants, but this time through the lens of Western science and Latin taxonomies.[3]

Cat found her way to the Oakland Food Policy Council, which seeks ways to provide local, healthy, and sustainable food to all Oakland residents. This is when Cat realized how important mushrooms are. "I'd been focusing on plants, planting things in all kinds of dirt as part of my work as a landscape architect. But I didn't know the first thing about healthy soil. And mushrooms. Mushrooms are key to healthy soil." Carrying a backpack full of guidebooks on a long hike in the woods is tough. "When a friend told me about iNaturalist—an app I could put on my phone that would let me leave the guidebooks at home—I was hooked. I don't use a lot of apps, and I'm not very techy, but this one was for me."[4]

Cat uses the iNaturalist app almost every day. She takes photos of mushrooms when she's hiking. She participates in butterfly counts—walking over a specified area with other people, counting every butterfly they see, snapping photos, and uploading them to iNaturalist. She uploads high-quality photos and blurry ones. When she can, she'll include her best guess at identifying the mushroom or butterfly. "But that's just the beginning," she tells me. "Once the photos are uploaded, the online community checks them out. They suggest identifications. If enough people agree, the photo is tagged as identified. If it's a good quality photo and it's properly identified, it gets marked as 'research grade.'" Those photos are then marked in the iNaturalist database in ways that scientists can use them. Even if a photo is not research-grade, however, it's likely that Cat learned something. She's no longer just adding her own photos and identifying those of strangers. "My father passed away, and I want to clean up, tag, and add the seven thousand photos he has from around his house in the Texas hills. He got into iNaturalist too late in his life, or he would have added them himself."[5]

Every photo is a donation of digital data. The iNaturalist dataset contains more than fifty-eight million photos, videos, and audio recordings. The app, the database that powers it, and the community of three million users includes experts and amateurs in every field of natural sciences. Birders, bug lovers, hunters, hikers, gardeners, and mushroom-loving landscape architects like Cat combine their knowledge with that of professors of dendrology (study of trees), science museum entomologists (study of insects), and amateur and professional malacologists (study of mollusks).

The uploaded photos are sorted by the metadata (information about the location, time, and date of the photo) that phone cameras automatically embed in photos. Scientists use iNaturalist's dataset to track change over time in ecosystems around the world. Amateurs use iNaturalist to quickly get the name for something they've seen, share what they've learned, and help answer questions. The photos are all donations; the time people spend helping answer questions is all volunteered. The results are extraordinary. Millions of people get their curiosity sated, an incomparable biodiversity database is built from donated photos, and communities of like-minded people connect online and off in *bioblitzes*—social events designed to bring lots of people together to take pictures of everything in a certain park or outside space on a designated day. The iNaturalist data has contributed to scientific breakthroughs. At least one new species has been identified. One photo captured a snail that scientists, who knew of its existence from Captain Cook's eighteenth-century diaries, had never seen. Other communities, such as those that use an iNaturalist-type app called eBird (more in chapter 6), have helped build a database from which hundreds of peer-reviewed science papers have been independently published. When it comes to data donations, small contributions can add up to a big impact.

SEEING THE GIVINGSCAPE

We're surrounded by opportunities to give. The menu of options is long and diverse, a mix of old and new choices. It includes consumer choices, charitable donations, choices about political time and money (not to mention voting), investing, boycotting, protesting, making loans, and giving our data. It's a world full of direct options, such as handing a dollar to a man on the sidewalk or donating money directly to people on the other side of the planet via a program called GiveDirectly. There are more abstract and long-term options, from investing some of your retirement plan in affordable housing developers or donating your time to political issues, the strategies for which require lengthy time frames and no promise of success.

This landscape of giving products is what I call the *givingscape*. It includes different products and vendors selling products that help people give money, data, and time. The vendors are also diverse. Products are sold by nonprofit organizations and political groups, banks and mutual fund companies, crowdfunding companies (both for-profit and not-for-profit), social media and text-based giving applications, online payment companies, retailers selling charity-branded products, social businesses seeking both profit and purpose, and quasi-governmental organizations. In many cases, the choice facing you involves a combination of these. Let's consider a few common scenarios.

Scenario one: You go shopping for shoes. At the store is a display table of TOMS shoes, a company built around the buy one, give one (BOGO) model, promising to donate a pair for each pair purchased. On the next table over, there are hiking boots and a sign noting that the brand being featured donates "10 percent to the environment." Both options depend on some kind of partnership to benefit people other than you. TOMS works with partners around the globe; the hiking shoe company will probably note a nonprofit partner on the package. What neither TOMS nor the hiking shoe company will make it easy for you to do is check on what happened with your money. Note that the second company's 10 percent claim doesn't indicate 10 percent of *what*. Is it 10 percent of the purchase price? Of total sales? Total profit? These kinds of arrangements make it easy to fold an act of charity into a purchase. The good feeling that accompanies the act may last slightly longer than the basic retail therapy boost, but even that's not guaranteed.

Scenario two: You pass an older woman sitting on the sidewalk outside the drugstore. You go in the store, get your stuff, and approach the cash register line. When your turn comes, the cashier asks if you want to make a donation to "help cure cancer." You say yes, and she adds a dollar to the amount you owe. In return, she puts a playing-card-sized Thank You card into the bag with your toothpaste and razor blades. When you step back outside, the woman asks for your change. You drop it in the cup she's holding toward you, meet her gaze, and say "take care of yourself." She thanks you and wishes you well. As you walk away, ask yourself: Which interaction will do more good—the dollar disappearing into the pharmacy till or the change in the hands of another human being? Both were easy to do, but it's hard to know what either accomplishes.

Scenario three: While sitting in the waiting room at an urgent care clinic, you're handed a tablet with a stylus attached. It's opened to the electronic equivalent of the old paper forms that you would have been handed on a clipboard a dozen years ago. You scroll through pages of information on your health, family background, current symptoms, and drug use. Several pages of fine print precede large blank boxes in which you're asked to scrawl your signature. You know that at least one of these blocks of text is informing you that data from any tests your doctor orders may be used for research purposes. What you don't know is what happens if you don't tick that box, what kind of research might be done and by whom, and for how long they plan to keep your data.

THE GIVINGSCAPE AS PRODUCT MARKET

Every one of these options is a product choice. Most of us have to choose between these products. Should I hand a dollar to the guy outside the grocery store or donate to a political candidate that I think can help pass meaningful laws and budgets to help ease the crisis of homelessness? Can I afford to do both? And what about buying products that claim to donate funds to causes I care about? If I recognize each of these ways of giving as a different product (being sold to us by a different set of companies), then I can ask myself how to choose between them. Are there some to emphasize and others I want to avoid?

I call these choices *products* and use the term *selling* deliberately. There are companies selling these offerings and costs that accompany them. The costs are often buried in the details, hidden underneath the promises of "doing good." The providers of the products, whether they be banks or community foundations, nonprofits or crowdfunding sites, are calculating those costs. When you choose a specific product, you pay some of those costs, although the provider will do whatever they can to distract you from those fees. Crowdfunding sites, for example, ask you for a "tip" on top of your donation to pay the cost of using the site. If you don't add a few dollars to your contribution, many sites simply subtract it for you. You either add $2.50 to your $50 gift (paying $52.50) or the site subtracts the costs (You pay $50, but only $47.50 goes to whatever you were supporting and $2.50 goes to the company that runs the crowdfunding site). For donor-advised funds, you pay a fee for the account. Some percentage of each donation to a nonprofit organization or political group goes to managing the organization, often called *overhead costs*. One of the reasons we don't think of these choices as products is because of how hidden the costs are. But there are costs, and you pay them.

Once you start thinking of these as different products, you'll also realize how often you are asked to choose. In a given day, you may be asked for a direct donation outside the grocery store, receive an email from a friend about a crowdfunding campaign, choose between milk from an organic dairy that's structured as a B Corporation or a generic store brand, and get a text message from a political candidate asking you to show your support (by buying a bumper sticker, for example).

For each of the three resources—money, data, and time—that we have to give, there are different products. Most of the product choices currently available have to do with money—so I'll lay out that part of the givingscape first. Then I'll look specifically at data, then, finally, at time.

PRODUCTS FOR GIVING MONEY

The first step is to scan the landscape of product choices for how to contribute money. Table 2.1 sketches out the different products available. The left-hand column shows the products. They are arrayed against the types of recipients that each product legally can be used to benefit. For example, you can donate money directly to a nonprofit, a political campaign, or an individual (top row). Prior to 2020 and the economic fallout from the coronavirus pandemic, few people might have thought to donate money to commercial businesses. The desire to keep local shops alive and to keep retail and restaurant employees safe and paid led to a boom in precisely this behavior, facilitated by crowdfunding sites and the ease of direct donations. GoFundMe's CEO estimated that one-third of all new campaigns on the crowdfunding site by March 2020 were for pandemic-related expenses associated with loss of income.[6]

Thinking about a direct donation as a product choice may seem strange. Giving cash directly to another person hardly seems like a product choice. But as you move away from that immediate exchange, and down the left-hand column of table 2.1, you'll notice something happens. The other choices all involve some form of intermediary—whether it's the organization that sets up the donor-advised fund, the crowdfunding site that facilitates your contribution, or the actual product that you buy (or don't buy). For example, banks, mutual fund companies, and nonprofit community foundations and some universities all "sell" donor-advised funds (DAFs). The product is the same—a designated fund that you put money into and from which gifts to nonprofit organizations can be made. They are the fastest growing product on the givingscape, growing 7.6 percent in

Table 2.1

Product choices for giving money

Product types	Type of recipient			
	Charitable nonprofit—501(c)(3), public agency, religious org	Political cause, candidate, or political nonprofit—501(c)(4)	Commercial business	Individual, group
Direct contribution of money	X	X	****	X
Donor-advised fund	X			
Crowdfunding	X	X	X	X
Political donations		PACs, super PACs, 527s		
Product purchase—direct support to cause	X (e.g., buy a T-shirt, tote bag)	X (e.g., buy a T-shirt, tote bag)		X (e.g., cookie sales)
Product purchase—indirect support to cause			X (BOGO,* branded products,** PoS***)	
Boycott products/companies			X	
Invest in shares			X	
Invest in pooled funds (mutual funds, DAF investment options)			X	

*BOGO: Buy one, give one; TOMS shoes or Warby Parker glasses, for common examples.
**Branded products: Red iPhones, pink batteries—products that promise a donation to a cause.
***PoS: Point of sale transactions; add a dollar at checkout to support a cause or round up your bill to donate.
****Campaigns to raise donations for small businesses or to help their employees—usually on crowdfunding sites—boomed in the United States during the coronavirus pandemic.

2016 compared to a 2.7 percent annual increase for all charitable giving.[7] Legally, once the money is transferred to the seller of the DAF, the donor is only advising on where the money ultimately gets distributed. In practice, so long as the donor is advising a legal use of the money, the DAF seller rarely says no.[8]

Depending on who is selling it, the details of the product change. National banks, for example, will set up an account for you, require a minimum deposit, offer certain investment choices for the funds, and allow a certain number of grants to be directed per year, all for a certain fee. That mix of characteristics is what distinguishes their DAF product from one sold by your alma mater. A university-based DAF will differ on the account size and frequency details, and probably include some element that links the fund directly to the purpose or goals of the university. It's very much like comparing one checking account to another; the product details differ depending on who's selling it to you.

These intermediaries are the vendors that sell the products. Table 2.2 shows the range of products and the range of vendors that sell them. Looking at the vendors selling givingscape products reveals three things. First, there are profit-seeking and nonprofit vendors. Second, the vendors include some of the world's biggest institutions. And third, the vendor and the intended beneficiary or recipient of the donation are not always the same. Banks sell (and profit off of) DAFs, for example, but they are intermediaries to hold the funds until they are distributed to charitable nonprofits.

I mentioned giving a dollar to the man outside the grocery store. I do this even though I was raised in an era when giving directly was a no-no. You have probably been told not to give money to the person on the street and to instead give it to a program or shelter. The logic was to "trust the institution, not the person." It's no longer clear that this is the best advice; the number of people living on our streets continues to grow, and their plight seems ever more miserable. In many places, practices of collective

Table 2.2
Products (for giving money) and sample vendors

Product	Sample vendors	
	Nonprofit	Commercial (for-profit)
Donor-advised funds (DAF)	Community foundations, colleges	Investment banks, mutual fund companies—via nonprofit partners
Crowdfund donations	DonorsChoose	GoFundMe
Loans	Kiva	
Political contributions	Nonprofit 501(c)(4)s, PACs, campaign contributions	Fundraising consultants, campaign bundlers
Impact investments	Community foundations, some credit unions, some nonprofits	Banks, investment funds, mutual funds

care or mutual aid—in which communities have created alternative, often informal and out-of-the-public eye networks to pool and lend money along with other resources—have long-standing practices to protect and lift up their own, or to provide care during disasters. One of the fastest-growing nonprofits of the last few years is called GiveDirectly, an antipoverty organization that facilitates direct cash transfers via mobile phones. In the time since we were taught not to reach out directly to the panhandler on the street, the organizational landscape around us has changed. And our trust of "the organization" has become much more complicated. Digital tools—such as shared documents—make previously "invisible" practices of collective care visible to outsiders in a variety of ways.

There are now all kinds of enterprises claiming to provide social services. Some are long-standing informal networks and others are nonprofits, commercial businesses, or some mix of the last two. Why does this matter? Because each type of organization has its own set of practices for building trust and oversight systems for accountability. If your concern as a potential donor or volunteer is that your money or time be used to help people, you need to know how to find out basic information—like what's being done with your money, how many people are being helped, and how well. Nonprofits have to make that information available. Businesses don't.

It's easier than ever to track down information on nonprofit organizations, but first you have to know if what you're dealing with is an actual nonprofit organization—specifically, a 501(c)(3). Why does this matter? Because different organizations do different things, offer you different incentives, and have to follow different rules when it comes to reporting on their activities and their money. If you want to give your time or money to an organization that has to report publicly on what it does and how it uses the money it receives, then the nonprofit you want is a 501(c)(3) organization. This information should be clearly displayed on the organization's website and you can verify it online.

There are an increasing number of businesses that operate to both make money and pursue a social purpose. The irony is that most of these businesses don't have to report what they're actually doing with the money they earn. If the organization is a business with a social purpose, you'll probably have to take it at its word that it's doing good—there is no Consumer Reports or Securities and Exchange Commission to hold social businesses accountable. To fill this need, there's a relatively new designation for businesses, *benefit corporations*. These companies enroll in a voluntary reporting process. They will be able to tell you not only about their profits and losses, but also about their progress on social goals.

If you decide to give money because a friend asked you to do so on social media, Kickstarter, or GoFundMe, then you can ask your friend about the end result. Depending on what platform you used, you may be able to get information on how much money was raised and whether or not it was delivered to the right recipient. But any information beyond that, such as what the platform did with the fees you paid or with the data you generated by logging into its system, is out of reach.

These reporting requirements are the legacy of old ways of thinking. In this view, charitable giving to nonprofits was not just a piece but almost the whole of doing good. Other types of action were cordoned off—either not counted at all (such as gifts to individuals) or seen as unrelated activities, like shopping, investing, or political engagement. While tax laws and reporting regulations still treat them as separate domains, people choose between them as comparable products for taking action. This is problematic.

REUSABLE MONEY

We have created ways to give money away and get something back. Loans and some types of investments also do this. Kiva lets people make small financial contributions that get packaged together into bigger loans. These funds are then loaned out to help someone start or expand a small business. Kiva started by packaging loans to entrepreneurs in countries where there were few bank loans available. It now works worldwide, including in forty-eight US states. Donors contribute the money, the loans get made, then people grow their businesses, make money, and pay back the loans. The original Kiva donor gets to reallocate their original contribution to another entrepreneur.

Loaning money and donating data are perhaps more similar to donating blood than they are to donating money. When you give blood, your body regenerates what you donated within days. You contributed something, but you can also still use it. When you upload a photo to iNaturalist or eBird or other such apps, you're contributing it to a greater cause, but you also still have your photo.

Loans like those from Kiva start to look a bit like investing. In general, an investor is looking to both buy a small piece of a business and earn back that money (and more) over time from the profits the business earns. Investments in renewable energy or affordable housing, and other areas that people see as socially productive, are quite common. Since tracking started decades ago, *socially responsible investment* products have become extremely popular. They account for about $12 trillion a year, which is 25 percent of all money managed by US investment companies.[9] These products help people invest in enterprises that produce things they care about, such as affordable housing or environmentally sustainable products, and they also screen out whole industries of which they may disapprove, from tobacco to weapons to fossil fuels. Those that screen out certain industries are generally described as *socially responsible*; those that actively seek out environmentally or socially positive industries are called *impact investments*.

Investing as a way of using your money for good increases the total amount of money you can dedicate to the causes you care about. As you are making decisions about where to give away your money, you might also think about what kinds of investments you want to hold, whether through your retirement account (if you're lucky enough to have one) or through other mutual funds, stocks, or bonds if you own them. These products give you a way to use more of your money in ways that match your values. And if you use a loan program with a good repayment rate or make investments that earn money, you'll be able to reuse your money again and again.

All told, there are several considerations for choosing the right giving product beyond its simple cost. Some choices, like giving circles, are designed specifically to encourage collective action. As we'll see through the rest of this book, options that help people come together and pool their resources are the best avenues for getting the most out of your giving. You'll also want to think about the derivative data that your particular product choice generates, especially if you wish to protect your privacy or simply limit downstream uses of personally identifiable information.

PRODUCT CHOICES AND DATA

Another reason to think about the vendors in table 2.2 is to think about the data being exchanged when using these products. Almost every financial transaction (except giving cash directly to another person) generates data. Throughout this book, it's important to think about two kinds of digitized data: that which are intended for a purpose and are deliberately donated, such as Cat's photos. I call these *donatable data*. Then there's the data that are generated by every online transaction, from credit card payments to the clicks that indicate you like something online. I call these *derivative data*. The information from the STEM Squad's discussions and purchases are derivative data. Table 2.3 lays out some of the products and actions that produce donatable data. Note that any of these actions that use digital systems also produce derivative data.

It's important to keep the idea of derivative data in mind when you're making choices about giving time or money, as well as when you're donating data. That's because every online action will automatically generate

Table 2.3
Products for donating data (and sample derivative data)

Product	Type of donatable data	Examples of derivative data
Phone apps (iNaturalist, eBird, cameras) or website tools (spreadsheets, databases)	Photos Spreadsheets of collected data Audio recordings Video recordings	Location, time, date, possible name or account ID
Digitized, networked personal health devices (pulse oximeters, thermometers, blood sugar or heart rate monitors)	Personal health information, such as temperature, heart rate, exercise level, oxygen level, etc.	Location, time, date, possible name or account ID
Fitness apps	Exercise amount, type, frequency	Location, time, date, possible name or account ID
Swab kits	DNA from lining of cheek	Name or account ID

derivative data. This information is captured by credit card companies or payment processors, as well as whatever vendor is selling you the giving product. The derivative data may or may not be passed on to the intended recipient of the financial gift, but it will always be captured by (and used) by the intermediary. Table 2.4 shows how payment processors, third-party platforms, and businesses act as data middlemen between certain product choices and the final recipient of the funding. Note that this table looks *only* at the first round of transactions. It doesn't examine second level effects—when organizations sell the data they collect from these transactions.

Table 2.4
Derivative data and giving products

Product choice	Who gets your data (email, address, phone, account numbers)	Who doesn't get the data
Cash donation to nonprofit or individual	No one	N/A
Credit card payment to nonprofit or individual	Credit card/payment processors; recipient; donations can be anonymous	N/A
Credit card payment to political group or campaign; political donations	Credit card company/payment processors; donations above a certain limit must be identified publicly	N/A
Donor-advised fund	Vendor that sells the DAF; payment processors	Recipient nonprofit *may* or may not get name; won't get contact information for follow up
Crowdfunding	Payment processors; crowdfunding vendor	Project or campaign organizers *may* get names; may not get information for follow up
Product purchases from nonprofit or political campaign	Payment processors/credit card company; vendor; political parties (if political purchase)	N/A
Product purchase, indirect support via product selling company	Payment processors/credit card; product vendor	Organization or cause
Point-of-sale transactions	Payment processor/credit card company; vendor	Organization or cause

Tables 2.3 and 2.4 show how your data, including your name, email, location, time/date, and payment information, is part of every financial transaction except handing someone cash. In most cases, the data that accompanies the financial contribution is captured not by the group, cause, or person you are trying to help but by the vendors selling the products that let you make the gift. For example, a donation on a crowdfunding platform sends your name, address, and credit card number to the company running the platform, not to the people raising the money. Similarly, buying a piece of clothing that promises funding to fight cancer, for example, will send some money to the cause (see chapter 7 for how this works), but all of your data stays with the vendor who sold the product. Any transaction that involves a credit card or an online payment involves your data. In most cases, your derivative data goes somewhere other than where you're intending to send your money.

HOW DATA DIFFER

Digital data doesn't work like time or money. One of the most important characteristics of digitized data is that innumerable, exact copies can exist simultaneously in different places. That's why you can have the same email message on your laptop and phone, and how everyone in your family can admire the same holiday photograph that your cousin shared on social media. We don't really "give away" our data when we contribute it; we still have it. If you give your data to several different researchers or databases, they will each have it, as will you. Money and time don't work that way. You can't give away a dollar and still have it, and once you've spent an hour on a task, you can't get that time back.

The characteristics of digital data are key to understanding its value. A digital photo that you share with family has emotional value. Shared with the iNaturalist dataset, it may have scientific value. Scraped from your social media account and added to a facial-recognition database, a digital photo adds value to corporate/government surveillance systems, which in turn devalue individual privacy and control. Cell phone videos have helped move long overdue White outrage about police killings of unarmed Black people.[10] As legal scholar Jasmine McNealy explains, individual digital data can be valued in many ways, all of which involve seeing the data as indicative of relationships: you and your family, you and your health or place, you and your community, you and the government, you and corporations.[11] Any individual data point—be it blood sugar level, daily steps taken, photo and location data on forest mushrooms, or a photograph of your family—derives value from the relationships it represents and the relationships drawn between it and other individual data points. These many nuances to valuing digital data are why we are seeing so much experimentation with institutional forms and data governance. Thinking about "owning" our data centers a market perspective over the relational and personal identity value of digital data. This transactional view is likely only to further enrich already wealthy corporate aggregators of data, while misleading individuals into selling their digital identities.[12]

Cat has some concerns about donating her data to iNaturalist. She knows that her photos document where she is at any given time. She read the site's policies and decided that because the site is meant for educational purposes and is sponsored by two well-regarded nonprofit science organizations, she trusted their promise to use the data only for those purposes.[13] Donating data requires us to consider a different set of issues than donating our time or money.

One of those considerations has to do with how data can be used by many people at the same time. Think about Cat's photos again. Remember, she has them on her phone and can do whatever she wants with them. Once she's uploaded them to iNaturalist, the photos also become part of a massive database. While the individual photo still has value to Cat, the value of the database is in its aggregate size. Researchers can see many photos of the same creature and discover variations. They can see changes in population numbers over time, which helps to understand the effects of climate change. With a single action—uploading a photo—Cat has helped in two ways: she's added one useful photo, while also making the whole database more useful and valuable. That's pretty good math—two outputs from one action.

GIVING TIME, MONEY, AND DATA

We all have experience giving time and money. The users of iNaturalist are early explorers of the new practice of giving our digital data. Because digital data are so different from time and money, we need to think individually and act collectively about how we want this to work. One goal of this book is to get us all thinking about how we use these three resources together. Let's look closer at intangible factors—such as joy, control, and scarcity—that shape our giving.

Giving time and data are similar in one way: you tend to get as much as you give. When Cat spends an evening identifying other people's photographs, she's more focused on what she is learning that on what she is giving. People who volunteer at community organizations, engage in political door knocking, teach Saturday or Sunday school, or help school kids and elders safely navigate the streets of a busy city often talk about the joy, the learning, the spiritual satisfaction, or the feeling of making a difference they get from spending their time in these ways.

Scholarship on volunteering and generosity identifies evolutionary roots; biological benefits; contributions to healthy childhood development; and physical, psychological, and relationship benefits. One metareview of the scientific literature examined more than 350 peer-reviewed studies focused on the reasons for, and the personal benefits of, giving our time and money to others.[15] In short, giving time makes us feel good.

Unlike our data, our time is limited. We can use it once, and that's it. Every moment spent doing one thing is a moment spent not doing something else. So we make our choices carefully.

MORE CHOICES, FEWER GIVERS?

Many of the previous examples focused on giving money to charity and it's this space that makes the most claims to innovation. Ironically, with all these new tools and products and ways to give, and with so many of them focused on making the act of giving easier, the actual rates at which we give have not changed. For decades, aggregate giving by Americans has hovered at around 2 percent of the country's gross domestic product (GDP) year after year. It shades above 2 percent some years and dips below in others. It seems like no matter how easy a company or product or sector tries to make giving, we still give at about the same rate.[16]

That average is important, but it obscures a critical chasm. When averaged across the entire population, the percentage has stayed the same, and the top-line number keeps growing, but in the last two decades fewer people have been giving more, and more people are no longer giving. There is now a "missing middle" of givers, at least as counted by those who track charitable donations.

Over the last two decades, a chasm has grown between the very wealthy and the rest of us. Measures of income inequality in the United States have been rising since the 1990s. They recently hit their highest rate since recording began.[17] Even as annual totals of charitable contributions go up every year, and each new presidential election sees more campaign donations than ever before, these funds are not coming from a representative cross-section of the country. As the wealthy get wealthier, their individual ability to make the total giving number grow increases. It takes only a handful of mega-multi-million-dollar gifts to tip the annual giving total up by billions of dollars. That's what's been happening. Total charitable giving increases year over year, but the number of people participating in that giving has been going down. Analysis of charitable giving data from 2000 to 2019 revealed that more than twenty million households that used to give had stopped doing so.[18]

We don't know why this is happening. We do know that charitable giving is only one of many ways that we give. We won't be able to understand why one type of action—charitable giving—is changing without seeing it in context of the broader givingscape.

Many of the products that make giving so easy you forget about it end up doing much less than they promise. They may be lulling us into thinking we can do good by doing nothing. Just as you rarely get something for nothing, you rarely give something for nothing. This is especially true of digital data. So much of the digital data we generate gets used by companies to make money even as they try to assure us not to worry about it. Think about that online petition you signed based on a tweet you saw from an old friend. Petitions hosted by Change.org, for example, are data-harvesting products. Have you ever wondered how the site stays in business? It does so by selling both the data (email, name, address) you generated when you signed the petition and the insight about you that your signature indicates. The petition site bundles your name, email, and the insight about your interests (you just signed a petition about something you care about, remember?) and sells this information to data brokers, advertising agencies, subscription houses, and political campaigns.[19] When you sign an online petition, the chances that you've just handed over your data for someone else to make money from them are higher than the chance that the intended legislative recipient of your petition will ever see it.

A quick rule of thumb: it takes time to make a difference. This is actually a good thing. Research shows that giving our time makes us feel as though we have more of it, a concept called *time affluence*.[20] This is the feeling you get from doing something for other people or for connecting to communities, or from working toward a shared goal: it takes time, but you end up feeling more energized. Some approaches to giving time, money, and data are both quick and fulfilling, while others are like junk food: cheap, easy, and bad for you (and the world around you) in the long term.

Finally, remember that the givingscape and its many products are simply tools. They are not all that matters. How we organize ourselves to use our time, money, and data matter more than the tools. We can mix and match the tools. For example, neighborhood groups, PTAs, mutual aid networks and bail funds all use crowdfunding platforms because they make it easy to manage the money coming in. The people in the groups do the hard work of organizing, making decisions, and allocating funding; the crowdfunding platform is an easy on/easy off tool for bringing donations in and holding them before they're disbursed.

Pia Mancini, a democracy activist from Argentina, recognized an opportunity to hybridize digital technologies and collective decision-making traditions. She launched Open Collective, a turnkey software program that lets any group track its finances in accountable and transparent ways. It lets people—from small groups of software developers to theater artists who've come together for a single production—accept donations and track the money coming in and going out in a simple, online way. The group makes its decisions collectively, determining production timelines or assigning roles to people, and managing the funds is almost automated. Open Collective allows groups to get projects done (which may last for weeks or years) without having to set up a formal organization, hire managers, and establish boards of directors. Established organizations can offer to host new or adjacent projects via Open Collective, providing the legal or insurance coverage to the project for a fee while nurturing new ideas (without adding a lot of management weight). This is an example of the organizational innovation that marks our moment as transitional, between an old, fully analog, top-down world of nonprofit corporations and an emerging, more fluid, digitally enabled world of collective action. It's one signpost for the future. The next six chapters offer more.

3   CROWDFUNDING AND ITS ANCIENT COUSINS

Javon Brame is an administrator at Arapahoe Community College, outside of Denver. He spends his professional days working to improve educational options for Coloradans. Javon, who grew up in Denver, sees the effects of underfunded public schools on young adults every day. He also remembers growing up in the area and trying to succeed as a young Black man when the odds were stacked against him. Several years back, he joined the Denver African American Philanthropists group, a giving circle of Black men in the region.

Javon is one of an estimated 150,000 people across the United States who participate in a giving circle. These groups are rapidly increasing as people seek to make a bigger difference by working with others, both politically and charitably. Giving circles are often groups of like-minded people, usually several dozen, each of whom contributes an agreed-upon amount of money into a shared pot. The group then makes decisions about how to put the money to work. Some people organize circles around their identity, some around particular places, some around political visions, and some around causes. There are more than one thousand giving circles in the United States, three times as many as were known a decade ago.[1] There are groups focused on African American men, people in southern Iowa, and people who identify as evangelical environmentalists; there are women-only groups, groups for young Jewish professionals, and giving circles embedded within corporations' ethnic affinity groups.

Giving circles hold their money in a wide range of the products discussed in earlier chapters. Some use simple bank accounts, others set up donor-advised funds, and others partner with local organizations or national networks. Some are affiliated with nonprofits, such as community foundations or churches; some operate mostly online; and others are deliberately informal, focusing more on the act of collective decision-making and perhaps less on how to manage the money.

Giving circles are an old form of collective decision-making that's experiencing boom times right now. This growth is powered in part by deliberate efforts to promote these circles. Some of this comes from within communities themselves. Asian Americans and Pacific Islanders in Philanthropy (AAPIP), for example, started promoting giving circles as a way of increasing giving participation in their community. Big foundations, such as the W. K. Kellogg Foundation and the Bill & Melinda Gates Foundation, have also encouraged the growth of giving circles by providing financial support to researchers, consultants, and giving circle networks. In 2020, Philanthropy Together launched with the specific goal of incubating more giving circles. Some of the growth is more organic, led entirely by the energy and commitment of groups of friends or neighbors. Technology plays a role in both spreading the idea of giving circles and, in some cases, making it easier than ever to manage them.

THE HUMAN UTILITY: CURATED CROWDFUNDING

"Life, liberty, water, and the pursuit of happiness," said Tiffani Ashley Bell. "That's what independence would look like in a more just society." Tiffani and I were sitting in a café in San Francisco on an unusually drizzly May afternoon. I'd just asked her why she had started the Human Utility, the nonprofit crowdfunding program she created to help Detroiters get their water turned back on. "I was angry. The people affected by this—mostly Black, mostly women—look like me. I read about it and I couldn't sit by." Tiffani thought back to 2014, when she first heard about the decision by the Detroit Water and Sewer Department (DWSD) to cut off water service to thousands of people who were behind on their bills.

Tiffani looked me in the eye and picked up her water glass. "Imagine not having this. You can't drink, you can't cook. Can't shower. You can't wash your children. Or take your medicine. You can't use the toilet. For weeks. Months." I looked at my own water glass. Californians live in a perpetual drought/deluge cycle, so we tend to think about water. But what Tiffani was describing was of a different scale and cause. This wasn't nature's work; this was a set of policy decisions that were making people poorer. And making them sicker. And ruining families.

"They take your children," Tiffani continued. "You have to have running water for your house to be seen as a safe household for kids. So people who get sick and miss payments, people whose pipes leak and can't afford a plumber, unemployed people—their water gets cut off and then the state takes their kids!" She's soft-spoken, but her voice rose in pitch, if not volume, and she shook her head in disbelief. Tiffani's eyes held me tight. I let this sink in. The government cuts off people's water for getting behind on government bills, and then another government agency comes and takes their children. Disgusted as I was by the moral elements of this story, I was also stunned by how little practical sense it made. "That's not right," Tiffani said. "Water is life, and providing it is a basic city function. This is about human dignity. I had to help." The DWSD has some of the most expensive rates for water service of any city in the country, and it charges high interest rates on overdue bills. In 2014, fifty thousand water accounts were overdue, and DWSD shut off service to 28,500 of them.[2] Everything about this is broken.

Born into a military family, Tiffani grew up all over the United States. She went to high school in North Carolina and taught herself software programming skills as a preteen, before taking computer science classes in high school. By the time she got to Howard University, she knew she wanted to be a software developer. Right out of college, she created an app for small businesses, and then she turned to public service, joining Code for America in Atlanta. That's where she was when she heard about the water in Detroit.

Within a weekend, Tiffani and a friend, Kristy Tillman, had written the basic plan for what started as the Detroit Water Project and is now known as the Human Utility. Most of the bills people owed were small, as it was city policy to disconnect accounts that were $150 or sixty days in arrears.[3] Tiffani and Kristy reached out to their networks to raise money, use it to pay off the overdue water bills, and get families' taps flowing again. In a matter of days, they built a basic website via which anyone could pledge a few dollars (or more) to help.

By this time, outrage over DWSD's shutoffs had captured the media's attention. Alerted by local welfare advocates, the United Nations sent a delegation to Detroit in October 2014 to investigate, referring to it as a humanitarian crisis.[4] As the news coverage ramped up, pledges started to roll into the nascent project. Kristy and Tiffani hadn't even finished the paperwork to establish a nonprofit bank account (the Human Utility is now a sponsored project of a 501(c)(3)), so they asked people to pledge money—but not to send it yet—while they worked on these details.

As the pledges rolled in, Tiffani turned her attention to the people of Detroit. How were she and Tillman, based in Atlanta and the Bay Area, going to pay people's bills in Detroit? Other people's bills. And lots of them. How were they going to find and build trust with the people who actually needed help?

This was hard. The financial help started rolling in as soon as word about the site went out on social media. "But the people who needed help, they weren't sitting in front of computers all day." After just three days, they had money, but no families to help. "Then one of Kristy's friends posted on Facebook and we had forty people the next morning who signed up for help."[5] They quickly got to work contacting people in Detroit, assuring them that the help was real. They began gathering bills to pay.

Tiffani thought to try the analog version of social media: postcards. She used the US Postal Service's website to identify the zip codes and postal routes assigned to the neighborhoods where water shutoffs were happening. She ordered 150 postcards from a print/mail shop that detailed how to apply for help. The printer was so taken by the effort that they made and mailed 350 more cards than Tiffani had ordered. This experiment resulted in five hundred postcards being mailed to houses in the 48228 zip code and generated a few requests for help. Tiffani kept trying—reaching out to churches, nonprofits, and schools in the area to spread the word. Working at the speed of social media to raise money, within weeks they had

$600,000 in pledges, which Kristy and Tiffani tracked in a spreadsheet. At the same time, they were moving at the speed of postcards, word of mouth, and trust to find families and households who would believe that two strangers and a website were going to pay off the bills.

Five years later, the Human Utility is working at both speeds. The organization continues to raise funds from the public, most of whom are not in Detroit or even in Michigan. "They give for religious reasons, out of outrage and anger, or to 'stick it to the man.' Some people remember growing up without heat, or they know someone else who did," Tiffani tells me. "And our donors are loyal. We have a recurring donation program, called the TAP. People give ten dollars a month or more. And they tell their friends." The Human Utility has paid more than one thousand bills, keeping families together and in their homes, and Tiffani is now able to focus on research, advocacy, and policy engagement to change how cities charge for water.

CROWDFUNDING AS GIVING INFRASTRUCTURE

The Human Utility is just one of many crowdfunding platforms in the givingscape. You've probably heard stories of remarkable amounts of money being raised online: The social media post that motivated $25 million in contributions to pay bonds for asylum-seeking families separated at the US border. The crowdfunding campaign for people in Houston that had eighty-three thousand donors within a few hours of Hurricane Harvey hitting the city. Or the global phenomenon called Giving Tuesday, a one-day giving campaign set on the Tuesday after (American) Thanksgiving—which has facilitated more than $4 billion in giving since starting in 2012. You may also know of, have given to, or even run one of the hundreds of thousands of GoFundMe campaigns to help a neighbor, a friend, a family member, or even a stranger. Between March and May of 2020, during the early months of the COVID-19 pandemic, the CEO of GoFundMe noted that the platform was being used first for protective equipment for frontline workers, then for employee and small business relief, and then for food, shelter, mental health, and burial expenses. That trajectory mirrors both the trail of the pandemic and what one would have expected to see functioning public systems providing.[6]

Crowdfunding has become an infrastructural part of the givingscape. There are crowdfunding platforms for every choice. Some only support schoolteachers; some are just for water bills. Others are more open, supporting artists, product designers, writers, activists, or specific campaigns run by nonprofits. In 2015, the Smithsonian raised more than $750,000 to pay conservation costs for spacesuits worn by astronauts Alan Shepard and Neil Armstrong.[7] By 2020, museums and nonprofits—as well as bookstores, cafés, and cobblers—across the United States were hoping crowdfunding could help them keep their doors open.

Most crowdfunding campaigns succeed not on the basis of the platform, but on the hard work of the person or people organizing the campaign. Their ability to reach out, build excitement, and motivate friends of friends and then the next circle out from there is what makes the small donations add up. Disasters, as we will discuss in chapter 9, and other events that get a lot of media attention are surefire catalysts for crowdfunding campaigns. Being good at pulling on strangers' heartstrings is an important part of these efforts.

But browsing through GoFundMe feels like perusing other people's pain. Crowdfunding for people's basic needs is morally confusing. How do you choose which person to support in the aftermath of a fire or mass shooting or during a pandemic? What criteria would help you choose between two people with different life-threatening illnesses? There's something unsettling and inherently unjust about using a website to weigh decisions that influence the life and death of other people. And so we do what we've always done: we give to those who ask us or to those we know.

From the giver's perspective, crowdfunding taps into some basic human instincts. The social element of giving is one of its most interesting characteristics—you do something for others, enjoy yourself and feel good, and may even attract others to join you. Biologists who study altruism and what's called *prosocial* behavior see this as one of the ways in which our individual actions and happiness are interwoven with our collective actions and happiness (or at least survival). Giving is, and always has been, a social act. We give to be part of something, and we give because we're asked to. The design of crowdfunding campaigns, their dependence on social media, incentives, online networks, thank-you gifts, and celebrations makes it feel like you're part of something, even if you never meet any of the other givers (or the recipient) in person.

BEHIND THE SCREEN

The Human Utility is a carefully curated crowdfunding platform, focused only on a specific issue in designated locations. Well-known platforms such as GoFundMe, Indiegogo, Kickstarter, and Patreon are more generalized, hosting nearly every type of project imaginable. For the Human Utility, Tiffani and her team of three make sure donations are used to pay off water bills. In this case, the technology platform and the people who run it are actively involved in making each project (paying each water bill) succeed. This is unusual. In most cases, the platforms are distinct from the projects listed on them.

Each project on Kickstarter or GoFundMe is designed and run by a different person or group who is responsible for developing the idea, posting the ask, reaching out to their social networks to ask for money, and deciding what, if any, perks to offer donors. They are also responsible for thanking the people who give, communicating the results, and carrying out whatever action was promised. A recent scan through these sites uncovered fundraising calls for developing a new kind of dog toy; feeding hungry women and children in Yemen; creating customizable, light-up doormats; paying surgical costs for a beloved school bus driver; launching a café using only coffee beans from Chiapas, Mexico; providing physical therapy for a gunshot victim; and offering self-defense training to families in Chapel Hill, North Carolina.[10]

Not only are the projects diverse, but there are also different business models behind each crowdfunding platform. These business models hold clues to the organizing incentives and priorities of the different companies. Those that are run by nonprofits, like the Human Utility, can focus on a single service. Those that are investor-funded need to get as big as they can, as fast as they can, to start earning profits to pay back their investors.

Crowdfunding platforms are used to facilitate all kinds of public-purpose actions, from rebuilding after disasters to raising funds for charity or building public infrastructure like bike lanes and community gardens. When these funds are raised the "old-fashioned way," through offline fundraisers or the issuance of public bonds, there are protocols and reporting mechanisms to protect the public's interest in knowing where the money comes from and where it goes. Just because some of the funds are now raised on crowdfunding platforms doesn't mitigate the public's interest in that information, but it does make it harder to ensure we can find out. That information (and much more) is now contained within the data that each platform generates and holds on to with every transaction. The different business models incentivize different approaches to managing, reporting, or sharing that data.

Kickstarter went live in April 2009, had a million "backers" by 2011, and hosted its first million-dollar project (a project called Double Fine Adventure) in 2012.[11] As of 2019, more than sixteen million people had pledged money on the site; five million of those are repeat backers. Nearly half a million projects have been launched and 168,000 of them have reached their funding goals, collectively raising more than $4 billion.[12]

Underlying all of this fundraising is a company: Kickstarter, PBC, owned by three founding partners. They originally incorporated the company, raised $10 million in venture capital in 2011, and reincorporated in 2015 as a public benefit corporation (hence the PBC at the end of the name). As a PBC, the company is a commercial enterprise with a set of publicly stated values and intentions that go beyond being profitable. In Kickstarter's case, these values include building tools to help creators achieve their visions, trying to limit the environmental impact of its services, hiring and promoting an inclusive and diverse staff, and "not lobby[ing] or campaign[ing] for public policies unless they align with its mission and values, regardless of possible economic benefits to the company."[13] Despite this progressive posturing, Kickstarter management fought against its employees' (ultimately successful) efforts to unionize and it carefully curates the information it shares publicly about projects and donations.

Other crowdfunding sites, such as GlobalGiving and DonorsChoose, are run by nonprofits. They follow the same public reporting rules as other nonprofits, and both GlobalGiving and DonorsChoose have shared their data with researchers. Still others, such as GoFundMe, are commercial corporations built on venture capital investments. GoFundMe stands out among other crowdfunding platforms as the place to go to raise money for individual needs, such as medical or housing assistance. Since its founding in 2010, the company reports that its platform has been used for more than one hundred and fifty million donations, totaling more than $5 billion, and one-third of all the fundraisers on GoFundMe are for personal medical expenses.[14]

Crowdfunding platforms are structured as commercial businesses, nonprofits, and everything in between, yet they provide similar services and operate in essentially the same way. Crowdfunding campaigns are designed to aggregate lots of small contributions. Individuals pledge to contribute a certain amount, but they don't need to pay until the campaign creator has received pledges for the entire project budget. Once a budget is reached, the campaigns keep all the money they've raised, except for the fees that the platforms charge for hosting. These fees are all remarkably similar, hovering around 5 percent of a project's total budget, plus credit card transaction fees and small fees on each donation. Individual projects succeed by being able to raise small amounts from lots of people; crowdfunding platforms succeed by convincing lots of people to host their projects and aggregating lots of small fees.

The different business structures matter in terms of what information they make public. Those that are organized as nonprofits file the same public documents as other US nonprofits and may make the data generated on their platforms available to researchers. Kickstarter (the public benefit corporation) reports some data in aggregate, such as the numbers of campaigns and total funds raised. Commercial platforms like GoFundMe release the least amount of information, instead making unverifiable claims about dollars raised at the end of each year.

Just the platforms named in this chapter take credit for having moved more than $9 billion. That's a lot of money. But for most of the platforms, we have to take their word for what they've done; without access to the data, there's no way to verify what they claim. Given how pervasive crowdfunding has become, it's time that policymakers and researchers get reliable access to what's happening with all that money.

As the use of these platforms has grown, so have the problems. In response to fraudulent campaigns, for example, GoFundMe now offers a donor protection guarantee so that people can get their money back if the campaign they supported turns out to be a scam. The first consumer protection lawsuit against a crowdfunding project was filed and won in 2014, and since then the National Association of Attorneys General and the Federal Trade Commission have issued guidance, filed suits, and worked together to determine appropriate oversight of these companies.[15] In 2020, the California Association of Nonprofits worked on legislation that would have required crowdfunding platforms to abide by established practices for responsible nonprofit fundraising.[16] The range of business models, from nonprofit to venture capital–backed start-ups, and the different types of fundraising that they support, from personal to charitable to business investments, make things particularly challenging for regulators. Crowdfunding companies cross all of the preexisting boundaries between nonprofit and commercial organizations and between charitable giving, consumer spending, and investing.

CROWDFUNDING AND COMMUNITY BUILDING: IOBY

Some crowdfunding platforms, such as Ioby, are more about the crowd than they are about the funding. Ioby, which stands for *in our backyards*, is a way for neighbors to work together on local issues. Erin Barnes, one of its three cofounders, explains that the money-raising side of Ioby is just part of the picture. The real goal of Ioby is to help people step up and take action in their communities, something that requires time, courage, and conviction and maybe a little money.

Paradoxically, the interest in helping neighbors came out of experiences Erin and her cofounders had as graduate students in a program that required them to spend time overseas. "So, all of us were basically shipped off to different places to do research, and the thing that struck [us was that] whatever we were supposed to contribute as field experts, to the people living in these places, was meaningless," Erin remembers. "The knowledge that people had of their own places was just extraordinarily more important than whatever some supposed White, American graduate student was going to offer them. I think that this, for us, this bizarre bias of feeling like you can help somebody far away, where you actually have almost no information whatsoever about the local context, but the idea that for some reason outside expertise is going to help you, just struck us all as absurd."

The challenge was reconciling proximity and local knowledge with the power of an online platform. Eventually, the pitch that worked to get them the start-up money they needed to launch Ioby was to refer to it as "Kiva, but local." This captured only part of what they were after, however. What they hoped to do was help people who wanted to improve their local communities. For many people, the biggest barriers to taking those steps aren't necessarily financial, as these projects often don't cost very much. The opportunity was in making fundraising easy enough that people wouldn't let it stop them from navigating their local systems and making change happen.

Unlike other crowdfunding platforms, Ioby provides people with tips to work with their local government, as many of the projects are about street safety, clean parks, bike lanes, and other neighborhood issues. Ioby has an "etiquette guide" for working with government officials, tips on navigating bureaucracy, and helpful hints on asking permission, as well as how to bring people together without formal city permits or other requirements that can be deal breakers for some communities. Tips and tricks from people in one community are available for people in other parts of the country who may have questions about permits, planning, or marketing. Community action liaisons are on the ground in five US cities, helping community groups plan and implement their projects.

Reverend Eleanor Williams, a retired special education teacher, pastor, and neighborhood activist in North Pittsburgh, has run three campaigns on Ioby. "It works, and they help us," she states very simply. The Northside Partnership spent years negotiating with the Pittsburgh school district to use an abandoned school building as a community resource hub. The small crowdfunding campaigns that the partnership ran during this time allowed the already active volunteers to reach out to friends, raise little bits of money, and show progress while the bigger, more complicated negotiations were going on.[17] Ioby enables the partnership to keep reaching out, building the network of people who support it. Because Ioby is designed to help people build community, they have staff people dedicated to helping organizers such as Reverend Williams use the data from their campaigns to build their networks. Where other platforms take donors' data (email addresses) as their own, Ioby is designed so that projects can use that information to stay in touch, keep people up to date, and get people involved.

Yancy Villa, a Mexican American artist in Memphis, had just such an experience. "I was raised to work and then you earn money. You don't go and ask for money." Yancy's project, *Barrier Free*, is a traveling sculpture installation that entices people to see themselves in community together, to reach out to each other and tear down the (literal and figurative) walls between us. It's an example of artivism—a mixture of art and activism. The work consists of a series of life-size photographs printed on white screens— the size and shape of the portable barriers that are used in malls or airports to redirect pedestrians around construction zones. The portraits show people from Memphis—people of many races, ethnicities, and abilities, some standing alone, others in every possible arrangement of family and friends.

Placed near these winding mobile screens are statues made to look like real people by using three-dimensional prints of photographs. Both the mobile wall and the statues include quotes from the people pictured—who they are, why they participated, how they feel about their community and place in Memphis. There's room for viewers to write their thoughts and add them to the wall. Yancy had no idea what would happen when she put out calls for people to participate. Would anyone show up? Would they be afraid to be seen? As it happened, people came from all over the city. She thought the installation would last for a year, "but people keep coming. They want to see it and be in it. Museums want to host it. We're taking it to other states. Ioby made this possible."[18]

Ioby is focused on neighbors, but some of its most important partners turned out to be city agencies. It launched in New York with support from the Office of Long-term Planning and Sustainability and within a year had a similar relationship with the Office of Sustainability in Miami-Dade County. At the same time that Erin and her cofounders were out talking to people on the streets and in community meetings about what it would take for them to bring their ideas to fruition, the civic tech movement was kicking into high gear. *Civic tech* is a wide-ranging term for projects that aim to help governments use technology to better serve their constituents.[19]

These projects were often designed with and for professionals in city governments, and many of them were about improving services. The government "customers" of the civic tech efforts were all trying to reach out to residents, and Ioby was reaching out to residents to help them get things done in their cities. "We're the other side of the civic tech coin," Erin says. "[Ioby] was designed to encourage people to step up, and I think a lot of governments continue to reach out to us, because they feel like they don't have enough capacity to actually be able to meaningfully engage their constituents."

Yancy Villa's experience in Memphis bears this out. A year after launching the *Barrier Free* project, Yancy submitted a project to the Memphis City Planning Department. "City planners have hard times connecting to communities; they wanted help reaching community members to provide input into planning. [I can help them] use art to connect neighbors to the city planning process." She'd like to do more. Yancy wonders, What if artists could help cities not just plan for creativity but creatively plan? She's hoping her work will "integrate art and creativity into the processes of how the city works. Not just what you're seeing, but offer a new, creative way to be in the governmental process."[20]

Ioby's projects are more about civic and political engagement than money. Ioby is a civic engagement program masquerading as a crowdfunding platform. It focuses on relationships before, during, and after a project, and it provides supports such as community liaisons that crowdfunding platforms focused on efficiency and scale will never offer. For Ioby, the campaigns that matter are not just the ones that fulfill their fundraising goals, but the ones in which individuals take action, realize they can change things, and rally others to do the same. While other platforms focus on the funding, Ioby focuses on the crowd.

LATINO COMMUNITY FOUNDATION GIVING CIRCLES: CHANGING CHARITY

"Before we get started let's take a moment to think of the people who made it possible for us to be here today." As she says this, Masha Chernyak, who until this moment hasn't stopped hugging and smiling and greeting people, lowers her voice and speaks slightly slower than before. There's a pause and the room goes quiet; the only sound is the buzz of the fluorescent lights. "All right!" Masha says, her voice back to its above-the-party volume. "This is the fun part, when you all come together, all the work you've done all year. Get ready to welcome our guests, our community. Here we go."

It's a Thursday evening in a suburban office park. The temperature is just beginning to drop from a high in the mid-90s. Two dozen or so business-attire clad people crowd into a set of offices used by a charter school during the day. The fluorescent lighting and office desks clash a bit with the abundant food and music. Cans of soda, a few bottles of wine, and one of tequila are available on a back table, near the copy machine and recycling bin. Tonight, members of the Contra Costa Latino Giving Circle are meeting with three community groups. Two people from each group, an elder and a younger leader, get time to talk about their programs and answer questions from the people in the room. The process is as orderly as any pitch session or demo day, although the warmth and friendliness filling the room distinguishes this gathering from similar settings defined by competition. Each presenter seems to know a few of the people in the giving circle. Each pitch is met with hugs and laughter all around. The presenters are there to raise funds for youth soccer groups and leadership programs. As they finish their pitches, members of the giving circle clap loudly, thank them, complement them on their work, and call out, "Why don't you join us?" The pitching is going both ways—community members seeking funds for their programs and the giving circle recruiting future participants. "We're *familia*" is probably the phrase I hear most frequently over the course of the evening.

The Contra Costa Latino Giving Circle is one of hundreds, possibly thousands, of such groups around the country. The idea is simple. People come together, pool some money, and make decisions together about using the funds. On that hot summer evening in Walnut Creek, California, the focus was on programs that help young people. The giving circle members are Latinx, the community groups are led by Latinx neighbors, and the young people served by the programs are mostly, though not exclusively, Latinx. Other giving circles focus on international giving, women's issues, African Americans, LGBTQ communities, Jewish groups, Muslim groups, Christian groups, environmental groups, and every imaginable combination of these.

By the end of the evening, the circle members have decided how much money to give to each group. There are quiet sidebar conversations about politics, a bit of professional networking, a few toasts, and a lot of laughter. "I knew we could do it," says Natalie Tocino, who sits across the table from me. "This is our first round. We can do so much more."[21] I ask Natalie how the group got started. "I did it," she says. "I volunteer with a group that got money from a Latina circle in San Francisco. I asked that circle how to start one over here. They told me to find fifteen people who can each give $1,000 a year. So I did. And look at us." I smiled. I'd counted twenty-three people sitting at the tables around us.

Not all community giving needs an online platform. Latinos are the largest demographic group in California, but they still hold few positions of public, private, or philanthropic power. The statewide Latino Community Foundation (LCF) is focused on changing that. One of its most successful tools for doing so has been supporting the Latino Giving Circle Network, which includes groups like the one in Contra Costa County.

Giving circles have been around for generations but have captured the attention of philanthropic and political researchers in the last few decades.[22] The idea is simple: a group of people gets together, pools money, and makes joint decisions about how to give it. Some giving circles require monthly contributions of four dollars per person; others raise thousands or tens of thousands of dollars. At least one US giving circle has an individual contribution level of $2 million per year![23] The key is not the amount of money, but the process of coming together and making shared decisions. Giving circles exist in every state and in Puerto Rico, and networks such as Amplifier, the Community Investment Network, and Philanthropy Together are emerging to help people start their own.[24] People organize these groups by just about any identifier you can imagine, including age, religion, ethnicity, gender, and employer. There are so many individual giving circles that they've developed shared networks to connect them across geographies.

The Latino Community Foundation's giving circle network includes twenty groups across California. Several have emerged out of corporate-sponsored employee groups. As Amber Gonzalez-Vargas, who coordinates the giving circle network for LCF, notes, "For a lot of [corporate employee groups], there's not much of intentionality with the gatherings. A lot of the times, it's a taco Tuesday during Hispanic Heritage Month and that's it."[25] In contrast, when these people start working together to give, they have a reason to meet on a regular basis. They get to work on something that matters to them individually and collectively. These groups naturally tend to catalyze other groups, Amber notes. The first giving circle the foundation sponsored was created by professional Latinas in San Francisco. After it had been running for a few months, their male counterparts wanted a circle of their own. Soon people wanted circles in the East Bay and the San Francisco Peninsula. The foundation took the idea and ran with it. "I'm from

Stockton," Amber says, "and we're a statewide foundation. We're getting circles going in the Central Valley and down south."

These circles give away money, but just as raising money together is a means to an end for Ioby, the money is one step in the larger aspiration of the giving circle members and the Latino Community Foundation. "This is about change, not charity," says Masha Chernyak, vice president at LCF. "People bring their whole selves to these meetings. They bring their traditions from home, and realize they've been 'philanthropists' all along, just in ways that aren't recognized here in the United States. Remittances, mutual aid, serving on boards—these are all ways of giving."[26]

Masha is a Russian immigrant who learned Spanish from Cubans in St. Petersburg, and Amber is a Peruvian American born in Stockton, California. The giving circles are about community and collective power. The members teach each other and treat their money and the nonprofits they fund as part of the circle. Many giving circle members join boards of the nonprofits they fund and seek to be the connectors between these Latino community organizations and the bigger, whiter nonprofits and foundations in the state.

Once the circle members get to know and trust each other, they start doing more than giving.[27] Living up to their aspiration of "change, not charity," they discuss the news, power, politics, and public policy. Before the 2020 Census, people who had met through a LCF giving circle organized their own study sessions to learn more about the Trump administration's proposed citizenship question and how decennial census numbers affect state and federal budgets. People organized themselves to reach out to rural Spanish-speakers, recent immigrants, and multigeneration Californians about their fears associated with the count. These offshoot political groups invited candidates to speak to them and mobilized across California for a get-out-the-vote effort. Tech workers and farm workers, professionals and homemakers, students and elders come together in these circles and across the network. Members help members within and beyond the circles, creating new networks around politics and employment. "They're becoming philanthropists," Amber and Masha tell me. "But we are also changing what philanthropist means."

4 GIVING IS POLITICAL

Democracy is a form of government designed around crowds. Elected officials earn legitimacy, at least in theory, because they're selected by a majority of voters. As long as democracies depend on "one person, one vote," large groups of people aligning their votes can make a difference. If organized and channeled toward political action, numbers are a source of power.

Of course, real life is never as neat as theory. All too often, those who gain power start changing the rules so they can hold on to it. Democracies are designed to be run by majorities. To prevent tyranny, they must also protect and sustain a space for the ideas, expressions, beliefs, and gathering of those not in the majority. That's where civil society, and philanthropy, come into play.

Elected officials, acting (theoretically) in the interests of the majority of voters, determine what gets done in the name of "the public." Education, health care, infrastructure, and public safety are large, familiar categories of services that are administered by democratically elected governments. How much, for whom, and at what cost are the details that separate one set of political choices from another. By shaping what the public sector does or doesn't do, our political choices indirectly influence what gets done, by whom, and how in the adjacent civil society spaces of community action, nonprofits, charity, and philanthropy.

If theory holds, public decisions should reflect the interests of a majority of voters. People may choose to extend the public priorities by dedicating their voluntary contributions in ways that align with the public choices (augmenting the budgets of public schools or hospitals, for example). Or we may choose to provide options not being provided by the majority system (e.g., by supporting religious schools or churches). We can also choose to direct our attention to create alternatives to, or pathways into, the public system (which is where advocacy or political protest comes in). And many of us get involved to fill gaps that public choices don't address, perhaps prioritizing cultural expression, celebrating certain traditions, or fighting for fair treatment and equitable inclusion within discriminatory public systems. There are many different options, but most of them are influenced to varying degrees by the shape and scope of either government decisions or the desire for something not available in the marketplace.

Since the 1980s, the primary policy trends in the United States at the national level have been lowering taxes on wealthy individuals and corporations and allowing them more leeway in their operations (deregulation). During this same time period, wages for workers have stagnated, the wealth gap has reached unprecedented proportions, and wealth in Black communities has been systematically destroyed. A 2018 economic study found that "no progress has been made in reducing income and wealth inequalities between Black and White households over the past 70 years" and that the ratio of White family wealth to Black family wealth is higher now than it was one hundred years ago.[1] The policy choices that enable the accumulation of wealth and some big philanthropy come at the expense of shared prosperity and functioning public systems. There's been a fairly remarkable celebration of the former without simultaneous consideration of the latter.

Political action and voluntary philanthropic choices are dynamically linked. What happens in the public sector shapes what people do in the social sector. And what happens in the social sector may align with, oppose, or stand as an alternative to those public priorities. As Rob Reich, author of *Just Giving*, argues, we pass and enforce laws in the public sector that draw the boundaries of civil society and philanthropy. The laws, corporate structures, and rules that delineate and privilege certain types of giving are artifacts of the public sector.[2] The actions associated with political organizing, running for office, and voting and those we take as community organizers, issue advocates, or service providers are distinct, but the spheres in which they happen interact with and influence each other. And our own individual giving—of time, money, or data—cuts across these two spheres. Increasingly, our giving is also linked to the marketplace, to how we shop or invest, which we'll discuss in coming chapters.

BLURRY BOUNDARIES

The lines between political and charitable action are not very clear. Here's an example: Perhaps you care about high school students having artistic opportunities. Many public schools no longer provide art or music classes as a regular part of the school day, and often those that do have to raise the money to do so from donations, not from the regular school budget. Parents, students, and teachers will raise money for the arts by selling ads in a program, hosting fundraising events, even going door to door to sell tickets. The students put on shows to demonstrate their work and to raise awareness and more support. In the course of all this, some of the people they'll reach out to will be school administrators and school board members. The students may even speak at school board meetings, trying to convince the board to augment the arts budget. Where exactly in this scenario should the lines be drawn between raising awareness for teen art programs by providing them, advocating for more such opportunities, and influencing policy on school programming? Those lines are unclear. And success in any one of these actions depends on and influences success in the others. Defining some of these actions as charitable and some as political matters in theory and in the law, but for the sake of arts education they're all necessary.

If you're concerned enough to do one (raise awareness), chances are you're also interested in doing the other (change the relevant public policy). But most of us don't take those next steps. In a time largely defined by increased polarization and a news cycle that makes it nearly impossible to avoid politics, only a tiny percentage of the US population engages in the political process in meaningful ways. According to Eitan Hersh, political scientist at Tufts University, "Among daily news consumers in 2016, less than 4 percent reported doing any work whatsoever on behalf of a campaign or party that election year. Even among those who reported that they were afraid of Donald Trump, only 5 percent reported that they did any work to support their side."[3] The Bureau of Labor Statistics runs time studies on how adults in the United States spend our time. On average—across race, sex, and age—twenty minutes a day is spent on civic, organizational, or religious activities.[4] That's a broad category and not a lot of time. How can we make those minutes really matter?

Some issues are so all-encompassing that they require every type of action possible. In the fight for racial justice, for example, all tactics are on the table and all types of action matter. Rashad Robinson, executive director of Color Of Change, exemplifies how weaving together political and charitable choices (as well as consumption and investing) and giving people options for small and big actions (alone and together) add up to change.

POLITICAL ACTION: COLOR OF CHANGE

Rashad has been involved in politics since going to the polls with his grandfather on the far-eastern shore of Long Island, New York. He grew up in Riverhead, a farming town with a large Polish population, located seventy-six miles east of Manhattan at the last exit on the Long Island Expressway. "As a kid, I'd go into the voting booth with my grandfather and read out the candidates' names," Rashad tells me. "I couldn't pronounce many of the Polish names, they're not always phonetic. Granddad would correct me, and then pull the lever to mark his vote." His family talked politics, race, and sports at the dinner table. "My grandfather moved to New York from Southern Virginia. He supported the Mets, because the Yankees had passed on Jackie Robinson."[5]

Rashad took this political awareness with him to Riverhead High School. The town had only a small African American population when Rashad was growing up. He realized early on that shops would let in groups of White kids and then forbid more than one Black student at a time from coming in to buy chips and soda. Rashad learned at a young age that race was a factor in who ran for office, who got to play professional baseball, and who could shop where.

Today, Rashad runs Color Of Change. Van Jones and James Rucker founded the organization after Hurricane Katrina, as a response to the damage done to New Orleans's African American population by the ineffective and insufficient government response to the storm. They modeled the group on MoveOn, where Rucker had previously worked. Rashad joined Color Of Change in 2011, after leading media strategy for GLAAD.

Rashad has helped grow the membership of Color Of Change to more than seven million people. Membership costs four dollars. You can sign on to their advocacy efforts, share their campaigns, and add your voice without being a member. Color Of Change uses the web, email, online petitions, social media, and online donations to quickly aggregate the voices of African Americans and allied racial justice advocates. Digital tools make it easy to reach large numbers of people. In-person meetings organized by members across the country make the work small, personal, and fun.

Color Of Change helps people take both charitable and political action. It helps get corrupt elected officials out of office by raising funds for opponents, it organizes people to make phone calls and sign petitions, and it holds brunches where members eat, talk, and send text messages to get voters to the polls. The Color Of Change community has spearheaded consumer boycotts of companies that advertise on television shows, websites, and radio programs that traffic in race baiting or xenophobia. The organization helps mobilize people to boycott and draws media attention to the numbers of people who've signed on. Meanwhile, staff work behind the scenes with advertisers to impress upon them the power of African American consumers and the changes they want.

Color Of Change confronts head-on the complexities of fighting for justice. Social media helped the organization grow as big as it has, and its strategists know the power of digital connections. The organization was also fully aware of the Janus-faced nature of media platforms—specifically, Facebook—which enable connection while also spreading lies, harm, and racist tropes. In 2020, Color Of Change and several civil rights organizations ended several years' worth of effort to convince, cajole, and work with Facebook on it is policies about hate speech and political propaganda. Having convinced the company to conduct a civil rights audit, it couldn't get senior leadership of the company to abide by either the audit's findings or the coalition's demands. The result was to organize a massive advertiser boycott of the platform. The #StopHateForProfit boycott involved more than 1,100 advertisers in July, 2020.[6] Like many boycotts (see chapter 7), the financial hit to Facebook was miniscule, but the effort contributed to a growing public reckoning about not just the social media giant but also the role of big technology corporations in democracies. Public policy reckoning is still slow in the United States, but the "techlash" took a giant step forward when civil rights groups got involved. By late 2020 state and federal governments in the United States were filing lawsuits against Facebook and Google—a far cry from the kid-glove treatment afforded the technology giants for the preceding decade.

The staff of Color Of Change leads on some issues, but the organization also depends on—and makes it easy for—their members to take the lead. Taking full advantage of the power of networks, members suggest issues, develop petitions, and organize at the local, state, and national levels. Members get together locally to have coffee or drinks, watch political debates, and send mass mailings of postcards or text messages. At the same time, the organization's staff and fundraising capacities are structured to work at a national level, representing the full force of 1.7 million people, each of whom is a potential giver, voter, and customer.

Color Of Change represents a hybrid option in the givingscape. Color Of Change is one community, supported by two organizations. To comply with tax law, it operates both a (c)(3) and a (c)(4). When Color Of Change is raising funds for a policy issue, it clearly communicates that the actions are political and the donations aren't tax deductible. When they're raising funds to educate consumers, on the other hand, they use a different accounting system and provide tax receipts to all givers. The different technology platforms are mostly invisible to the giver, but the language on the sites and the provision of a tax receipt help Color Of Change and the donor keep track (if she's so inclined). Color Of Change has to keep two sets of records, one for political reporting and one for charity.

Color Of Change runs two systems to make things as easy as possible for donors and to respect the law. Many other organizations—working on every kind of issue—do the same thing to manage their charitable (c)(3) and their political (c)(4). While it may seem like overkill to run two different systems, it's a manifestation of those underpinning values about transparency and privacy.

POLITICAL ACTION: SAFE PASSAGE

I arrived at the office of the Tenderloin Community Benefit District at five minutes to two, ten minutes later than I'd intended. A tall, smiling African American man greeted me once the door was buzzed open. "Hi. I'm looking for Greg or JaLil," I said. "Kate said I could tag along with Safe Passage today."

"Welcome, come join us for orientation. I'm JaLil." I shook his outstretched hand and turned to look where he was pointing with his other arm. "We're just getting started."

JaLil showed me to a table where about a dozen people were gathered, two in motorized wheelchairs. There were people who appeared to be in their twenties and others who were closer to sixty. African American, Latinx, White, and Asian, some with the accents of recent international immigrants and others whose speaking cadence signaled roots in the American south. I introduced myself to the group, but before everyone could respond, JaLil rejoined us and took charge.

Fifteen minutes of orientation followed. A multisided die was rolled from person to person. Each recipient went on to say something to the effect of "team two, southwest corner, Turk and Leavenworth, code orange." They'd then roll the die to someone else, who'd offer up a similarly cryptic sentence. JaLil would gently prompt anyone who skipped over any part of the message, which I eventually realized were walkie-talkie check-in codes. Once everyone had practiced, JaLil sorted people into pairs, double checked his map, and assigned the pairs to different street corners. "You come with me," he said to me. "We'll be roamers today." An older man sitting near me reached behind himself to a coatrack and pulled down a green reflective vest. He handed it to me, saying nothing.

With that, our group of fifteen left the building. We walked together for a few blocks, with JaLil and Greg, another roamer, using walkie talkies to check in with one person from each pair as we did. "Remember, I'm checking on you all the time," JaLil reminds us. "When you hear me on the walkie-talkie, check in. Respond. It's important. I'm going to be checking all through the shift." When we reached the corner of Turk and Jones, one of the vested pairs ducked inside the corner building. They emerged with brooms and began sweeping the street corner. Noting a pile of broken wood and cardboard, one of them called over to JaLil, "Hey, call the cleaners, can you? We need to get this out of the way." JaLil pulled out a cell phone and made a quick call. "They're on their way," he called over to the sweeping man.

I followed JaLil for three more blocks, watching a similar scene at each intersection. One pair from our group was assigned to each intersection. They immediately began talking kindly to people as they cleared any trash on the street, saying hi to shopkeepers, and checking in via walkie-talkie. As we walked, JaLil made eye contact with everyone, greeting people by name regardless of whether they were standing or sitting, paying attention to him, or staring off into space. He always smiled as he repeated, "The kids will be coming soon. Thanks for making way. Children coming soon, thanks for cleaning up." It was now 2:50. "Ten minutes, everybody!" JaLil called out. I could hear Greg's voice coming in over JaLil's walkie-talkie. I realized they weren't talking just to the corner teams, but to everyone within earshot.

That's when I noticed the quiet shift taking place around me. Everyone JaLil had said hello to or who could hear the "ten minutes" call was now packing up their things and moving out of the way. A woman with a bedroll, a two-liter soda bottle, and a dog pushed herself to stand. She looked around where she'd been sitting, knelt to pick up some food wrapping she'd left on the ground, and walked off. Others were a bit slower, but everyone was on the move. I heard JaLil say, "Hey, thanks. The kids will be here soon," to a group of men huddled around a dirty tent. The men began passing the word down the street as they walked, away: "Hey everyone, kids coming. Kids on the way." "It's time," JaLil said to me. "Let's go."

He and I picked up our pace and approached the farthest corner we'd walked to, where one of the vested volunteers in a wheelchair was waiting with a hand counter held high. His partner was standing in the intersection, holding a stop sign in one hand and stretching out her other hand in classic crossing guard fashion. On the opposite corner was a young woman, holding a clipboard and the hand of a small child. Lined up behind her were another ten or so children, waiting for her signal. With a loud "let's go," the vested crossing guard and the young woman led the line of kindergartners into the intersection and across the street. The man in the wheelchair clicked his counter as each child passed and began counting down the seconds until the light changed. "Two, one, that's it, hold it up, wait everyone!" both volunteers shouted. The last of the children scurried to the sidewalk, and I noticed another line forming on the opposite corner. The woman and her line of kids waved thank you to the two volunteers, several said hello to JaLil, and they moved on down the block.

This scene repeated itself for another thirty minutes. Lines of kids came, waited, crossed, and moved on. The volunteer pairs stopped traffic, counted heads, and made sure no one was in the crosswalk when the lights changed. I noticed the traffic seemed to get more aggressive. "It's Friday," the man in the wheelchair told me. "All these cars, rushing to get out of town. Or at least outta the TL." (TL is local shorthand for the Tenderloin.) Turk Street is a one-way straight line connecting the city's business towers downtown with its residential neighborhoods and suburbs to the north and west. "Every day at three, the traffic picks up," JaLil tells me. "All these folks want to beat the traffic to the [Golden Gate] Bridge. Just as the littles get out school." The volunteers had helped clean the sidewalks of drug debris and trash while also protecting the kids from rushing cars. The drug dealers and users had made themselves scarce as the children walked by. It was easy to see why the whole program, known as Safe Passage, was necessary.

TAKING BACK THE STREETS

Neighborhood moms started Safe Passage in response to tragedy. After a missing child scare in 2008, local resident Margarita Mina and her neighbors were determined to find ways to keep their children safe. There were all kinds of threats. Drug users and dealers occupy the neighborhood streets all day, every day. Used needles, trash, and feces fill the gutters. All too often, there is a human being lying still on the sidewalk.

The Tenderloin neighborhood is also home to the highest concentration of children in the city. Somewhere between 2,500 and 3,500 children live here. A missing child is a parent's worst nightmare, but it wasn't only the extreme forms of trauma that moved Margarita and her neighbors to action. They wanted to make their neighborhood a place where going to and from school was safe, not a daily excursion in sadness and trauma.

To achieve this, neighborhood moms took it upon themselves to approach local nonprofit groups, public agencies, and the police. They asked for help. They asked for ideas. They met. And met. And met. Staff people from the housing authority, the park, the Boys & Girls Club, and the local police precinct came. After two years of weekly meetings, the group had identified its core concern—safety—and had agreed to mark out its territory. Its members went door to door, talking to neighbors and other parents. How do you get to school? What route do you take? Where do your kids go after school? What makes you feel safe? They mapped families' paths to school against the street grid. Then they went out and painted the route yellow, sending a clear message to everyone that this is "kid territory," that families live here. The simple act of painting a "yellow brick road" through the area changed the visual and emotional presentation of the TL to residents and outsiders.

But it wasn't enough. Marking the territory made it visible, but it didn't make it safe. Different people had different ideas of what safety meant. Cities are increasingly relying on official eyes on the street in the name of safety: more police, more cameras, more patrol cars. These systems gather information and store it or stream it to remote third parties—sometimes the police, sometimes distant landlords. These measures allow people far away to watch what's going on. They provide a way of documenting and are often sold as preventive. For those outside the neighborhood, the ability to pull camera footage to see what happened offered a sense of keeping a watchful eye.

The people in the neighborhood experience this quite differently. As stated by Tawana Petty, an author, researcher, and community activist with the Detroit Technology Community Project, surveillance equipment makes residents the watched, not the watchers.[7] Surveillance isn't safety, Petty often says, and it's not what the moms wanted.

Eventually, the group landed on the idea of having a group of people help the kids navigate the streets. Trusted adults, on the street, with the kids—that wasn't surveillance, and it might keep kids safe. The question was, Who would do it? The nonprofit and government professionals thought the neighbors would do it. Their response? No way. They lived there. They were not going to risk confronting armed drug dealers or those sleeping rough on the streets, people who they had to pass by every day. Even if things went well one day, who's to say that revenge or retribution wouldn't eventually come?

Finally, a few of the nonprofit staff people offered to escort the kids home from school along the yellow brick road. One of the first people to take up this task was Kate Robinson. At the time, she was a recently returned Peace Corps volunteer working as program staff in one of the housing authority apartment buildings. She remembers feeling culture shock on first coming to the Tenderloin. "I didn't know anything about the place. And while I worked there, I was coming to realize I had no idea what it meant to live there."[8] Keeping with the community's desire for the kids and families to be seen, they borrowed a set of yellow reflective vests, like utility and road repair crews wear. No one knew what to expect. Would the kids come with them? They cleared it with school officials first. Would the drug dealers and sidewalk sitters harass them or make space? Was it even safe to try this?

Wearing their vests, they chose a key intersection. They stood on the corner, and as the kids arrived, in pairs or small groups, the adults called out, "kids coming, coming through," and acted as crossing guards. Some of the drug dealers ignored them; others paid attention. As the call of "kids coming" kept ringing out, some began to move away or at least temporarily hide the tools of their trade. Some of the neighbors who had attended the meetings watched from the windows or the street. But they didn't join in.

The first shift ended. Nothing had happened. Some strange looks had been exchanged, but no one got hurt. Everyone got home safely. Walking back to her office after that first shift, Kate remembers feeling a palpable break in the tension, revealing just how uncertain the whole thing had been. What if they'd been harassed? Ignored? Shot at? Any one of those could have occurred. But nothing had happened. So, maybe, something different was possible.

LISTENING TO LOCAL EXPERTS

A few more shifts were set, and again it was the nonprofit staff who took to the streets. The residents insisted it was not safe for them. Besides, they asked, what was it really doing? Slowly, everyone was realizing that monitoring the corners would only make a difference if it happened as a regular and reliable thing. An occasional gathering on the street corners wasn't going to change the kids' experiences, nor was it going to have much impact on the street corner's habitués.

The adults finally asked some young people for their advice. They asked a group of teens from the Boys & Girls Club for their ideas. The adults had already borrowed some of the club's tools when they created the yellow brick road, including a safety code. This code allowed the club members to communicate with each other when something was going on, without having to shout out the details. A code orange, for example, might mean there was a medical problem and that emergency responders needed to be called. The volunteers borrowed this language when they were on the street corners, allowing them to discuss and triage the different events they were witnessing, from public defecation to drug deals to overdoses, without alerting everyone around to what they were saying.

The teenagers made it very clear that the effort would only work if it was there every day. They'd already taken it upon themselves to set up something similar for the younger kids at the club, the youngest of whom were only six. The club closed at 7:00 p.m. Parents had to choose between having the kids stay home all afternoon, to avoid walking through the neighborhood in the evening, or finding a way to pick them up right at closing time. The latter wasn't an option for many working parents. And so the teens, many of whom had grown up facing the same choice, created their own system for walking the younger kids home. One of the things they made sure of was that the system was reliable, so that parents and kids could count on it. That was not only key to making it work, but also key to building a feeling of safety. The dangers of the neighborhood were compounded by uncertainty. While a one-time crossing guard can help a kid cross a street, it doesn't help her feel safe in her neighborhood. Safety required reliability. The monitors had to be there all the time.

From this, the parents and nonprofit staff knew what they had to do: find a way to make the corner monitors dependable. They also needed to cover more corners; one wasn't enough. And ideally, they'd need to find a way to not just wait for the children, but be able to go get them and escort them the whole way. They'd built the yellow brick road; now they needed to be the ones to use it.

TEN YEARS ON THE STREETS

The Tenderloin neighborhood is bounded by tourist-filled Union Square on the east and the gold dome of San Francisco's city hall to the west. Every day, Monday through Friday, at 8:00 a.m. and 2:00 p.m., groups of volunteers leave the office of the Tenderloin Community Benefit District at 512 Ellis Street and fan out across intersections, as they did they day I shadowed JaLil. They sport bright vests, wear walkie-talkies, and carry big, orange signs. They escort parades of small children, who wave and say, "Thank you!" or "Hasta mañana!" to the vested adults. Preceding each cluster of kids is a quiet ripple of adults, clearing themselves and their belongings out of the way so the children can pass. As the children pass the sidewalks behind them close back in. A woman goes back to sitting on the ground. Several men move back from the shadows. The green-vested escorts and the groups of children are like human ice boats, breaking a path through the dangerous reality of their neighborhood streets. The passage lasts just long enough for the kids to get home from school. In their wake, reality returns to the sidewalk.

That Safe Passage has been going on consistently, twice every school day, for ten years, is impressive. This isn't a one-time march or protest, but a daily routine built for safety. One sign of how important the program has become is the support it receives from the local merchants. Safe Passage is now a program of the Tenderloin Community Benefit District, which provides it with office space, funding, and the crossing guard materials it needs. It enables the program to provide stipends to some of the *corner captains*, providing much-needed income to residents of the neighborhood.[9] The corner captains and volunteers temporarily take the corners back from the drug dealers. They negotiate peace, for at least an hour each day, so the little ones can get to and from school without getting shot. When tech companies started moving into the TL, the group recruited company employees to teach them how to collect data and present it to city officials.

One such volunteer built a custom database and trained everyone to use it. After every shift, there's a fifteen-minute debrief, during which each pair reports on the cleanliness of their corner, how many children crossed the street, the approximate number of negative interactions they had with people, and whether they had to call in any security, hazard, or cleanliness codes to the roamers. From these verbal debriefs, they've developed a longitudinal dataset of numbers served and attitudes on the streets—both of which help with building the culture of safety that the founders of the program sought back in 2008.[10] The program has expanded to create Safe Passage Senior, escorting neighborhood elders to the community center and park. Building a culture of safety requires ongoing practice of deep civility among parents, drug dealers, users, and neighbors. It saves lives. And it's been copied across the country.

Safe Passage gathers a lot of numbers. One person in every corner pair uses a hand counter to track crossings. Every pair on each shift reports on five factors having to do with health, safety, and cleanliness. They track if they had to call for the *clean team*, a special maintenance and sanitation crew paid for by the benefit district. They track the presence of police and whether or not anyone from Safe Passage had to call for an ambulance. Volunteers and paid program participants who want to can learn how to enter these numbers into the program's database, pull them out to do aggregate counts, or compare them to previous weeks, years, or other corners. Residents use the data to advocate for more city services. They've bolstered arguments for traffic abatement, enforcement of laws regulating the sale of alcohol, and maintenance of the neighborhood's single public park. For Safe Passage, the time commitment comes first; the data come second.

Time and data often go hand in hand when volunteering. The volunteers of each Safe Passage shift collect and debrief data about the conditions of the neighborhood. Because Safe Passage is focused on making the streets safe for all, it's careful to collect data that can't be connected to a particular person. It tracks issues like calls to the clean team or incidents of violence, but never tracks people's names. These data practices are indicative of the community's complicated relationships with the police and city government. Negotiating safety on the streets requires treating everyone with respect, working with police and drug dealers, and not becoming a potential source of conflict between those already at odds. Safe Passage collects the data it needs to improve its programs and advocate for services, using proxies or rough measures to ensure no volunteer is ever put in the position of documenting individual people. These data collection practices have developed over time, from experiences on the street. They are constructed so that volunteers can gather the data while keeping the children safe. They don't require any visible data collection mechanisms other than hand counters (which track how many, not who), but can still provide useful insights for the program, especially when looked at over time. For safety's sake, Safe Passage asks volunteers not to carry cell phones, cameras, or electronic equipment when they're on their shifts, yet it still manages to collect, store, analyze, and advocate with the data it does gather.

Committed moms got Safe Passage up and running. It now depends on both volunteered time and financial support from the Tenderloin Community Benefit District. Being able to pay TL residents to be corner captains is important. If Safe Passage had to rely on volunteers, it would wind up with many people like me—people with the kinds of jobs that allow them to take two hours out in the middle of a weekday and who don't live in the neighborhood. But Safe Passage is intended to be of, for, and by the TL. This is important in building respect on the streets and for getting things done at city hall. I can best help by following the lead of those in the TL, just as I followed JaLil up and down Turk Street.

5 INVESTING ACROSS GENERATIONS

From colonial times on, some Methodist communities in the United States have refused to invest any funds in slaveholding ventures. Religious Quakers don't invest in weapons manufacturers. Civil rights activism and war protests in the 1960s motivated many communities to align their investments with their missions. At first, this was done by screening out companies that built weapons, those that invested in nuclear power, or those that supported the apartheid-era government in South Africa. By the 1970s, the financial industry was creating products specifically geared toward these "socially responsible investors," including mutual funds "reflecting faith-based values, civil rights-era sensibilities, and environmental concerns."[1]

The socially responsible investment field that developed from these actions has grown significantly. It's also spun off a more activist field, one in which people seek out opportunities to invest in things they want more of rather than just avoiding things they don't want. This field is called *impact investing*, and while most of its money comes from big pension funds and endowments, more and more opportunities are being created for people of modest means.

INVESTING AS REPARATIONS: SOULS GROWN DEEP FOUNDATION

Boykin, Alabama, is home to about three hundred people, almost all African Americans; four churches, three of which are active; one post office;

an elementary school; a ferry terminal; a senior nutrition center; and the Gee's Bend Quilt Collective. Surrounded on three sides by the bridgeless Alabama River, Boykin occupies the tip of an inland peninsula. The nearest store is ten miles distant; the high school and closest town are forty minutes away, whether you drive the thirty-seven miles or take the ferry, which will cost you three dollars each way and runs five times a day. The area has long been known as Gee's Bend, named for the first White resident who settled in the area in 1816. Thirty years later, Mr. Gee's descendants sold the land and its enslaved inhabitants to a cousin named Mark Pettway. Today, Boykin is home to Mary Margaret Pettway, a Black quilter whose skill and artistry goes back at least three generations and whose family history in the area goes back centuries.

"You need a lot of quilts here. Each house has, probably, five beds. Each bed needs four quilts," Mary Margaret tells me. This is the practical, working view of the quilting she's done since she was eleven years old. "Every girl learned to sew and quilt." The value of the quilts is clear; they keep you warm. "All my kids had their own quilts from birth. My daughter had a king-size quilt, which she used into her teens. Wore them right out, wore the backing right off of them."[2]

The value of these quilts as family and household items is timeless and measured in memories. Of course, there are other ways to think about value. Mary Margaret's mother, Lucy Pettway, helped found the Gee's Bend Quilt Collective as a way to capture some of the financial value from these quilts for the women who make them. Her 1981 adaptation of *Birds in the Air*, an abolitionist-era quilt pattern, is now owned by the High Museum of Art in Atlanta. Pettway's unique twist on a design that was once used to mark safe houses on the Underground Railroad inspires quilters like her daughter, as well as artists around the world. In 2016, fashion designer Michelle Smith reproduced the pattern and coloring of Pettway's quilt for the dress former first lady Michelle Obama wears in her official portrait hanging in the National Portrait Gallery. Gee's Bend quilts are now recognized as valuable art works, cultural treasures, and historic symbols. Just as value takes many forms, its financial benefits accrue to many people. The women who founded the quilt collective did so as a way to profit from their skills. Mary Margaret continues that quest today, seeking financial investments that will not only keep the art form alive, but also help the artists and their children stay in this place they've called home for two hundred years.

REPAIRING HARM DONE

It's not often (enough) that a discussion about art collecting and museums turns out to really be a conversation about reparations for slavery. Nor do most inquiries about endowment investing turn toward questions of righteousness. If Mary Margaret Pettway, Max Anderson, and other board members of the Souls Grown Deep Foundation (which includes actor and activist Jane Fonda) are successful, both frames will become more common.

Several decades ago, a White Atlanta art collector named Bill Arnett started buying quilts from the women of Gee's Bend, often right out of their houses and off their beds. Arnett later created the Souls Grown Deep Foundation (SGD) to protect and promote the quilts as art. This isn't unusual; many individual collectors, artists, and estates use similar tactics. Increasing the financial value of an art collection is in the interest of the collector. SGD is trying now to tweak this art market tactic so that the beneficiaries of the financial gains include the artists and the community from which they come.

Here's how the market has worked. Arnett bought the works, promoted them, and helped build interest and value by lending pieces from his collection to visiting exhibitions at museums around the country. This is how I came to see the quilts at the de Young Museum in San Francisco in 2006. These exhibitions, and accompanying coverage on television and in newspapers, brought attention to the quilts and expanded a market for the work of African American artists from the rural South.[3] However, because Arnett bought the works before there was art market demand for them, he didn't pay the high prices that the quilters' works now claim. In other words, the value of the collection increased, but that value wasn't shared with the artists.

As president of the Souls Grown Deep Foundation, Max Anderson has pushed the foundation to do more than just raise the profile and value of the art. Rather than lending pieces to other museums, it now sells works from its collection directly to them. This helps those museums permanently diversify their collections and makes sure the quilts are preserved for public viewing. Works by Black artists make up a tiny percentage of the holdings of most major museums.[4] It makes the other museums permanently responsible for and invested in the art form. Souls Grown Deep uses the money from these sales to care for the remainder of its collection and makes grants to help artists continue their work. Artists from the Alabama Black Belt, which includes Boykin and other communities, use these grant funds to buy supplies or travel to see their work on exhibit.

The board members of Souls Grown Deep and Anderson wanted to do more than this, and Anderson wanted to use the endowment to make it happen. He also wanted to avoid the kinds of financial tensions familiar to philanthropy in which an endowment is invested in companies that are at cross-purposes with the purported mission of the organization. Recent years have seen protests and outrage at museums, universities, and other endowed institutions that have taken gifts from people who made fortunes by manufacturing weapons or opioids. As one opinion writer put it, "museums have always been exceptionally good places to convert roughly obtained private wealth into social prestige."[5] In SGD's case, the tension was slightly different. It had helped build the financial value of the art in its collection, but the benefits were flowing to the foundation, collectors, and museums, not the artists. Quilters could get higher prices for new work, but they were not reaping the benefits of the work they'd sold years before.

SGD's goal now is to direct foundation funds away from the regular market for stocks and bonds and into the systems and businesses that support artists and their communities. The Souls Grown Deep Foundation helped build interest, awareness, and a market for the work of these African American artists. Now it's seeking ways to make sure the financial rewards of their labor reach the 160 families who created the art. Think of it as a philanthropic twist on the idea of a circular economy. It's not an easy thing to do. Rather than parking its money in mutual funds, stocks, or bonds, the board now needs investment partners who can take an active role in the economic development of small, rural communities.

Mary Margaret Pettway sees this strategy as a way to keep the "kids from having to leave Boykin to find a job and a life" and to keep her community intact. Max Anderson sees it as a moral obligation. The impact investing community that is watching the effort hopes that Souls Grown Deep's strategy might inspire change among other museums, which, in 2019, held $58 billion in investable endowment funds.[6]

The work of these artists has been undervalued for so long for the same reasons that African Americans have been structurally disadvantaged in so many other areas of American life. Making reparations for centuries of harm requires seeing this bigger picture. And finding ways to invest the proceeds of their art into the artists' community is what SGD is trying to do.

Max turned to Laura Callanan and Upstart Co-Lab for help. Why not invest some of the foundation's endowment directly in the Black Belt communities where the artists lived? Better yet, perhaps they could invest in growing the artists' businesses or distribution partners or community resources in ways that would bring the revenue from sales back to the artists. Buying art directly from the artists had been Arnett's first step in this direction, with an eye toward increasing the recognition (and market value) of the work. Directing the financial benefits of that marketplace and the art's increased value to the artists is another step toward closing the loop from creator to beneficiary.

The mechanics of how Max, Laura, the Souls Grown Deep Foundation, and Upstart Co-Lab will do this draw from the mostly unregulated world of art sales and the highly regulated world of investment finance. They're taking advantage of several trends. First is the decades-long growth and formalization of financial investments that focus on producing positive social or environmental outcomes. Second, people who used to be viewed only as potential beneficiaries of philanthropy are increasingly involved as actual decision-makers. Two artists sit on the foundation board, including Mary Margaret Pettway, who serves as the president, a role she took on so that she "could find out what was happening with the quilts and make [her] voice heard."[7] Third, as we've seen throughout this book, people are starting to look at all their resources and think about how they use them in line with their values. Museums, Max reminds me, face pressure and public protest about certain donations. Taking money from industries that don't align with your mission is one problem—and the public is increasingly calling museums out for this. Traditionally, museums have not done much to align either donors or investments with their mission. Max points out, "We're small. One million dollars isn't a lot of money. We can try this." That's the practical side, the rational, financially responsible argument. Then he notes, again, "It's our moral obligation."

FOR GENERATIONS TO COME: NDN COLLECTIVE

What is your idea of a long time? Is it five years? Fifty? Fifty thousand? Aboriginal people have inhabited Australia for more than sixty-five thousand years, a tenure made possible by ways of knowing, communicating, and connecting to the land that sustains them even in the face of colonization and genocide. Native Americans have lived in the Americas for a shorter period, but their survival in the United States can be credited to knowledge systems and connections to the land that defy White settlers' deliberate, sustained attempts at destruction. Today, as climate change reveals the error of modern extractive processes, Native Americans' ability to survive genocide and forced removal from the land offers paths forward. As scholar Nick Estes, a citizen of the Lower Brule Sioux Tribe notes in his book on resistance to the Dakota Access Pipeline, "our history is the future."[8]

For years, Native American water protectors have been holding their land against construction crews and militarized police forces. In 2016, both were present just north of the Standing Rock Indian Reservation, determined to build an oil pipeline that the community had been fighting in the courts. Prosperous White landowners had used the legal system to divert the pipeline away from their property. The proposed "alternative" route ran the pipeline right through Native American land and water sources.

People who have thrived for millennia in harsh geographies and climates often experience the relationships among land, place, living things, and people in ways that the English language can barely communicate. Their wisdom and cultural systems are both the cause and effect of long-term habitation. Many Indigenous peoples value relationships between people and their environments that Western, White, property-owning economics systematically destroy. The Sioux peoples' fight for their water sources are rooted in worldviews so long-lived and interconnected that it makes colonizer talk of sustainability and systems thinking superficial in comparison.

If you start from a mindset that assumes interconnections and long time horizons, you develop a different set of strategies for making change in the world than if you start with a focus on short-term extractive profits. These perspectives require looking beyond immediate challenges, searching for the deeper systems at work, and assuming that change takes time. Meaningful interventions are needed that work on multiple timelines. Yes, there will be actions that are immediate and opportunistic, visible, and perhaps purpose-built to use social media and television to generate awareness and attract support. And there will also be arduous, behind-the-scenes, root-based work focused beyond the TV moment, on the legal, cultural, and economic incentives that drive the decision-making calculus of your opponents. Native Americans and Aboriginal Australians have been fighting to protect their lives and lands from cultural and economic outsiders for centuries. Their fights for justice reveal the importance of multiple time frames.

FIGHTING THE FUNDING PIPELINE

Nick Tilsen is a citizen of the Oglala Lakota Nation. He was born and raised on the Pine Ridge Reservation in South Dakota. From Pine Ridge, the awe-inspiring (and sacred to the Lakota) Black Hills are visible on the horizon. Prairie grass extends for miles and green-brown land and blue sky seem to swallow everything else in sight. Outsider accounts of Pine Ridge usually start by noting statistics about unemployment and life expectancy, while simultaneously eliding the centuries of war, settler colonization, and broken treaties that created poverty amid such cultural and natural abundance. Tilsen has worked since he was in his twenties to build the Thunder Valley Community Development Corporation (Thunder Valley CDC), an Indigenous-led planned community that provides training and jobs, healthy and sovereign food systems, energy-efficient sustainable housing, and culturally legitimate healing ceremonies for those who live on the reservation. His commitment to community wealth and sovereignty extends beyond his day job. In 2020 he was arrested and charged with three felonies for protesting President Trump's visit to Mount Rushmore on the Fourth of July. The monument is carved into the sacred Black Hills.

After building the Thunder Valley CDC, Tilsen helped launch the NDN Collective to help other Native communities expand on the CDC's work. In the course of doing this and in alliance with those at Standing Rock, Indigenous leaders like Tilsen have come face to face with another powerful system of interconnection: modern-day finance. The water protectors at Standing Rock recognized that fighting the companies doing the drilling wasn't the whole story; their fight was with the banks that financed the companies doing the drilling. Organizing around the slogan "Kill the Funding, Kill the Pipelines," Sioux leaders and others created the Mazaska Talks initiative (*mazaska* means *money* in the Lakota language). Mazaska Talks is a divestment campaign, aimed at pulling money out of banks that fund fossil-fuel extraction. The model is analogous to divestment campaigns used against apartheid-era South Africa, and it aligns with a broader fossil-fuel divestment movement that claims commitments from more than 1,200 organizations worldwide, with $14 trillion in investable funds.[9]

Tilsen and the water protectors haven't stopped at divestment. Simply taking money out of fossil fuels may slow the growth of climate- and community-damaging extraction, but that money still needs to be invested in something. Just as SGD now invests its money in African American artists' communities, the NDN Collective gives the Lakota (and others) alternative investment options. These include direct investments—moving money from banks that fund fossil fuels to banks that invest in community development, for example. Nick is quick to point out that many of us can make choices about where we bank or from whom we buy insurance. Taking your money out of damaging companies is a good start. But the real goal of the NDN Collective and Thunder Valley CDC is to give investors options that support positive financial and economic outcomes for Native communities.

For the water protectors in North Dakota, the pipeline was the immediate problem, but the roots of the challenge ran much deeper. Native Americans and the people of Canadian First Nations have been fighting for their lives, freedom, and land since Europeans first arrived in North America. They're fluent in searching for and exposing deep connections between short-term actions and hidden systems. The Native activism to protect land and watersheds galvanized not only physical sit-ins in front of earth-moving machines but also efforts that reached far beyond these machines. They looked past the pipeline and earthmovers to the companies that owned the machines. They then looked further again to find the financial institutions that provide those companies with working capital. In doing so, the water protectors of North Dakota sparked a national protest against banks that fund pipelines and other parts of the extractive fuels industry. They connected the immediate threat of one pipeline to the larger threat of climate change, bringing new allies to their fight and joining themselves to a global movement.

Making the connections between a threatened water system and a bank's investment policies requires two things: an understanding of systems and a long-term commitment to see change through. Some might argue that mobilizing people to move their money to different banks was a distraction from the immediate goal of stopping the pipeline. An integrated worldview argues just the opposite. This perspective points out that stopping one pipeline without changing the financial system that powers it is condemning yourself to a lifetime of playing whack-a-mole. Taking on the banks while also taking on the pipeline builders and their political allies also provides more ways for more people to join the fight. Some people will be able to hold the physical line against the earth-moving machines. Many, many more will be able get involved by moving their money away from the banks that finance the machines.

IMPACT INVESTING BY THE REST OF US: CREDIT UNIONS

Several hundred miles west of Standing Rock, Marilyn Waite spends her days thinking of ways to make it easier for people who don't think of themselves as investors to use their money to mitigate climate change. Marilyn is a triple citizen, holding passports from France, Jamaica, and the United States, and credits her interest in climate finance to three things: her island heritage, her identity as a Black woman, and her experience in venture capital and other parts of the finance industry. "Islands," she says, "are already being hurt by climate change. Poor people are already being hurt. People of color are committed environmentalists—they're trying to save themselves and their communities. And I know how capital markets work."[10]

She pulls up some research she's done on where the trillions of dollars that make up the global economy are held. One slide shows three circles, each one representing the size of different kinds of financial institutions, including multilateral organizations like the World Bank, investment and commercial banks, and global insurance companies. "Credit unions," she says, pointing to part of the middle circle, "are here." Compared to the other circles, Marilyn's finger is pointing at what looks like a small piece of the graph. "It's a trillion dollars," she says. I laugh; only on a graph of financial institutions could one trillion dollars look small. Marilyn continues, explaining that credit unions in the United States have about one trillion dollars in assets. "They do the same lending [as the commercial banks]. They do the mortgages, they do the auto loans, they do small business lending." And they're responsible to their members, not to Wall Street. Credit unions, especially those set up as community development credit unions, are inclusive "in terms of rural communities, people of color, immigrant communities." Just by banking at a credit union, a person becomes a type of impact investor, Marilyn points out, because the members set the investment policies.[11]

Credit unions often have their roots in particular geographies, businesses, or identity communities. They compete against the big banks by working together, sharing a global network of ATMs so that members can access cash without fees, and sharing ideas on sustainable investing through national networks such as Inclusiv, formerly known as the National

Federation of Community Development Credit Unions.[12] They need to make the most of both their community identity and global convenience to compete. One way to do this is through sharing systems and knowledge. A new credit union, focused on climate change, is doing this. The Clean Energy Credit Union is dedicated not only to making no investments in extractive fuel industries, but also to actively seeking to make the kinds of loans that the clean energy world needs. This is what Marilyn describes as the *distributive infrastructure*, including things such as solar panels, roofing materials, and energy-efficiency solutions for buildings. The Clean Energy Credit Union intends to build this investing expertise and then spread it to other credit unions.[13]

These kinds of opportunities seem harder to find than they really are. That's partly because investment policies and the inner workings of the finance system are not usually how banks markets themselves to customers. But activists are changing this. People on the ground at Standing Rock and coordinated fossil-fuel divestment efforts are drawing much more attention to financial industry practices. And credit unions, online-only banks, debit card purveyors, and financial tech start-ups (known as FinTech) are beginning to advertise their investment (or divestment) strategies directly to customers. I ask Marilyn, who spends her professional time understanding these systems, How do "regular" people keep up? She laughs, and offers up a link to her personal website, where she shares information on how she manages her own money. "That's how I help the people who ask me." She smiles. "But my day job is really about helping these kinds of options grow in size and awareness so that everyone knows about them. And can find them. And use them. If you're already using a bank, there's an option for you."

Not everyone has access to banking services. The Federal Reserve notes that 6 percent of Americans were "unbanked" and another 16 percent were "underbanked" in 2018. These percentages are higher for Latinx (11 percent and 23 percent, respectively) and African American (14 percent and 35 percent, respectively) communities.[14] Payday lenders, check-cashing services, and high-interest loan servicers target these populations. These firms are unlikely adopters of socially or environmentally friendly practices. Building the capacity of credit unions and community banks to better serve all communities will make financial systems both more accessible and more sustainable.

Companies that sell investment products to wealthy people and endowments are getting guidance from Laura Callanan (who also helped SGD) and others to begin slicing their products into smaller pieces for everyday people. This is the same story behind the creation of mutual funds: packaging big investments into small pieces so regular people can buy into the market. Calvert Financial, a mutual fund company, has a nonprofit affiliate called Calvert Impact Capital. The nonprofit sells a product called the *community investment note* that slices up big holdings in affordable housing, renewable energy, education, and health into investment products that can be purchased for as little as twenty dollars.[15]

In many cases, impact investing models require a mix of a few people with deep pockets working with lots of people with much smaller bank accounts. Mitch Kapor and Freada Kapor Klein run the Kapor Center in Oakland, California. The center uses a mix of investing, philanthropy, and policy advocacy to pursue its goal of a more "diverse, inclusive, and impactful" tech sector.[16] It invests in start-ups founded by Oakland residents that hire people from the city and actively promotes these investment opportunities to others who might help get the companies off the ground. Through this work, the Kapor Center is seeking the social and financial benefits of a more inclusive local economy. But it's also changing the investment opportunities in Oakland. The Kapor Center does the upfront due diligence work and supports the entrepreneurs, and then it helps attract other investors.

Buyer Beware: Commodification, Not Democratization

The creation of mass-market products for small investors is at the heart of the commodification and productization of giving that I described in the opening chapters. It's critical to remember that every one of these products—from a community investment note to a donor-advised fund—comes with costs. The companies that sell these products usually make their money by charging fees on your account. You have access to something that was only previously available to wealthy givers, but that doesn't mean you have as much power as they do.

The power of a group like NDN Collective or organizations like community credit unions comes from their form of governance—controlled by members—not from the products they sell. This is also what sets mutual aid networks and informal lending collectives apart. Similarly, Ioby is an example in which the community comes first and is supported by products such as a crowdfunding platform. The same is true of many giving circles, which pool their funds and hold them in DAF accounts. Communities can pick products, but this doesn't work the other way; products don't build communities. Keep this in mind whenever you hear a marketing pitch for a new way to democratize giving. Chances are it's just a slimmed-down version of a product once marketed to the wealthy. And commodities aren't communities.

SMALL BUDGET INVESTING WITH BIG PHILANTHROPY FEELS (AND FLAWS): DONOR-ADVISED FUNDS

Bringing impact investing to small investors means finding big pots of money that can be divided into lots of small pieces and that don't cost more to manage than they will earn in profit. Banks and mutual fund companies are experts at this. They've already seen great success in commodifying charitable products to sell to people lower on the wealth scale. Since the early 1990s, the fastest growing product in the givingscape has been donor-advised funds, a kind of charitable checking account pioneered by community foundations but made ubiquitous by nationwide mutual fund companies. Today, you can open a DAF with no minimum deposit at a mutual fund company, investment bank, community foundation, or other nonprofit (including, possibly, your alma mater). As soon as you open the account, you are eligible for the charitable tax break on those funds. But the money sits and earns investment income until you "advise" that a gift be directed from the fund to a charitable organization.

The companies that sell donor-advised funds are starting to mix and match their product lines. It's possible to designate that the money in your DAF be invested in an impact investing pool. The promise is twofold. First, by investing the money in impact-creating companies, your money is supporting socially positive activities. Second, this growth means that over time, you will have more money to allocate in charitable gifts from the fund.

The allure of DAFs comes from their simplicity and their ready availability. They're particularly appealing to people for whom tax issues still matter to their charitable giving planning. They also appeal to people—at all giving levels—who want to protect their identity when they make donations. This is good for people who want to do their giving anonymously. However, the overall effect of DAFs' popularity is making it harder to track who is funding what. DAFs are available to people wanting to give $100 or $1 billion. In 2018, the cumulative value of all US DAFs was $121.4 billion. These are the funds sitting in the accounts—not the amount being donated to create change in the world.[17]

The growth of DAFs is double-edged. They protect individual donors' privacy, but the aggregate result is a less transparent and understandable givingscape. DAFs are easy to set up, but there are few rules about when the money in them has to leave the income-earning account and be donated. They create an inviting and comfortable resting place for a lot of money. The money sitting in each DAF account earns fees for the company managing it. If it's invested in impact investing ways, it may capitalize some socially positive activities. Otherwise, the billions of dollars in DAFs are doing wonders for the capital markets but little social good. This is beginning to catch the attention of regulators, and I'd anticipate seeing new regulations at the state level if not nationally in coming years.

DAFs raise another important consideration. The rules on how money flows in and out of them benefit wealthy DAF holders. For example, foundations can fulfill their legal requirements by making grants to DAFs. This means a wealthy person can put money first in a foundation, then move it to a DAF. In doing so, they get the tax break when it goes into the foundation and credit for meeting their grant payout when the money moves to the DAF. So they meet the legal requirements for giving away the money even as they effectively keep control over it. It's the equivalent of shifting money from one pocket to another, but getting tax benefits along the way. It's not dissimilar from the 2015 media adulation Mark Zuckerberg and Priscilla Chan received for "giving away" 99 percent of their fortune when all they really did was put their funds into a limited liability company they controlled.

The number of choices in the givingscape means we need to think about not just individual products but the dynamics between them. We previously discussed how products interact in chapter 4, when we looked at the fuzzy lines between charitable and political activity. Once-distinct products are now being mixed and matched in ways that elide the written rules about control and disclosure.

Different products provide different values to different people. Impact investing is still a rich person's game, although the long-term horizons and the focus on systems are ways of thinking that can improve everyone's giving.[18] Bringing the same values that shape how you donate your money, give your time, or make household purchases to saving or investing your money is something any of us can do, but it takes time to do it well. Those who engage deeply in mutual aid networks, with the intention to both meet their community's needs and create alternative economic frameworks for at least parts of their lives, also know this. This happens out of view of mainstream banking and investing; it is shaped by a collective intentionality and set of values. The mainstream options are built around products; the mutual aid and alternative banking approaches are about collectivity.

More and more mainstream companies make claims of responsible or sustainable practices. (It goes without saying that all marketing claims deserve scrutiny.) The easier opportunity for most of us will be finding a trusted source who has done the work of scrutinizing those claims. That might mean looking for a community development credit union instead of a bank.

Impact investing is in a transitional phase from being a strategy for wealthy people to an industry selling products at more affordable prices. This is an example of the commodification process underpinning so much of the financial side of giving. It focuses on producing something that can be sold quickly and easily to as many people as possible. This very process de-emphasizes community and collective action and focuses on individual purchasing decisions.

6 THE GOOD, BAD, AND UNKNOWN OF GIVING DATA

Unlike Cat Chang and others in the iNaturalist community, not everyone is interested in collecting data, let alone thinking about sharing it as part of their giving practices. Not one of the 338 people we spoke with in our mapping conversations brought up the idea of donating their data without being prompted to do so. When they were specifically asked about data donations, they tended to respond with looks of either confusion or disdain. Many people commented on their data being "taken" or "leaked" or "sold" by companies. The idea that they had any data that they could control well enough or make a choice to contribute was foreign to almost everyone. Upon reflection, people most often brought up the way they thought their health data was being used, based on what they vaguely remembered from the form in their doctors' offices, which they had admittedly skimmed. Two people also mentioned that they were regular blood donors and thought there was "data involved" in those donations.[1] Some communities, such as the Navajo nation and other Indigenous peoples, have laws that set clear limits on whether or not individual data can be collected, used or shared, because of the community-wide implications.

There are many possibilities for using digitized data for public benefit. They are rife with moral questions, short- and long-term equity issues, and opportunities to further entrench already powerful and dangerous extractive relationships. They also offer the potential to imagine very different futures—with positive potential for more equitable approaches to digital data in every sphere of life. People and communities interested in economic systems that value collective health over individualistic advancement, those who seek to reinvigorate a commons approach or resource stewardship over corporate extraction, and cultures where humans live in relationship to both the physical world and shared knowledge traditions have much to offer in terms of approaches for using digitized data for human betterment. To date these worldviews have been largely kept to the fringes by policy debates and marketing campaigns led by already powerful people and institutions. Changing this won't be easy, but one step forward is for each of us to imagine ourselves having a stake in the effort.

Aggregated digital data can have enormous value for solving shared public problems, from climate change to medical research. Re-empowering individuals with regard to their data can start with considering the uses of digital data for collective action. We can use today's edge cases to understand why people contribute their data, how they build enough trust to participate, what protections they require, and what new kinds of collective action safe data donations can enable. This understanding then needs to inform the regulatory process so we can protect the collective good of digital data and to provide better individual and community protections. There are some uses of digitized data that we know cause harm. These should be banned, as is beginning to happen with facial recognition and predictive policing data collection and use.

This is a transitional moment. Choosing to give access to your digital data to a cause you care about is a new opportunity. The qualities of digitized data mean that "giving" it is really about granting access, not about relinquishing your hold on it. Our assumptions about ownership are challenged by this—and so are our assumptions about philanthropy, giving, and control.

BIRDS, BUGS, AND PHOTOGRAPHS: DATA AND THE ENVIRONMENT

Leo Salas's eyes light up and he gives me a big smile at the mention of an indigo bunting. Spotting one of these small, intensely blue birds "is what turned me on to birds," says David Leland. "I was nine or ten at the time," he continues. Leo, David, and I are sitting in a small conference room at Point Blue Conservation Science, a forty-five-year-old nonprofit organization on the edge of Shollenberger Park in Petaluma, California. Housed in a nondescript office park, the building reveals nothing of itself to the street; but pull around the back of the building, to Point Blue's main entrance, and you look out over acres of marshlands. In the distance, you can see the traffic on US 101. It might seem odd to squeeze an internationally recognized environmental science organization in between a major north-south California traffic artery and generic suburban blacktop, but the location is a visual tell for Point Blue's work. People, our buildings, our cars, our economy, and our politics are putting unbearable pressure on the earth. Even the picturesque marsh, a jumble of greens, blues, and browns, with the occasional wildflower pop of yellow, is the byproduct of a man-made channel dredged by the city of Petaluma in the 1970s to manage the flow of the local river.

The spark of joy in Leo and David's eyes is contagious. We're all smiling now, as David remembers that first sighting. "I got lucky," David says. "Our neighbor was a birder who participated in the Audubon spring count. Through her I learned about birds and counting. No one else in my family cared."[2]

Decades later, David is still counting. I'm here at Point Blue to talk with Leo about the work he does creating and managing huge datasets of satellite imagery to help count seals around the world. Leo is a Colombian-born quantitative ecologist who has been leading data-intensive research projects at Point Blue for more than a decade. He coordinates a community science project in which 350,000 volunteers from around the world use satellite images—pictures from space—to locate migrating seals. Satellite imagery is a key tool for environmental scientists, providing a vantage point that makes it easy to see changing landscapes over time. Pictures from space are not so helpful when it comes to getting accurate counts of a species; that's much better done by tagging individual animals and counting them when they come to shore. Leo's research takes advantage of both techniques—he combines space photo data on migratory patterns with hand counts of tagged seals to understand what is happening to the species and its habitats locally and globally. This research is not only scientifically valuable, it's readily available for use by planners, policy makers, and environmental advocates.

Leo is part of another Point Blue project, the Soundscapes to Landscapes (S2L) team, on which David volunteers. For months, David and others on the S2L team have been placing hand-sized sound recorders (called AudioMoths) in designated spots around Sonoma County. The team programmed each AudioMoth to capture one-minute snippets of ambient sound at precisely set times before dawn and at dusk. Over the course of several months, the team collected three hundred thousand of these one-minute recordings. They've finished loading all this audio data onto Point Blue's servers, and more volunteers are helping the scientists to organize the snippets, find patterns in the sounds, and analyze the data for insights about bird populations and their breeding and migration patterns. Expert birders identify the bird calls from the recordings, tag each sound appropriately, and use that coded data to train machine-learning models that can be applied against the entire dataset. In this way, the project both identifies all of the recordings and trains algorithms that other science organizations can use.[3] The scientists also teach interested volunteers how to create the machine-learning models, the perfect data nerd opportunity for David and his ilk. Ultimately, all of the ground-level sound data, the dataset, the algorithms, and the insights will be analyzed along with data collected by NASA, taking one more step toward developing high-quality remote-sensing mechanisms for protecting the environment.[4]

David smiles again. "Birding excites me because of both the birds and the data. Volunteering on these projects, I get to watch birds and play with data. I used to keep my lists in notebooks, then on spreadsheets, then on a laptop-based bird-tracking program. Now I use eBird on my phone. I instantly share my sightings with the world. Then I come here and help create machine-learning programs to make sense of all the soundscape data."

Birders often are, by their own admission, data nerds. They're easy converts over to digital data systems. The eBird app that David uses was built by the Cornell University Ornithology Lab and is now used by hundreds of thousands of people. In 2019, there were more than five hundred million observations in the eBird database, a number that increases by one hundred million per year. "Birders are also competitive," says Leo. "In 2012, eBird redesigned the app, gamifying the experience for app users. The number of observations people submitted skyrocketed after that."

David chimes in, "I'm not that into the game or competitive side of it, but the app has changed how I think about what I'm doing. I've been observing and noting birds for decades. But now, with eBird, I know that each of my single observations can go into this massive database. Each single observation I contribute is part of something so much bigger—it's like adding a grain of sand that's now part of the whole beach. It's really motivating. Something I love doing can build something really useful on a global scale."

Leo's projects and David's contributions are in some ways the inverse of the iNaturalist model. They are driven by scientists, working through hypotheses, with an eye toward methodical accuracy and data quality. Volunteers are carefully trained in data collection techniques, analysis, and—if interested—developing advanced algorithms. At Point Blue, science comes first and community comes second, whereas iNaturalist is designed to delight, engage, and connect people to each other and the natural world.

The tensions between experts and amateurs are a big issue in citizen science. It's representative of a number of tensions—agenda setting, inclusion, neutrality—most of which are really about power. The very term *citizen science* is contested—with some arguing that the term is inherently nativist and exclusionary, while others claim to be taking back the word *citizen* to mean something more like *responsible participant* than *person with certain papers*. In chapter 2, Christine Liu and Tera Johnson reminded us that science is political. Who gets to do it, what they study, how it's used and by whom—these are questions of participation, expertise, agency, and activism.[5] The tensions of citizen science pervade much of giving and volunteering; they are all political.

FROM DATA TO COMMUNITY

Ken-Ichi Ueda built the iNaturalist app and database after moving from New England to California. He wanted to learn about the flora and fauna he was finding near his new home in Berkeley. Like David Leland, Ken-Ichi had spent a lot of time playing in the woods as a kid. When he moved west, he realized he didn't know the plants or animals, nor did he have a community of friends to help him learn the way he had playing outside as a kid. The original version of iNaturalist was just a blog. He turned it into an app, trying to keep a balance between useful data and community participation. iNaturalist is now a hosted project of the California Academy of Sciences and the National Geographic Society.[6]

The first time Mira Bowin used the iNaturalist app, she just wanted to know the name of an insect she'd noticed in her backyard. Mira grew up in Queens, New York, and moved upstate as an adult. Mira used to work as an advocate for people with mental health issues, and she manages her own life paying careful attention to what she and others can access. She tends to keep close to home, where she's discovered that her backyard holds wonders. Lavishing attention on local plants and the insects they attract, Mira describes herself as "a crazy gardener person whose garden has turned more into a lab for iNaturalist observations than an actual garden with any cohesion."[7]

Mira found iNaturalist after first using eBird. "I wanted an eBird for praying mantises like the ones in my yard. And lo and behold, I found it in iNaturalist." After using the app for several months, Mira began to wonder, "Who are these people who can identify things even from my crappy photographs? How does this work?" So she logged into the iNaturalist website, where she found she could track all her own observations, reach out to the people who were identifying photos she was uploading, and follow other people's posts and photos. "This one guy kept identifying my micro moths, which are a very difficult taxa to identify, and they're mostly ignored by people looking at the big pretty moths; they ignore these tiny, tiny little things. And I don't ignore any tiny thing."[8]

The guy turned out to be the head of a university's insect collection and he invited Mira to visit his lab. Mira spent a weekend with the professor and his students. "I tear up thinking about it. I cried several times, just overwhelmed emotionally at how many people had had their hands in this process in the actual physical collection [at the university]. And then I realized how many more hands were involved in iNaturalist."[9]

iNaturalist does more than facilitate scientific breakthroughs. It builds community. As Mira remembers, "It's just amazing to me. [The professor's] generosity. He was candid with me that it's an investment. He sees amateur naturalists playing a big role in this kind of research, especially when they're things that nobody else is interested in. So I get it, it's not just like he's super nice, it's an investment in the community, but I take that seriously. And that started because of this tool." These kinds of connections can be as meaningful as the face-to-face community that the Safe Passage volunteers experience with the children they escort. That's encouraging from the perspective of encouraging people to share data.

Not everyone who shares their photographs knows what they're looking at. When Ken-Ichi Ueda created iNaturalist, it was these people he had in mind. People who see something, want to know what it is, and get on with their lives. iNaturalist provides a quick way for that to happen. Once a photo is uploaded to the site, it's up to the community to identify it. These identifications come from the other one million users of the site. If they can, they will tag the photo with a species—and you'll have learned what type of mushroom, insect, or tree you're looking at. Research-grade photos can be added to the Global Biodiversity Information Facility, a key resource for scholarship.[10]

This is crowdsourced information at its finest. And, also, at its worst. There can be heated disagreements about proper identification. Some of iNaturalist's most active users are people who will argue for days about the proper subspecies or classification of a certain animal or plant. Fights over taxonomies are a regular part of scientific progress, and the moderators on iNaturalist (and eBird) work hard to keep these discussions civil. While arguments about taxonomic categorization might appeal to only a small subset of dedicated enthusiasts, these people can get just as nasty with each other as people anywhere else online. Tony Iwane, iNaturalist's communications staffer, credits his previous work experience with severely emotionally disturbed children for his success as a community moderator. "I don't get angry easily. I'm good at finding some way to settle things down."[11]

These skills are particularly important on a site like iNaturalist, which attracts both experts and one-off visitors. With a laugh, Tony notes that school students being forced to use it in their classes are a consistent source of problematic comments on iNaturalist. "They love to post pictures of other kids and tag it as a type of bug." Tony takes this in stride and trains his volunteer curators to do so also. "They're kids being goofy," he says, while telling me they will usually just take down those photos. As the iNaturalist site has gone global, however, this has gotten harder. "I don't speak Korean," says Tony. "So if someone reports someone else for uploading a photo and tagging it as a snake, how am I to know if that is a really derogatory term in Korean culture?" Once again, trusted volunteers become the solution to helping the site adapt to different cultures and languages.

For the most part, people on iNaturalist are there because they want to be. Helping create a positive community vibe is the best part of Tony's job. He calls out "cool observations" of the day, writes blog posts about "super identifiers," and encourages people to find and follow others with shared interests. He's wowed by the engagement of some on the site, including the person in Germany who's identified more than three hundred thousand beetles. "Beetles are really hard," says Tony, with admiration in his voice. The site's success in keeping things civil is what keeps users like Cat Chang and Mira Bowin coming back every evening.

Apps like eBird and iNaturalist rely on a few paid staff and extensive global networks of volunteers who do everything from keeping conversations civil to keeping the software running. Software coders are invited to help maintain and build new features of iNaturalist; the site's code can all be found on GitHub. This makes iNaturalist part of the open-source software community, which has long relied on unpaid contributions.

iNaturalist's focus on community complicated the decision to begin using artificial intelligence to speed the time it takes to identify photos. Putting an algorithm in between the person contributing a photo and the people identifying it didn't immediately sit well. The compromise was to begin using artificial intelligence but not limit the community aspect. Now you can get identification suggestions from both people and machines.

These machine-driven identifications are a boon for the casual user of iNaturalist, who can now sometimes get their photo identified "automatically." The team keeps working on ways to get people to stick around and share and learn. "We're trying to recreate the feeling of wonder that we had as kids, playing outside," Tony and Ken-Ichi agree. Tony tells me that he lost touch with nature when he grew up, got a job, and moved to a new part of the world. "But then I got a digital camera, and I went back out into nature. Good digital cameras can make naturalists of people. It rekindles something that they lost when they grew up."[12]

FROM BIRDS TO BLOOD PRESSURE: OPEN HUMANS AND SAGE BIONETWORKS

There are lots of ways you can contribute your personal data for health research. So many, in fact, that it can be hard to keep track of what's really going on. Imagine that you wanted to contribute data about your blood pressure, heart rate, insulin count, DNA, or level of daily exercise for medical purposes. You can do this via a commercial service, such as 23andMe or Ancestry.com. These two organizations sell you a product—information about your genealogy—in exchange for cash, data, and consent. You give them a swab from the inside of your check, a check for about a hundred dollars, and a click on their consent page. These actions allow them to include your digitized DNA data in a dataset that they then charge pharmaceutical companies to access. You will receive a pie chart revealing the places your ancestors *may* have come from. You'll also get frequent updates as their databases expand and diversify. You've paid for the service of learning about your ancestry, and in consenting to the company's rules, you help them profit by selling access to that dataset. Quite simply, you've paid the company in both money and data.

You don't have to go through a commercial company to do this; in fact, doing so is the most financially expensive way to go. You could contribute DNA data via nonprofit genetics websites or blood pressure and insulin information to any number of nonprofits or online communities. One of these is called Open Humans. It has a complicated history related to the Personal Genome Project (PGP), a Harvard-based effort that launched in the mid-aughts. Since then, Mad Ball, a former doctoral student, has been adapting the organization and its tools to help people share and learn from many types of health data.[13] Open Humans offers people a way to store, analyze, and share with others their genomic data, their Twitter feeds, movement information from any form of digital exercise tracker, or microbiome measures. Each person determines what data to share and with whom to share it. The Open Humans community creates software tools that make it easy to connect data from your devices (watches, Fitbits, insulin monitors, phones, etc.) to the online platform and lets you decide who has access and to what, with default settings that keep your data private to you (assuming the database can be secured).[14] Mad Ball and the Open Humans community are convinced that data from individuals can be useful for research and treatment; the challenge is to find trusted and safe ways for people to participate. Toward that end, the bulk of Open Humans' work is on building software and governance tools that appeal beyond the inner circle of do-it-yourself data geeks.

Open Humans is not alone in this quest; it's part of a much bigger community of people focused on creating new kinds of institutions that we might trust to hold our data and let us determine how it gets used.[15] This includes experimenting with new organizations such as data cooperatives, civic data trusts, and open collectives. These organizations are uncommon now, but some of them are bound to succeed and become as familiar as nonprofits are today. Think about it: nonprofit corporations proliferate in the United States as trusted institutions to put donated time and money to work creating change. We're seeing great efforts to create new forms for this—purpose-built institutional structures that enable safe and trusted digital data donations.[16]

In 2015, Apple introduced ResearchKit, a software framework that allows people to share—by choice—data from their phones with medical researchers. Apple's launch of ResearchKit called out five initial studies, covering asthma, breast cancer, diabetes, heart health, and Parkinson's disease. The study on Parkinson's disease was called mPower and involved a team of researchers from a Seattle-based nonprofit, Sage Bionetworks (Sage was also involved in the breast cancer study). The idea was to collect movement data—how much a person moved around each day—to see how the tremors that mark Parkinson's disease changed over the course of a day and if there were relationships between tremors and exercise levels.

John Wilbanks, chief commons officer at Sage Bionetworks, remembers the excitement about the initial mPower study. "The numbers were off the charts. We couldn't believe how many people signed up."[17] In December of 2015, nine months after launching the study in March, the mPower team reported that 48,104 people had downloaded the app and that more than 9,500 not only completed the study but agreed to share their data with the research community.[18]

John has built his career around the potential of scientific studies such as the mPower project. Well before we were all carrying cell phones (data collection devices) in our pockets, John was working to open up science to regular people. He knows as well as anyone that the challenges of encouraging broad participation in scientific research are more social than technological. "Trust is key," he notes. "How do you encourage people to share information, really personal information, for the potential of science?"

This question has bedeviled scientific research for decades. And for good reason: the research community's track record on building trust and respecting the rights of people who participate is historically bad. Travesties abound. From the Tuskegee syphilis experiments, in which African Americans were deliberately infected as specimens rather than treated as humans with a disease, to the story of Henrietta Lacks, a young Baltimore woman with cervical cancer whose tissue cells were taken from her without her knowledge, the worst violations often subject African Americans, Indigenous people, people of color, and women to direct and lasting, multigenerational, physical and emotional harm.

The team at Sage Bionetworks spends its time working on ways to build trust, respect, and protection into research procedures. This is hard enough to do when there is a face-to-face relationship between the researchers and the people participating in the study; doing it for tens of thousands of people through an app is another level of difficult.

Vanessa Barone, research scientist for outreach and engagement, is John's colleague at Sage Bionetworks. She holds a master's degree in public health and has spent much of her career in clinical research doing recruitment and outreach, participant monitoring, and project management on "everything from kidney donation to oncology."[19] Before starting at Sage, Vanessa had not worked on any form of mobile health studies. Her professional experience had been on clinical trials in which she could develop "a pretty personal relationship with the research participants." Her job was encouraging people, in person and with email or phone follow-up, to get involved. She spent time listening to their concerns, talking them through the protocols, and answering their questions. She was attracted to the job at Sage because she knew mobile health would "be an interesting way to engage with people on a different level but also deal with some of the things that are commonly known with recruiting people to research, whether it be ethical challenges or just overall recruitment and retention, which is a beast in itself that no one can really solve completely."[20]

Vanessa is very aware of the field's transgressions of trust. "I'm a person of color . . . I got into this work to address health disparities . . . it's an ethical concern for me. We're not going to further science by studying the same populations."[21] But mobile health (often called mHealth) doesn't automatically solve any of these trust or diversity issues. Vanessa reflects on how familiar challenges persist and take on new forms. Recruiting digitally and on a national scale means she is no longer able to reach out to people in person. Sage could use the same digital marketing tools that advertisers use to get super specific in targeting its recruitment efforts. But Sage's focus on privacy protection and individual consent makes those tools suspect for research purposes. "No one can promise 100 percent security of your data," says Vanessa. The focus on integrity requires lots of compromises. Sage and its partners want to involve more people of color and other underrepresented groups in research. Doing so is critical to understand how diseases affect different populations, to better address medical issues specific to these communities, and inform and address political determinants of health. Digital marketing tools make such targeting easier than ever before, but the invasive data that power those tools violate Sage's commitment to protecting study participants identities as best they can.

Digital technologies and data create and complicate the promise of mHealth. Vanessa reminds me that not everyone has a smartphone. This means that recruiting via app stores will inevitably bypass certain populations. The ease of signing up (or downloading an app) also means these studies attract a lot of people who won't follow through. The original mPower study is seen as a watershed event, but even then 75 percent of the people who downloaded the app didn't take the second step, enrolling in the study. John and Vanessa note that the numbers of mHealth downloads have never again reached those mPower heights. This may be because app stores are now flooded with research studies, overwhelming potential participants with choice.

Vanessa and John think something else is also going on. The rise of consumer genetic testing services like 23andMe and Ancestry.com have changed the landscape for contributing physical specimens (spit swabs) that are then digitized and used for both medical and genealogical purposes. DNA testing that once cost thousands of dollars can be had for less than one hundred dollars and is even offered as an employment perk at some large companies. An estimated 220,000 people had used these services, known as *direct-to-consumer genetic testing kits*, in 2013; six years later, *MIT Technology Review* estimated that more than twenty-six million had done so.[22]

The mental calculus about these tests also keeps shifting. People give DNA swab kits as gifts and get together with friends and family to discuss the results. At the same time, more of us understand that the data behind those personal pie charts implicates other family members. Stories abound of police using DNA datasets to solve cold cases. Bestselling memoirs center around the discovery that a parent turned out to be someone other than expected.[23] African Americans, for whom genealogical research is vastly complicated by histories of enslavement and rape, have found both solace and rage from the ready availability of DNA testing.[24] Native Americans have been fighting for rights over their collective data for generations. They, along with Indigenous communities around the globe, are navigating age-old questions of identity and inclusion – as well as sovereignty - in this new marketplace of consumer-grade identity testing.[25] As a small number of companies come to dominate the market for digitized DNA, the potential uses of that information and the factors that shape how we think about it continually evolve.

For Vanessa and John and research writ large, the constantly changing public understanding about digitized data is a blessing and a curse. The marketing dollars that commercial firms such as 23andMe or Ancestry.com put into advertising their services have done more to raise public awareness about aggregating individual contributions into massive datasets than anything the nonprofit or publicly funded research community could ever afford. John, who has spent years working on legal policies and customer-facing graphic interfaces to improve the consent process for mHealth research, even has slight praise for the role some such companies play on this hot button issue and others. "They're raising awareness. People ask new and better questions," says John. "That's good." It's up to the research community to build on that awareness, offer trustworthy and rights-respecting opportunities to contribute, and distinguish themselves by their integrity.

This takes time and people, two things that many companies notoriously seek to avoid in their quest for efficiency. Vanessa remembers that she used to make at least five phone or email contacts with every participant during her days managing in-person clinical trials. "You call them to remind them of the process, to check in that they're following the protocol, to make sure they're doing what they need to do." Mobile health studies—especially those seeking participants from across the country—aren't set up to provide that kind of support. But they still have to do some of this work. mHealth promises to revolutionize research and healthcare. The truth is that, at least for now, the groups doing this work are grinding away to find the right balance between ease of participation and hand-holding, between recruiting diverse participants and not collecting any more data than absolutely necessary, and between building secure systems and being honest about the risks.

Buyer Beware: Data Philanthropy?

There are more unknowns than knowns when it comes to giving data. There are some domains, such as environmental science and medical research, in which aggregating data from lots of individuals can augment preexisting ways of studying the subject at hand. This isn't without controversy, however; debates rage about whether relying on volunteers for these critical inputs exacerbates existing divides in science.

As things now stand, most of the digital data that we generate using our cell phones, social media, search engines, and software is legally claimed by the companies whose products we're using. Buried in their terms of service (that thing you didn't read but for which you clicked the "I agree" button) is some legalese giving them the right to the data. They use these data in all kinds of ways, from improving their product to selling access to it after they've aggregated and analyzed it to develop insights about you, such as what your political affiliations are, where you worship, who you know, and what causes you care about. How these data can be used are issues of public policy. There are many ways to get involved in these debates—including advocacy and activism. You might want to engage directly in these issues for one of the causes you care about. Even if you don't, the decisions being made and the policies and laws put in place will shape your experience, even if you're not donating data but just generating it as you use your cell phone.

Finally, there's a term you may see in the media—*data philanthropy* (see appendix B). While it would be nice if this meant *sharing your data*, it mostly refers to companies providing controlled access to their massive datasets with researchers. This happens when cell phone records are analyzed to find travel patterns, something that's done frequently during pandemics. You won't be asked your permission for this to happen. Right now, you have very little say over what companies do with the data. They may call it philanthropy, but it's pretty much business as usual. Don't confuse it with your ability to contribute your data if you so choose.

INDIVIDUAL DATA AND COLLECTIVE GOOD

As the public and policymakers begin to pay attention to individuals' rights to their data, I realized the very issue I was interested in was going to make my ability to understand it more difficult. We have laws that limit how organizations can share people's health data. To better understand who donates their data to mobile health studies, I'd need to talk to people who do it, not just Vanessa and John (and others who receive the data). I knew the answer would be no, but I still asked both Vanessa and John if they could connect me to any health data donors. As expected, they said no (health data is highly regulated, and connecting an outside researcher to a study participant would violate the participant's privacy). So I reached out through my own networks, in person and via social media. This tactic was mostly a bust, gaining nothing but a few harassing responses via Twitter.

After months of trying, I finally connected with a man named Brady Rogers. By the time we connected, I had limited my social media outreach to LinkedIn, which was an easier platform for screening out creeps. I used a hashtag, "#medicalresearch," in my original post, and this may have helped display the request to groups that Brady follows. LinkedIn's algorithmic analysis of the content it shows on your home page helped Brady see my post; as far as he and I can tell, we don't know anyone in common. After a few tentative LinkedIn messages, we moved our conversation to email and eventually had a long phone interview.

Brady, it turns out, is more than just a data donor. While he describes himself on LinkedIn as a medical technologist, he's actually the program chair for a university training program that teaches and licenses medical technologists, the very people who do the data collection and management for hospital-ordered medical tests. He holds a master's degree in medical microbiology but spends most of his time now outside of the lab, overseeing associate and bachelor's degree programs. His students are the people in the hospital who do all the doctor-ordered tests:

> People who get transfusions or get a transplant, a tissue transplant, lung, heart, whatever, we're actually the ones to match to make sure that can donate to another person. We're also the same people who check to see what bacteria or virus is killing you or whatever. We're the people who look at the white blood cells to see what kind of cancer you have. Now an oncologist verifies those, but we're the ones who do the initial white blood cell count and then differentiation to determine what it is.[26]

Brady's career requires him to think about data protocols all day long. But that's not why he responded to my LinkedIn post. In fact, as he points out, the data that medical technologists collect in hospitals isn't for research, it's for diagnostic purposes. As he puts it, these aren't the "consent to research" tests, these are the "what's making you sick" tests. Of course, Brady reminds me, the tests that medical technologists run on sick people wouldn't exist and couldn't be trusted unless other people at earlier times and places had agreed to contribute their medical specimens for research purposes. "When you're diagnosing somebody, you can't be guessing that it's working, it has to be so standardized that there's no question that that procedure works."[27]

Brady, it turns out, was one of those contributors in an earlier time and place. As a child in Oklahoma, his mother had enrolled Brady in a research study. "The children's hospital in Oklahoma City was doing a study to see if dyslexia was genetic. And there was a theory that we had it, and so my sister and I were both enrolled and taken, and we did a lot of other tests, but genetic tests were part of it. Of course, they were trying to determine if it was familial."[28] As an adult, Brady has no idea what happened with the data collected from him or with the research that was done with it. He asked his mother about it once; she thought that the study might not have been published as the results weren't what the researchers expected.

Based on what he knows now, Brady thinks he might be able to track down the name of the researchers and possibly even the repository where the data were stored. His mother died years ago, and with the little information he has (name of hospital and approximate year, based on his memory of being in third or fourth grade), it has always seemed like too much effort. "I've never forgotten that event, and it's always been in the back of my mind. I don't know what ever happened to that or if it's still out there. I would say that the more I've learned about medicine, the more I became cognizant of what was happening then."[29]

The study itself seemed to have shaped Brady's life indirectly. He acknowledges that his dyslexia made school difficult for him and he had lots of teachers who dissuaded him from pursuing higher education. He had a chance to work in a science lab at one of his first jobs out of high school and rediscovered an interest in biology that high school had nearly destroyed. At age twenty-five, he decided college was for him, "So [the dyslexia] affected me, but I learned how to overcome it—in fact, I even learned how to embrace it; there's some really good things that I am able to do that other people are not. And so I lean on those strengths and just compensate for the stuff that I know is a problem." He goes on to describe how, as a program chair, he's careful to ensure that the training programs his university runs are accessible to students with many different strengths and abilities.

Brady tells me that if someone were to come to him today and ask him to participate in a genetic study on dyslexia, he'd jump in. He believes in the power of science. What nags at him, he says, is that he was enrolled as a child and it was his mother's decision, not his. And once you're in, you're in, he says. In thinking about the multigenerational implications of digital data collection, Brady immediately jumps from his genetic data to social media and back again:

> It's astronomical the amount of pressure we put on the people who cannot make a decision for themselves. And by the time it's done, it's done. There is no going back. I feel the same with the grandparents and the parents putting photos of their kids online. That's it. There's no way to ever take that offline. Even if Google says "we're going to destroy it" like they're trying to do in Europe. It's not gone. It just won't come up on the Google search. Sometimes, we as scientists go faster than we should because we don't know how to reel it back if we get to that point.

Brady's reflections touch on many of the issues that Vanessa, John, Leo, and Ken-Ichi address in designing their studies. What does real consent look like, who can give it, and given all the downstream uses of data given to one organization does consent even make any sense as a framework? What's the right balance between scientific accuracy and personal privacy? What does it mean to delete digital data? Answering these questions in trustworthy ways is key to creating a future in which people might safely donate their digital data.

The multigenerational aspect of digitized data is also important, especially when it comes to genetic information. When it comes to DNA, sharing yours is equivalent to sharing that of all your blood relatives.[30] Sharing other kinds of data also implicates other people. Text messages or social media data, for example, can be linked not only to you but to whoever receives or clicks on them. In the digital age, the data we generate not only says a lot about us but is revelatory about everyone we're connected to. This has led scholars and activists to think about *networked privacy*, in which you consider not only what your data says about you but how it inherently reveals the people you are connected to and information about them. This is one more consideration we need to design into systems for donating digital data.[31]

DATA: SPECIAL CHALLENGES

For decades, privacy scholars, lawyers, and technologists have been studying, writing about, and engineering software systems that protect individual people's data. Over that same time period, several industries and most of the world's foremost technology companies have been working overtime to create ways to claim ownership of and profit from the same digital data trails. Even as the public pendulum of awareness seems to have swung from "I don't understand" to "I don't care" to "I don't know what to do about it," the idea that a person could be in charge of how their own data are used is still new. Regulations in both the European Union (the General Data Protection Regulation [GDPR]) and in California (the California Consumer Privacy Act) have helped raise awareness about personal data, but the argument is largely framed as a battle between individual rights and corporate property. This battle is critically important, and those two choices don't represent the only ways to think about digital data.

Finding ways to return control of a person's digital data self is important. It is one of the most important civil rights issue of our time, a fundamental question of justice.[32] Putting us—and not companies or governments—in charge will require new types of technology, new laws, and new behaviors on our part. Ironically, getting people to think about how they might share their data willingly to accomplish things they care about may be a way to get us to care more (and act differently toward) other organizations that just take data from us.

It was much easier to connect with people donating photos and sound recordings of birds or bugs than people donating medical data. Some, like David Leland, have been passionately gathering data about birds since they were kids. It's a series of small steps from keeping your own list in a notebook and comparing your list with other birders to transferring your written notes into a software program. David made the transition decades ago and still keeps his notebooks, as well as the laptop with his AviSys database on it. When the makers of AviSys stopped supporting the software, it was an easy choice for David to move over to eBird. And once on eBird, sharing with the Cornell University Ornithology Lab is simple. You retain control over what you share (if anything), but the app makes it easy to contribute your sightings to the database, even as you keep a copy of everything for yourself.

The ability to keep and to share, to use and to remix digital data has been long understood by artists, writers, musicians, lawyers, and technologists. As a characteristic of digital data and technological systems, it's familiar to everyone who has ever shared a photo from their phone camera. Its familiarity hides its profundity. From the earliest days of public internet use, experts have been developing new licensing schemes and trying to reconfigure intellectual property law to support the possibilities created by this characteristic of digital data and networks. Software developers created and called for new types of software licenses that would require sharing and reuse. In the early 2000s, lawyers and artists created a suite of licensing options—called Creative Commons—that would allow people to choose from a range of sharing options for the things they created and posted online. In the decades since, Creative Commons options and software licensing schema have become as important to our ability to use and share information as the technologies themselves. They provide a legal scaffold that runs alongside our pervasive digital infrastructure. These technical and legal systems enable Cat and Mira to share photos with iNaturalist and they make it possible for families to hold on to their private keepsakes while also creating public digital archives of the American internment camps. Our ability to donate other types of digital data safely and intentionally will require continued innovation in these legal and technological systems.[33]

We're seeing some of this kind of innovation among open-source software developers who are calling for new "ethical licenses" that they intend to allow their software to be used, but not for acts of war, immigrant detention, or surveillance.[34] This mirrors what previous generations did in regard to investing their money: faced with choices they felt were immoral, they created alternative investment funds. We can do this again, with and for digital data. These innovations are likely to include changes to intellectual property law and licensing schema, as well as the creation of new types of organizations. All of this rhymes with our previous histories of creating legal organizations (nonprofits) to manage donations of private money for public causes. We need this same innovation—led by people from the communities most likely to be exploited—for the donation of digital data for public causes.

What about other types of data? What if the data on your daily purchases (tracked by credit companies or through loyalty cards), the data from your online searches, your social media feed, text messages, call records, or driving habits could be useful in modeling public transportation patterns, saving lives during disasters, or tracking diseases? Would you share it?

Would you contribute your data to help cure disease, build renewable energy systems, or feed hungry people? What assurances would you need to do this? Would you want to be asked first, ensured that the data would be used as promised, not sold or given to others, and that you could quit at any time? Those are the minimal conditions for volunteering time or donating money, so why shouldn't they apply to data? Sharing data with groups that you trust is even less painful and less of a sacrifice than giving blood. A day or two after giving blood, your body has completely replenished itself. You saved someone's life *and* you have all the blood you need. When you let researchers use your data, you don't even have to prick your finger; they can use it and you never even give it up.

Many people are either freaked out about all the companies and government agencies that have access to their data or they're so tired of worrying about it they've just given up. But what if we could control our data and our digital selves? Legal changes, advances in privacy-protecting technology, and, yes, widespread outrage about companies profiting off of our data and leaving us behind could be steps toward a future that works better for people and communities than the recent past. One of the greatest opportunities we face is to take control of our data so we can share it.

By our own choice, with the groups or organizations that we trust, to do things that we care about.

This is possible. If each of us begins to imagine a new relationship with our data and demand that we have the right to make choices about them, we can engage with and push forward technologies, laws, and social practices that serve communities rather than enrich companies. Each of us is rich in data. Putting that information to good use—adding it to our own giving portfolios—could make us all individually and collectively better off.

7 RETAIL THERAPY

Every November and December, I play a little game I call *how many asks*. It involves paying attention to how many times a day, and in how many different ways and places, I get asked for my money, time, or data. A typical day begins with checking email. A few requests are always in there. Then I go to work. Two or three times a week, on my way to or from the bus stop, I pass at least one pair of vest-wearing (red and yellow seem to be favorite colors), clipboard-carrying folks asking if I "have a minute for the polar bears [or children]?" If I go out at lunchtime, I'm asked to "add a dollar for juvenile diabetes" at the drug store or round up the cost of my grilled cheese sandwich "to help the hungry." More email and social media requests stream through my laptop or phone during the day. Heading home, I navigate past pairs of vested clipboard carriers and pass a bright-red Salvation Army donation pail and an enthusiastic bell ringer. I'm likely to meet another clipboard carrier down on the subway platform, wanting to know if I'm a registered California voter. Out comes a pen: "Sign a petition for high-speed rail? Safer poultry? Proposition X? Or Y? Or Z?" Arriving home, my first stop is the mailbox, which I empty while standing near the recycling bin. During the weeks when I play how many asks, I sort out the bills from the direct mail solicitations. I put the bills on my desk and the solicitation envelopes in a paper grocery bag. National averages suggest that my mail should be about 10 percent direct marketing requests.[1] In December, it seems as if that percentage flips to 90 percent. Most years, I fill at least one grocery bag, sometimes two, every week of the game.[2]

A few years ago, I realized I couldn't actually separate the bills from the requests. I've noticed that utility bills and tax notices are starting to include checkbox options to add a dollar or round up my payment to contribute to funds for the arts or wildfire protection. Since the middle of 2020, as nonprofits shift to face the long-term reality of the pandemic and economy, it also seems as if every month is December, at least as far as my mail solicitations are concerned.

There's nothing scientific about this game, nor is it about winning or losing; it's just a way to pay attention. I've noticed a few things. First, an awful lot of fundraising happens in the last eight weeks of the year. December is to nonprofits' annual revenue as the holiday season is to retailers—really important. Annual surveys and studies from online giving companies show that about 17 percent of all annual giving happens in this one month.[3] This is part of the reason that Giving Tuesday, a single-day event focused on encouraging acts of generosity, is scheduled for the first Tuesday following American Thanksgiving. It rides the rhetorical wave of Black Friday and Cyber Monday—both of which encourage, reflect, and have come to stand in as cultural and economic reference points for retail shopping trends.

Second, there are a lot of ways to tie together giving and shopping. In addition to being asked to round up a sandwich bill or add a dollar to my drugstore purchase, I can also choose between all kinds of branded products promising to "do good." The color pink (for breast cancer) starts appearing on everything from batteries to yogurt in October. By December, we can choose among special holiday versions of soda bottles, sweaters, and snack food, each promising to dedicate a small amount to a cause.

CAUSE MARKETING AND SHOPPING FOR GOOD

My game of how many asks also allows me to keep an eye on payment innovations and something called *cause marketing*. Making charitable contributions used to involve writing checks, charging a credit card, or dropping cash into a bucket or onto a plate. In the last twenty years, we've gotten used to clicking Donate Now buttons on websites. We can make donations by text message or Tweet, through Facebook, via PayPal, during videogame streams on Twitch, and by touching our phones to a card reader attached to the Salvation Army kettle bell. As for cause marketing, this is the industry term for all those products—batteries, T-shirts, iPhones, shoes, soda, and just about anything else—that indicate via a label, a tag, or a color that a "percentage will be donated to [fill in the blank]." In the years I've been playing how many asks, the number of items and places that offer to "make a donation to [fill in the blank]" has grown from a few to seemingly every-thing. It started in 1983 with a campaign by American Express to make a one-penny donation for every dollar that customers spent on their cards to restore the Statue of Liberty. It is now built-in business practice at checkout lines and for individual products.[4]

All told, it may be time for me to tweak the rules of my game. Rather than counting all the ways and places I'm asked to give during December, it might be easier to count the few transactions I undertake that don't involve a donation opportunity. This leads me to bigger questions about buying and shopping. First, what happens with all that money that goes to product purchases but that is promised to be sent on as a donation? Are there ways to track it? What does it cost—in real dollars and human psy-chology—to blend shopping with giving? Finally, from the perspective of giving, are some retail options better than others?

MAKING GIVING EASIER

For many people, the appeal of cause marketing is that it makes giving eas-ier and shopping more guilt free. You pick out the product you want, and the manufacturer or retailer has already chosen the cause or organization to donate to. Making giving easier has been a goal for fundraisers for at least a hundred years. In the spring of 1900, as a new century dawned, two brothers from Indiana, Arthur and Allen De Long, submitted an applica-tion to the United States Patent Office for a self-sealing envelope with a stub attached. The invention would "provide a practical and convenient device . . . for use in making stated or weekly contributions to church or other charitable institutions, societies, or associations."[5] Ten months later, the De Longs were awarded US Patent 776,426 for their invention. The breakthrough combination of a one-piece folding and sealing envelope on which a contributor's name and donation amount could be written would go on to become ubiquitous in fundraising. The brothers' patent expired in 1918, yet you and I still receive adaptations of their invention, inserted as the return envelope in direct mail solicitations.

The De Longs hold one of the first patents issued for an innovation in fundraising technologies, but the phenomenon didn't end with them. Today's innovations are focused less on mail-based tools and more on mobile apps, kiosks, text messaging, and point-of-sale technology. Walk into many a downtown sandwich or salad shop, chain drug store, or large grocery chain, and there's a good chance you'll be asked if you'd like to make a "donation with your purchase," "round up your bill for a cause," or "leave a tip for the community." These transactions, along with any purchase you might make that is branded to support cancer research, environmental preservation, or hungry kids, require some kind of tracking process. Patent applications for point-of-sale transactions date back to shortly after the De Long envelope patent expired. Just before World War I ended, a Hungarian immigrant named Joseph Garami filed a patent application for a device to help sell Liberty bonds and war savings stamps at neighborhood stores. By the time Garami and his coinventor Sarah Steiner received US Patent 1,311,601, the war had ended, but the trend of linking retail purchases with donations had only just begun.

Point-of-sale donations are now huge. If you've shopped at Walmart or Costco, chances are you've been asked to donate money as you were finalizing your purchase. These asks come in many forms. Usually, the cashier will say, "Do you want to add a donation for children's health [or another cause]?" You may be offered a paper icon or postcard to document your gift; these are often hung up behind the cash register or in some other prominent place.[6] In some places, you'll find a branded donation canister next to the cash register where you can drop your change (instead of the tip jar you're likely to find at independent coffee or sandwich shops). You may even be asked specifically to contribute that change, by rounding up your $6.47 to an even seven dollars, for example, and donating the fifty-three cents to whatever cause or organization is being promoted. Those cents add up. One study, looking only at point-of-sale campaigns that raised more than one million dollars each, counted a total of seventy-three programs that collectively raised more than $440 million.[7]

Those are big numbers. As such, these efforts tend to be dominated by big players. Most of the really big point-of-sale campaigns happen at chain stores. The beneficiaries tend to be large organizations, including groups such as the Children's Miracle Network (CMN), a single organization that raises money for 170 hospitals in the United States and Canada. CMN was born out of the old March of Dimes telethon model and has relied on star power and national reach from its inception. Pop singer Marie Osmond joined the initial Utah-based founding group at inception in 1983 and continues to serve on the group's board of directors. The "miracle balloons" that CMN provides in exchange for one-dollar donations at Sam's Clubs and Walmarts have raised almost one billion dollars since 1987. It is the biggest point-of-sale partnership in brick-and-mortar stores. Only eBay for Charity, which lets sellers raise money at checkout for any charity of their choice, raises more money per year.[8]

While big retailers and nonprofits dominate point-of-sale giving, they neither invented nor have a lock on it. Wander into an independent coffee shop, hardware store, or bar in any community following a natural disaster and you're likely to find a jar next to the cash register. It may be the typical tip jar repurposed to go to recovery efforts or a special jar put there just for that particular disaster effort. It will be in the same place you often find a small clear plexiglass box with a coin slot in the top, asking for your spare change.

FOLLOW THE MONEY

What happens to the coins or dollars that your purchase is supposed to generate as donations? There is no easy answer to this question. Imagine the following scenario. You buy a pair of sneakers, branded as contributing to a cause, at a department store. The sneakers promise "a percentage" will be donated. You buy the sneakers. The department store takes its profit as a percentage of the shoe sale. The number of pairs sold is communicated to the sneaker company, and they calculate the percentage to donate. Funds are transferred to the partner organization, which had been chosen in advance and (one hopes) vetted by the company's marketing team. The partner organization uses the funding to deliver on its mission. Someone somewhere (you hope) benefits from the organization's work. That's one possible way the money from your shoe purchase could be used for good. The problem is there's a lot of detail missing in that pathway and a lot of money leaking out along the way.

First of all, note that the marketing signs don't specify how the donation amount is calculated. What is it a percentage of? The price of the shoes? Retail price or wholesale? Or is it a percentage of the profit on each pair of shoes (a much smaller amount)? Or perhaps it is a percentage of all sales, capped at a certain level? Usually none of this is communicated to you, the customer. You're likely to assume (if you even think about it) that it's a percentage of the total price you paid (the retail price) because this would be the highest amount. In experiments run on customers to answer this question, many of them assumed the entire price they paid was donated.[9] In most cases, it's deliberately difficult to figure out what the real percentage is and what it's calculated against. Most retailers and brands don't publish this information—and certainly not at the point of purchase. In reality, it's possible that none of your purchase goes anywhere but into the retailer's pocket because many of these campaigns involve a capped donation from the company. After a preset (and not publicly announced) amount has been donated, the company keeps the promotion going but doesn't contribute any more funds to the cause.

This confusion is intentional. The brand wants you to feel good (and associate that good feeling with their shoes), so it's fine to let you assume the most generous choice. But the brand also has to make a profit (which is why you can be sure it isn't the entire price of the shoes that's being donated). Businesses like to be able to predict their costs, which is why it's also likely that the brand has negotiated a donation cap. This means the brand can plan for a donation up to a maximum amount and no more. This doesn't mean that it will stop advertising the shoes as donating to the cause. If the brand has promised a capped amount—say, $1 million—then the person who buys a pair of shoes after that millionth donated dollar isn't generating any additional revenue for the cause but only profit for the brand.

Most of the research on cause marketing focuses on the brand side of the equation. Promoters of cause marketing emphasize how companies that associate with a social issue can drive customer loyalty, make people feel better about their purchases, and even make people have more positive feelings about the companies that produce the brands.[10] None of these concerns have anything to do with how well the system works for the nonprofit partner or the cause.

If you want to find out how much money went to the cause, you'll have to do some digging. Big companies that sponsor these partnerships will often report their total contributions in their annual reports. Here again, they opt for the biggest, most eye-catching numbers. In reporting these, they still won't report what percentage (and of what price) each individual purchase generated, thereby making it impossible for you—the customer—to know how much you helped give.[11] They also won't report how much it cost for these donations to be made. Think about that for a minute. If there were actual donations per product being made, the companies would need to code their software to track these purchases, train their salespeople to tell the stories and make the asks, pay accountants to track the totals, and then write the checks to the partner organizations. Those costs would be counted against the total value of "your" purchase-based contribution, but you will have a hard time finding them reported anywhere. These granular systems changes are another reason to assume that there's actually a capped, negotiated agreement between the company and a nonprofit partner, and your individual purchase has almost nothing to do with that transaction.

When it comes to cause marketing, the front-end emphasis is on making you the customer feel good and generous about your purchase. On the back end, companies have every incentive to limit the total amount of the giving and to downplay what it costs them to move some percentage of your product purchase through their entire inventory and accounting tracking systems and make sure it gets delivered to the end organization. Those costs may not be huge for large companies that already have all the systems in place, but you can be sure that they are more than it would cost if you made a donation directly to the final organization—which is a perfectly fine thing for you to do.[12] Go ahead and purchase whatever shoes or eyeglasses you prefer, but be honest with yourself; that's a shopping decision. Then go ahead and make a direct financial donation to a nonprofit or spend some time working for the social or political cause for which your purchase signals support. Then you'll know what you are giving, how much, to whom, and for what.

RETAIL THERAPY OR GOOD GIVING?

The oldest trope in fundraising is "you don't get if you don't ask." So asking a lot and making it easy to give seem like no-brainers. But is it possible to ask too often or make giving too easy? Given the pervasive nature of donation requests and the many ways donations are integrated into other kinds of transactions, these seem like logical questions to ask. Research suggests that the answer to both questions is yes.

Giving while shopping seems to reduce overall giving. Most of the research on these relationships focus on the benefits to the companies that sell the product, not on how these partnerships affect either you—the consumer/giver—or the cause itself. There are a few academic studies of cause marketing that focus on the end result for the nonprofit partner or on how people's behavior changes after they've purchased one of these branded products. The most generous read of the research on cause marketing is that it is good for the marketer, not so much for the cause.

Scholars at the University of Michigan have run several studies that should make you think twice about buying products for good. The researchers set up two variations of a booth selling high-energy drinks for charity. In both cases, the booth was staffed by students from an on-campus fraternity known for supporting a major American cancer group. At one booth, passerby could make a donation for a cause. At the other booth, passerby could buy a high-energy drink for $2.50 per can; each sale would generate $.50

for the charity. You could also donate more with your drink purchase if you wanted to. When the researchers compared how much was raised in each case, the donate-only booth raised more for the cancer charity than either the soda purchase alone or the soda purchase plus additional donation.[13]

The research team then created additional test conditions to try different combinations of products, company financial matches, and types of causes. These two studies—run in labs, with students getting course credit, and not out on the campus square open to passerby—found that total donations to the causes or charities were higher when there was not a product sale involved. They also found that the higher the purchase price of the product, the lower the aggregate charitable giving, leading the research team to write "that people may mentally assign their CM [cause-marketing] expenditure as their charitable giving."[14]

At least three things are happening here. First, the total amount of money that goes to charity from these branded products (both from the percentage of the purchase and any company match) is less than if people just gave directly to the charity. Second, many people who buy products branded to help out a cause overestimate the good they've done, confusing the full cost of the product with the percentage that is actually donated. And third, people who buy cause-branded products may feel like they've done their good deed for the day and don't need to do anything else.

Economists call this phenomenon, in which doing one thing stops you from doing another, *crowding out*. In this case, the feeling that you've made a donation because you've bought a certain product crowds out your desire to make a direct gift to the cause. Some psychologists and economists study this even more closely, looking for something called *social licensing*. This is when we let ourselves off the hook for certain behaviors because we've already done our part. Studies of social licensing on environmental purchases, for example, show that we often give ourselves permission (or *license*) to drive more often because we're now driving a hybrid car, or we turn up the air conditioner because we've bought better insulation for the house.[15] It's a cycle that will be familiar to anyone who has ever tried to stick to a diet: eating an apple for breakfast licenses dessert after dinner. Doing this limits the impact of the healthy choice and makes it harder to lose weight. The same holds true for licensing wasteful behavior after making an environmentally sound purchase.[16]

These insights contradict the hype of cause marketing. The promise that's being made is that both products and causes will benefit. The reality is that it's the product manufacturers and retailers, the marketing part, that benefits, while the cause gets left behind.

Buyer Beware: Call It Shopping

It's tempting to try to do two things at once: to buy shoes and do good in the world. But there's very little evidence that this kind of giving is worth it. You might feel better about your purchase if it signals support for a cause, and that's OK. If more companies made real efforts to decrease the environmental damage or increase the social benefits of their operations and products, we'd all be better off. Those kinds of corporate changes require much more than a marketing partnership tied to the sale of their retail goods. In fact, it's all too common for corporations to use these kinds of partnerships to put a positive spin on their reputation without really changing their practices. So go ahead if you want, since you're already shopping, and buy branded products that make you feel good. But be honest about what you're doing: it's retail therapy for you. It probably won't make much difference in the world and may be a form of reputation management (sometimes called *charity washing*) for the company.

COMMODIFYING CONCERN

Just as pernicious, we often don't know where the money actually goes. For the most part, the companies that promise to donate the extra dimes or dollars associated with their feel-good products don't want us to follow up and ask questions. They do want us to associate their store and their products with doing good. They don't want us to hold them accountable for it.

Giving at the register fails on every front when it comes to good giving. Even people who do it seem to know this. In our mapping conversations, people almost always expressed some degree of derision for buying branded products. This was especially notable among groups that included more than a few people who worked in nonprofits themselves. One person indicated surprise at the discussion of point-of-sale donations, saying, "we would never do that."[17] Others scoffed at these efforts, noting that the companies and products aren't "very honest about how they do it" and that most people don't understand "how companies make money off of supposedly charitable enterprises."[18] Yet the practice continues to grow, so clearly people are doing it.

It's hard to know what happens with the money. And since most of us just feel guilty or pressured when the cashier asks us to donate, we don't even get a little hit of good feeling. We certainly don't get a big hit of feeling good; the companies take all the credit for the giving they do with your nickels. The result is a form of pseudogenerosity that is unfulfilling to both shoppers and society. It's possible that the opportunity costs of these omnipresent products are a reduction in overall participation and contribution rates.

RETAIL FOR GOOD: 826 VALENCIA STREET

Not every retail/giving alliance is suspect. Many causes and organizations run retail outlets or sell products directly. The Pirate Shop on Valencia Street is a front—literally—for the nonprofit writing program 826 Valencia, started by author Dave Eggers. People walk in off the street, enticed by the window display of message bottles, Captain Hook hands, and the promise of getting all their pirate needs met. The space itself is deliberately disorienting. Someone looking for an eyepatch after surgery is probably expecting a medical supply store, not a dark room dominated by a ship's prow. And everyone who enters is bound to ask, "What's going on behind the curtain?"

The disorientation is deliberate. The pirate shop, and the classrooms behind the curtain, are intended to help set the mood for good creative writing. Because 826 Valencia is a writing program for students, its staff is interested in sparking imagination, creating a playful and fun space, and nudging kids to try new things.

The shop itself is a bit of an accident. When the program was founded, it was hard to find an appropriate space to hold the regular tutoring sessions. The building at 826 Valencia was zoned for retail. When the program moved in (and adopted the address as its name), the founders had to meet the zoning restrictions by figuring out a way to "sell" something in the front of the building so they could use the back for writing classes. Legend has it that the idea for a quirky pirate shop was inspired by the unfinished interior of the building, which looked (vaguely) like the inside of a ship.

Once inside the quirky shop, you can't help but notice the tutoring going on behind the red stage curtain that divides the space into sales floor and classroom. There's no doubt that purchases made in the front of the room help pay for the activities going on in the back. Many cities are home to restaurants and cafes that are revenue-generating, on-the-job training sites run by nonprofits. Probably all of us are familiar with one of the longest-running of such retail efforts, Girl Scout Cookies. These examples share a certain quality: there's no distance between the retail sales and the program beneficiaries.

The 826 program has expanded tremendously and now includes three locations in San Francisco, as well as spin-offs in eight other US cities. Each location includes a retail front. These stores have become an integral part of the 826 look and feel, which has advantages and disadvantages. When 826 sought to expand to the Tenderloin neighborhood in San Francisco, the retail shop was an important positive from the standpoint of the program's new landlord.[19] In other locations, however, it can be harder to find appropriate programmatic space because of the need to also have a retail presence. But in all cases, the retail stores exist to serve the programmatic purpose. Any profit from the stores goes directly to cover program expenses.

That direct proximity is important. In cause marketing and point-of-sale donations, the distance between purchase and program is filled by several unnecessary middlemen. The cashier who asks you to round up your purchase total, all the costs the company incurs to track the dollars internally, and the marketing costs that went into building the partnership between the drugstore chain and disease research group are all intermediary steps between your donation and the cause you care about. They all cost money. It's very possible that more is being spent running the program then actually gets passed through in donations. This only makes sense when you recognize these brand alliances as part of the company's marketing and customer-acquisition costs.

Which should make you ask: Why bother? After all, even if all the money does go through to the organization as promised, you've handed all the good parts of giving to the company that sold you the product. They get the credit and attention and "good feels" for your donation. You'd make a bigger difference, and feel better about it, if you gave money directly to the cause yourself.

The second version of retail giving—the type in which a nonprofit earns revenue directly from running a pirate shop, a restaurant, or teaching girls sales skills with Thin Mints—is different. These activities align with and directly reinforce a social mission. The retail activity and the program purpose align and are run by an entity whose primary purpose is a social good, not a product sale.

There's an easy way to tell the difference between pseudogenerosity and retail that matters. If the product comes first—you're buying shoes or eyeglasses or rounding up your grocery bill because of a promise to send proceeds somewhere—then what you're doing is shopping. Don't count it as giving, count it as shopping. If you want to make your action about giving, take your purchase home, and then donate time or money to a cause.

CITIZEN OR CONSUMER?

Of course, buying things is only one way we can align our shopping behaviors with issues we care about. Another way is not shopping. Boycotting certain products or companies is nothing new—the Boston Tea Party, a boycott of British tea, is part of the founding mythos of the United States, and the Montgomery bus boycott plays an equally central role two centuries later. There is a long history of consumer activism in the United States that includes both boycotts and *buycotts*—avoiding certain products in the first instance, and rewarding companies for their behavior by preferencing their product in the second.

It makes sense to try to align your shopping habits with your values, as we spend most of the money we earn on consumer items, from food to entertainment to clothing. Consumption also makes up the largest part of the US economy. Most estimates of the US GDP credit about 70 percent of it to consumer buying.[20]

The phrase *conspicuous consumption* goes back to sociologist Thorsten Veblen's 1899 book titled *The Theory of the Leisure Class*. Nowadays, we see a focus on conscious consumption.[21] What we buy says a lot about us as individuals. Using our buying power to make a larger change in the world generally requires working with others. My own purchases reflect my values, but if I want to get a company to stop doing something or to start doing something else, I need to make my buying (or boycotting) decisions with a lot of other people.

Eric Shih spends a lot of time thinking about how we come together to make a difference as shoppers. Paradoxically, he comes to this after years spent organizing low-wage laborers in Chinatowns, many of whom worked in the garment industry or in restaurants. These are tenuous positions, and ones in which unions or collective bargaining power are rare.[22] At the time that Eric was doing this work, a lot of factories were closing down quickly as garment work moved overseas. Factory owners would often close up shop quickly, leaving the workers unpaid for work already completed. Eric and his colleagues knew how hard it was for these workers to demand this back pay. Shoppers, on the other hand, who were outraged by this, could be mobilized to demand better conditions. While the workers risked retribution from employers, informed customers could put pressure on restaurant owners by refusing to eat at their restaurants.

Eric runs a website called Spendrise that makes it easier for people to organize others to put pressure on companies to change their behavior. Social media, of course, makes it easier than ever for anyone to voice displeasure at certain corporate behavior; just think about how quickly the #DeleteUber hashtag took off after the company sought to profit off the Trump administration's Muslim ban in 2017. But getting from trending hashtags to changed corporate behavior takes persistence, coordination, and a specific ask of the company. Spendrise provides a place for people to identify and call out the specific change they want from a company and then organize their outreach around that. For example, food delivery company DoorDash at one point wasn't delivering to the Anacostia neighborhood, which lies just across the Potomac River from Washington, DC. Rather than accept this modern-day version of redlining, neighbors banded together using Spendrise to identify the problem, figure out the specific change they wanted to see, and organize people to pledge to stop using DoorDash within DC if it wasn't going to serve all neighborhoods equally. The effort worked, and DoorDash expanded its delivery area.

Changing our own consumer behavior helps us feel better about ourselves. Using our behavior to change how companies operate requires working with others. Even then, it's rare that even a big boycott hurts the bottom line enough to drive change. It's much more likely that a company's response to consumer pressure is driven by reputational concerns than by financial ones.[23]

The need to work with others, identify shared concerns, and express a common message to get a company to change is one reason that Eric is frustrated by arguments that pit our identities as *consumers* against our identities as *citizens*. He sees the two as potentially much more aligned. Practically speaking, the same kinds of activities that consumers use to shift corporate behavior (organizing, common messages, specific proposals) are what people can do to influence public policy. Eric believes we should be proud of our identities as consumers and make greater use of them. "We each make choices, every day, about what to buy and from whom. The reasons why people spend can very much be tied to how they want the world to see them . . . [we can] turn that into a basis for collective identity and then collective action."[24]

PROXIMITY MATTERS

Ironies abound when it comes to embedding giving opportunities into shopping transactions. On the one hand, consumer spending is what most of us do with most of our income. Linking giving with spending provides the greatest number of opportunities to "ask" for money. On the other hand, blending giving into spending masks the activity, erodes both the real and psychological values of the gift, and makes it harder to hold anyone accountable for the flow of funds. If you want to blend these activities, your best bet is going to be finding mission-specific businesses or nonprofits that sell goods directly, like a pirate shop. The proximity between the business product and the social mission matters, and they don't get any closer than when they come from the same organization. This is not unlike the work the NDN Collective is doing to create capital cycles that support businesses in Lakota country or the way that immigrants, Black people, and even "shop local" efforts focus shopping dollars on their own communities.

Your own proximity may also come into play. Look around your community. Chances are there are job-training programs in restaurants, soap or body-product companies run by people recovering from substance abuse, or moving companies that hire formerly incarcerated individuals. Supporting these and other local businesses is a time-tested way to use your dollars for good.

How can you make the most of the givingscape? One evening, I had a dinner conversation with a successful nonprofit leader. He's spent his career raising and spending money for arts organizations, from the most famous museums in the country to local dance groups dedicated to specific cultural traditions from around the world. We were gathered in late April, about a week after the deadline for filing federal taxes. "I came close to tithing this year," he noted. "I gave almost 10 percent of my income to charity. This made me feel pretty good. But it was the other 90 percent that bothered me." I asked him what he meant. "As I was doing my taxes, I looked through all the charges on my credit card for the whole year. I felt good about the 10 percent to charity, but all the other things I spend my money on—food, clothing, getting around town. In comparison to the amount I gave to charity, I felt like the rest of my spending could have been so much more aligned with what I care about."[1]

In counting his 10 percent, he was using what we now know is the most narrow definition of giving. He wasn't counting his time, his consumption, his investment, his professional choices, or his political involvement. He wasn't yet thinking about his data as a resource. Each of us, like my dinner friend, have an abundance of resources we can think about using to make the world closer to the way we want it to be.

Given all these choices, what's the best thing to do? As clichéd as it might sound, you need to start with where you are. This is a good time to put down this book and go get your checkbook, credit card statements, shoebox full of receipts, PayPal account, calendar, or anything else you use to track your spending and time. Reflecting on what you've been doing is the first step.

PLANNING YOUR GIVING

Mario Lugay is a tall, thin, Filipino American man who's lived on both coasts of the United States. A trained community organizer, Mario got his professional start working with MacArthur genius award winner Ai-jen Poo at a New York–based antiviolence organization. He is also the founder of Giving Side, a website that helps people track their giving. Here's how it works. First, you set up an account at Giving Side. Whenever you get an email receipt for a financial donation, you forward that receipt to your account at GivingSide.com. The program organizes your receipts, making it easy to see how much money you've donated and to which organizations. You can tag organizations according to issues, so you can see your giving by cause. You can enter in information about the time you spend volunteering in your neighborhood, at a nonprofit, or as part of a campaign. The site organizes this information into a pretty robust picture of all the ways you gave your time and money. Mario designed it not to be a perfect tracker, but to provide people a tool to reflect on their political journeys.[2]

Giving Side reflects Mario's experiences as a community organizer. He knows how to help people take small steps toward long-term goals. "Campaigns and thank-yous are a huge part of organizing," he laughs. Actions are important, "but organizing and social movements are built around identity." Helping people figure out who they are, what they care about, and connecting them to others who see the world as they do is what organizers do.

Organizing people to get involved for the long haul requires helping them connect to others who share their feelings, beliefs, and objectives. People who stay with the work, through highs and lows, do so because fighting for something with others helps people see themselves in community with others. "It's the emotional shift, the identity, that keeps you doing the work. That's the journey. That's the end goal."[3]

None of what Mario describes seems to have much to do with giving, so I ask him why he built a tool to help people track their donations. "It's a proxy, a start," he says. "Giving money is something we do that can be tracked and reflected back to us. That's what Giving Side does. It's meant to soften the ground, allow people to be prepared to be organized." Mario explains: "In order to get to collective action, people must first have . . . not shame, You could call it pride, but I would call it 'not shame.' So Giving Side is meant to provide people with 'not shame' by helping them see what they already do. This prepares you to look for others, and that's the key to finding a political or civic home."[4]

Giving Side shares similarities with the mapping conversations we held across the country. Those conversations revealed that each of us has our own categorizations of what's political or civic, voluntary or culturally obligatory, varying from place to place, person to person, community to community. For example, some of us view voting as truly voluntary and others recognize it as an obligation and even part of their identity, though one without the force of law behind it.[5] Some see helping their neighbors as a core part of who they are and their culture; others see it as optional. How we give is partly determined by how we see ourselves and how we fit into the norms of our own communities. These patterns are much more varied than the legal lines that privilege some actions as charitable and others as political would have us believe.

By bringing the sensibilities of political and community organizing to a tracking tool, Giving Side intends to help people act together. "Communities start with individuals," Mario reminds me. The goal is not to do more giving by yourself. More giving is not all that matters. Helping you consider how your giving reflects who you are and how you see yourself as part of broader communities is what matters. Your giving, as Mario says, says a lot about you. It's a proxy for your civic and political identity, for finding your people, for finding your crowd.

Giving Side isn't meant to be just another app to make it easier and more efficient to track your money. It's an organizing tool (lightly) masquerading as an app. Giving Side is a little bit of tech designed from the wisdom of generations of successful social movement organizers.

You don't need to use Giving Side or any software to do this; you can do it with paper and pencil. But tracking your current choices is the first step.[6]

SEEING ALL THE CHOICES AT ONCE

Once you have a sense of where you are, it's time to map out where you want to go. It's most likely that you'll be responding to discrete opportunities as they arise. Having been oriented to the givingscape, you should now have a better sense of what your options are. The next step is to compare them against each other in the abstract, so that you can make decisions in the moment when you're asked or as you're considering starting or joining something. In other words, it's worth comparing the options in advance so that you know what to do in a real situation.

To do this, let's use a thought experiment. Imagine there's a fire in your city. Two tall buildings burn down, and a hundred people lose their homes. (Luckily, no one dies. Thought experiments, unlike real life, make it possible to avoid worst-case scenarios.) The buildings included stores, market-rate apartments, and several affordable housing units. Even as the firefighters finish their work, social media explodes with claims about building code violations that may have contributed to the fire. Your city, like most in the United States, is notoriously short on affordable housing. It isn't at all clear where the people displaced by the fire will live.[7]

Just minutes after you learn about the fire on your newsfeed, your email and social media fill with funding solicitations from GoFundMe campaigns, at least one local nonprofit, and the local chapter of a national nonprofit like the Red Cross. You turn on the news and learn that several people have been hospitalized for severe injuries. Local television news shows local politicians calling for full investigations and promising to replace the lost units of affordable housing. Interviews with the property owner and real estate developers follow. They're all talking about their plans to rebuild better and safer housing in the future. Within a few days you've also received an email from the community recreation center that you walk past each day, asking you to come help sort donations of food, blankets, and clothing for those in need. You start noticing local merchants switching their tip jars to donation jars and hosting in-store events to raise money for those who lost their homes. Calls come in from the Red Cross asking for blood donations for those who were hurt. The people who lost their homes find themselves answering lots of questions from emergency responders and sharing lots of data with the city, nonprofits, and hosts of crowdfunding campaigns. They—and you—wonder what happens with all that data.

Disasters like this bring all of the possible choices into view—donations of money and time, political and investing options, and questions about the use of personal data. Here are some navigational guides through the choices.

NONPROFIT DONATIONS

A donation to a nonprofit (local or national) will spend some funds on the immediate victims; they may even provide people with cash or gift cards. In a disaster-related solicitation, the nonprofit should be clear about what they're planning to do with the funds. Some part of all funds received has to go to running the organization, just as some of all funds via crowdfunding platforms goes to credit card and company fees. Nonprofits should be able to give you a clear, honest answer about these costs. As a giver, you should know that hiring people and running programs costs money and that these overhead costs are part of quality programs.

There have been decades of debate over the right overhead costs for nonprofits. There's two parts to the truth about this. First, running organizations and providing services costs money. Even if the work is all done by volunteers, there will be costs for materials or space. The second part of the truth is that there's no magic formula or percentage, given the range of nonprofit activities, the difference in costs across the country, and the role of volunteers. But honest answers about these costs, easily justified and explained are possible. This is the very least you should expect as a giver. Keep in mind that running a nonprofit is like running a business. Businesses that earn money beyond all their costs call the remainder profit.

Nonprofits use all the money beyond their costs for programs and services. Here's a useful quick comparison. A small business in your community has a budget of one hundred dollars, as does a local nonprofit (it's easiest to divide into one hundred). For the business, all its costs for rent, staff, utilities, and inventory might add up to seventy cents. The thirty cents remaining is its profit (30 percent would be a very good margin for most small businesses). The nonprofit has rent, staff, and utility costs as well, and any additional funds are used to pay for more or better programs and services. In other words, the thirty cents remaining—plus the operating costs—go into programs; 100 percent is being spent on its mission.

Sometimes, nonprofits make promises such as "all donations go directly to programs." These claims can be legitimate; they usually mean the organization is getting some group of donors (usually its board or a circle of close donors) to cover the operating costs. If an organization makes such a claim, ask about it. Who is covering the costs? How much is the overall budget? Again, easy-to-understand answers about this should be readily available.

When it comes specifically to disasters, making a gift to a local nonprofit that's part of the affected community is key to ensuring that local knowledge is being brought to bear. If the group existed before the disaster, has been running effective programs or services, and is staffed and run by people from the community, you may have found useful proxies for trust, reliability, and local accountability.

Such an organization is likely to have a broader mission than disaster response. In the short term, it should partner with disaster-specific expertise because the nonprofit's real mission might be advocating for safer affordable housing or providing long-term shelter. These services will be useful past the short-term rescue period. The local chapter of a national nonprofit works the same way. Your donation will go toward the organization's mission, a portion of which covers the local fire victims and a portion of which includes the rest of the programs and services. In short, every penny of your gift goes to the mission, but not every penny will go directly to the victims of this particular fire. Given the many long phases of disaster recovery, this can be a good thing for communities over time.

POLITICAL CHANGE

Returning to our scenario, think now about calls from politicians. In the short term, they're probably not asking for money. The politician will be making certain promises about investigations or future public funding. You can keep these in mind when election time rolls around. At that point, she'll be asking for all kinds of support—financial contributions, volunteering on her campaign, and, of course, your vote. You'll want to revisit the promises she made during the disaster. Did she listen to the people who lost their homes? Did she work to provide more affordable housing? In short, did she deliver on her promises? You can then decide whether to vote for her or not and decide if you're moved to do more to help get her elected.

If you're not satisfied with the work of politicians, there are many ways to take action against them. You can vote for their opponents. You might attend public meetings to find out why promises weren't kept and what's being done. Still not satisfied? Help the opponent's campaign in other ways, by volunteering your time, sharing information with their policy staff, or helping them raise money. You might be moved to run for office yourself. In addition to voting and getting people ready to run for office, our political system requires many of the same inputs as other means of change—money, time, and data.

TAKE CARE WITH CROWDFUNDING

A crowdfunding campaign promises to send (most of the) dollars it raises directly to victims, minus the percentage of the money that goes to credit card fees and the costs of the crowdfunding platform. Crowdfunding prioritizes immediacy and directness. Chances are that the funding campaign will shut down once the money is raised; it's a short-term approach. There's rarely any way to be sure the money went where it was promised. This doesn't assume there's fraud, but it does depend on trust. Knowing the people running the campaign or being close enough to the situation to be sure the money gets to where it's promised is important.

Crowdfunding was one of the more divisive tools in our 2019 mapping conversations. People felt strongly that "they'd rather go across town and give [the money] directly to a person" or that they "didn't trust where the money went." They had concerns that a data breach at the crowdfunding site would provide access to all the giver's information and funds. Others noted, "[I] know that I'm not going to actually mail a check so will give to crowdfunding and cover the one dollar [fee]."[8]

Since 2019, crowdfunding has become an ever more pervasive part of the givingscape. As the pandemic-induced economic collapse wiped out jobs across the country and created massive personal health care costs, crowdfunding became the go-to tool for people, nonprofits, and small businesses. Even in desperation, crowdfunding can feel like a trade-off between trust and convenience. Platforms aspire to make crowdfunding trustworthy and easy, and some of them offer certain kinds of guarantees. But remember that in most cases the platforms aren't posting and running these campaigns; individual people are. You need a way to trust the platform and the people running the campaign. Communities that already know each other, who are working together to create something, often rely on crowdfunding platforms to make it easy for them to contribute funds and for each participant to ask their circle of friends or family. Not only do these campaigns, in which people are already working together or in which everyone probably knows at least one person directly involved, build trust through the face-to-face time, but that trust also gets signaled over the crowdfunding wires.

Crowdfunding platforms like GoFundMe allow project organizers to focus on the work of soliciting donations, working with communities, making sure the money is spent as promised, and thanking donors—without having to spend much time setting up systems to receive money. It's a huge time saving for those committed volunteers and allows them to focus on the human activities, not the financial and technological ones.

The competition among crowdfunding companies has forced them to build services that seem safe, secure, reliable, and trustworthy. Most of them now provide fraud protection, for example. This makes it a bit easier for people new to donating on these platforms. The bigger the crowdfunding brands get, the more likely you'll be asked to give on one you recognize, which makes it easier to do basic due diligence on the platform (read the privacy policy, read their fraud policies, search for legal actions against the company, check to see if you can give anonymously and how you can opt out of any future contact from the platform). Trusting the people running the campaign, who are separate from the platform, is still likely to come down to whether or not you know someone who is directly involved. If you don't, you might see if anyone in the campaign has run previous crowdfunding campaigns on the site, and whether those went well (or badly).

Perhaps you want to support this effort but, for privacy reasons, don't want to use a crowdfunding platform. Check to see if you can reach the organizer directly. Ask them how to make a donation offline—mailing a check, for example. If they can't help you with that, then that's a sign that the rest of their effort may not be up to snuff. If you do decide to support such an effort, don't click and walk away. Use the crowdfunding platform to check on progress and to see what the organizers do once the money is raised. How do they document what they've done? Can you contact someone to find out the final use of the funds?

My favorite quote about crowdfunding campaigns comes from someone who didn't start one. A few years ago, I read a news story about Anna Landre, a college student in Washington, DC, with spinal muscular atrophy who relies on the daily support of health aides. Cuts in Medicaid made these aides too expensive and she had to drop out of school. People suggested she start a GoFundMe campaign to cover the costs. She didn't. Instead, she pointed out, "A GoFundMe wouldn't help anyone but me." Her situation was a direct result of public policy choices, and it would take policy change to fix the problems. Even as her own situation became dire, she was concerned about others—the vast, dispersed community of people who were being hurt by public funding cuts. Rather than start a crowdfunding campaign, she took her story to the media, pursued legal action against her insurance company, and started working with policy makers focused on healthcare. When her insurance company offered a financial settlement to end the case, she wanted to continue to a court fight, hoping to set a legal precedent. Friends in the disability community convinced her instead to agree to the settlement so she'd have the care she needed to be able to keep fighting.[9]

INVESTING FOR THE LONGER TERM

In our thought experiment, shortly after the fire, local housing developers tried to raise public support for new construction projects. Some of these may have been in the works prior to the fire; others may be crafted specifically to respond to the loss of housing. There may well be public policy issues and political choices you can participate in regarding new buildings, which you can access via the political choices discussed earlier. But construction projects also open the door to another way of participating: impact investing.

Just as Mary Margaret Pettway and the Souls Grown Deep Foundation are developing ways to invest money in the Boykin community, there are real estate development opportunities designed to put local money to use in community projects. These tend to be developers with expertise in affordable housing who can navigate both the financial and political details. Some of these developers are themselves nonprofit organizations that can be supported with donations. Others are commercial developers seeking financing from impact investing funds (such as those from Calvert and other mutual fund companies, community development banks, community credit unions, or even project-specific impact investing funds). If you're interested in investing money in a project that will earn you some financial return and address your community's need for housing, these could be good choices for you. Be clear from the beginning that the impact of your dollars will come over a much longer time frame than making a donation for rescue or recovery options. New buildings take a long time to develop. Their impact can last a lifetime.

TIME AND DATA

You may also want to give your time, possibly to the community center where displaced families are being housed or to groups of neighbors gathering food, clothing, or school supplies. As you think about these opportunities to contribute your time, you'll have short- and longer-term opportunities. There may be a one-off food-packing day or a chance to join the neighbors planning longer-term interactions with city hall and the city planning department. In the aftermath of a disaster, both types of volunteering are helpful. These choices mirror, in some ways, the difference between using iNaturalist and marking a street corner for Safe Passage. Either can be time well spent; both will probably also involve some of your data.

Think back to Cat Chang's donations on iNaturalist and the time that the corner captains spend at Safe Passage. These seem like very different approaches to volunteering. But there are important commonalities between the two. Most important, even as Cat focuses on data, there's no doubt she's contributing valuable time to the iNaturalist community. The time she spends collecting, organizing, uploading, and identifying photos is of secondary concern to her. As she says, "Now I spend time most evenings scrolling through iNaturalist the way other people scroll through Instagram. I identify other people's photos."[10]

Tools like iNaturalist make it easy to volunteer for tiny bursts of time, literal seconds. But a subset of the iNaturalist community has also made more than twenty million identifications.[11] These are the result of people taking the time to look at, review, and perhaps cross-reference a photograph and identify the bird, bug, or plant in it by species and taxa. Some members of the iNaturalist community are superusers—like James Maughn (username, jmaughn), a poet and community college educator. As of December

31, 2019, jmaughn had contributed at least one observation to iNaturalist every day since March 28, 2013—for 2,470 days in a row.[12] This streak was almost two years longer than the next in line, and most of the people noted for their continuity were clocking in streaks of between one hundred and three hundred days. It might take only a few minutes to contribute to iNaturalist, but to do it every day for a year? That's commitment.

Short bursts of volunteering are the norm, but it's those bursts that make programs like Safe Passage function for ten years. It only works because enough people commit to short shifts every month. Volunteer-Match, a matching website, reports connecting one hundred million people to volunteer opportunities since its launch in 1998.[13] VolunteerMatch revolutionized volunteering twenty years ago when it made it possible to for anyone to find organizations nearby that could use a few volunteers for a few hours.

But our measures of donated time still focus on activities centered around religious or nonprofit organizations. No political volunteering is counted, nor are the countless hours people spend helping their neighbors. In our mapping conversations, donating time was the second most common activity, mentioned 16 percent of the time across all the discussions.[14] Notably, these mentions of volunteering were separate from people's counts of the time they spend cooking or transporting neighbors, working on political campaigns, mentoring others, donating blood, or doing advocacy work.[15] Time is a factor in all of our giving choices, and we routinely undercount it.

Both your time and your data can be powerful contributions toward a cause. Regardless of which one you focus on—the time or the data—there's a good chance you're actually contributing both. This is almost guaranteed if there's a cell phone, website, or app involved in your activity of choice, because nothing happens on these digital devices without generating a digital data trail. A system like iNaturalist clearly communicates to you what's being collected and how it's being used. This kind of clarity should be expected from all digital volunteering (or donating) tools. You should know what you're getting into so you can know what you want to give.

The disaster thought experiment helps us think through the different mechanisms for giving—the different kinds of *how*. The advantages and disadvantages of each type are true in everyday life, not only in disasters, so being able to compare a donation on a crowdfunding site to a nonprofit donation or decide whether to give blood or attend a public meeting of real estate developers (or both) will be helpful when those individual opportunities come along in other situations.

For any issue you care about, you now have these three resources to think about—time, money, and data. In some situations—such as Cat's experiences with iNaturalist—you'll find that you're getting as much as you're giving. This is a great feeling.

But you need to understand what you're giving, to whom, for what, and under what conditions. If you've finely honed your skills in sussing out fraudulent or misleading behavior when you're asked to give your money or time, you'll need to bring those skills—and update them a bit—when asked for your data. Because digitized data are so different from time and money, the ways they can be used—and misused—are also different.

At the individual level, making smart choices about using your resources requires understanding how the organization or cause you're supporting actually operates. Is it a business, a nonprofit, a government agency, or an individual person? Is it clear how it covers its costs—beyond your contribution? Just knowing that much is helpful. It doesn't equate to knowing the full details of the business behind the organization, but it helps. Nonprofit organizations operate under a specific set of rules about what they can sell, how much of their revenue they can earn that way, and what they need to report. Commercial businesses operate under a different set of rules.

These issues are important when it comes to donating digital data, because the rules are still unclear and because data are so different. Before you donate your digital data, you'll want to think about how digital data works, how organizations might use them (to improve their products or programs, to learn something, for research, or to sell), and whether or not you can stop donating them (or stop the organization from using them) at a later date.

Over the course of your lifetime, it's possible you'll use every one of the hows and more—some of which we can't even imagine yet today. But in any given moment you're going to have to make choices, between opportunities and between causes. The next sections discuss some additional considerations for planning your giving and making those choices.

Say Yes to Say No

While we have lots of digital data, most of don't have lots of time or money and most of us aren't very good at saying no. The better you become at knowing what you do support, what you are using your time and money and choices to achieve, the better you will be at saying no to those asks that don't fit, don't feel right, or don't add up to anything meaningful. The more clearly you can articulate the thing you want to see be different, the easier it is to see (and say no to) things that are outside of that sphere of influence. The inverse of this is, conveniently, also true. Say no to things that don't matter that much to you precisely so that you will have more time and money for the things that make you say yes. Back in the opening vignette of this book, I told a story of multiple asks and multiple nos. Saying no won't make you feel like Scrooge if you do it knowing that you're saying yes to other choices.

If It Seems Too Easy, It Is

If your action requires no effort, does it mean anything? I applaud you trying to make your giving easy, but don't do so at the cost of meaning. It's the joy and connection that will keep you involved. If you do go ahead and choose an easy giving option, remember two things: if it seems too easy, it probably is, and don't outsource your own reward. Giving is about building connections and being part of something bigger than yourself. If all the good feelings (or publicity or tax benefits) of your actions are accruing to the company that makes your shoes or the app that rounds up your lunch purchase, you're the one missing out.

Mind the Middleman

Most of the efforts to make giving easy pretend to do so by eliminating a middleman. After all, if you buy a certain branded item because the company promises to donate to a charity, you don't have to do the work to find an organization to support. Same with rounding up your purchase price, using a particular web browser, or any other daily transaction that incorporates a donation (or the promise of one). But be clear here: if you're no longer doing the choosing of the end recipient, then that means someone else is. That may be the retail chain whose cashier is asking you to participate, engineers building the apps, or head office managers negotiating partnership deals. These new middlemen are hard to see (on purpose), but they're there, adding costs and limiting your choices.

What Do You Have to Lose?

When it comes to donating digital data, you should be concerned about your privacy and your relationships. Your data—photos, text messages, emails, or DNA—link you to other people. If those relationships matter to you in the physical world, they should matter in the digital realms as well. We won't find answers to these questions by thinking in terms of ownership; after all, you don't own your friends or family members. Think about these relationships when faced with the choice of giving data: Are you giving information that is connected to someone else also? The answer to that question is always yes if you're giving your cell number, your email address, or your DNA. Remember to also think about the data connected to your online or text contributions when you sign online petitions or if you register for a video-streamed meeting or fundraiser.

TIMING AND DISTANCE

Disasters compress and intensify all of our choices and their trade-offs. If you've already tracked your behavior, talked about it with others, or thought about the givingscape, you'll be prepared when a disaster strikes. As you're doing this planning, keep in mind two types of filters. The first are filters of timing and distance. Just as real change takes time, disasters unfold in phases. There is an immediate response that includes finding and rescuing people who are hurt and getting them help. This is often referred to as *search and rescue*. Even as rescues are still happening, the next phase of relief begins. This includes providing people with shelter, food, and medical care, and reuniting people who've been separated from family.

The relief period can last for weeks or months. Then begins the early recovery and then long-term recovery/rebuilding phases. There's no easy rule of thumb for how long these phases last, but the patterns hold across events: there's an immediate harm, people are rescued, relief is provided, and then the process of recovering and rebuilding begins. Making a difference in a disaster requires knowing where things are in this cycle. Similarly, timing matters when you're making decisions about investing or crowdfunding, donating data, or volunteering your time.

So timing matters. People need different resources at different times. Make sure that the help you're giving is appropriate to the phase of the disaster or the type of change you're seeking.

The second factor to think about is distance, which has two components—geographic and social. You can be physically far away from a disaster, but if you have friends or family there, if it's your hometown or home country, even faraway events will feel very close. For events that are physically nearby, you may feel like family and friends have been affected even if you don't actually know the people involved. Both types of distance matter, especially in terms of how you might want to respond.

Use distance as a proxy for knowledge—the closer you are to an event or a cause, either physically or socially, the more likely you are to know (or be able to find out) what's really needed by those directly affected. If you're physically close, you can ask people what would be helpful. If you're socially close, you're likely to be in direct contact with people who can tell you what they need. If you're neither physically nor socially close to the event, the most useful thing you can do is provide money and let those doing the work take the lead.[16] Local knowledge, relationships, and accountability matter. It's important to make sure that the people closest to the situation have a say in the process.[17]

GIVING PUBLICLY OR PRIVATELY

Besides time and distance, there is a second filter you can apply, one that is rooted in personal preference. It has to do with your individual preference about anonymity or attention. For some people, this doesn't matter one way or the other. You may not care if your name is listed as a donor or if it's collected by a crowdfunding platform or third-party payment processor (remember, data about you travels with every online donation you make or petition you sign). You may want to signal your support and concern by purchasing a T-shirt or some branded item that explicitly commemorates a certain event. Some people want to show the world that they were involved or perhaps use the items to help us remember.

On the other hand, you may prefer to keep your name off of certain donor lists or out of certain databases. You might want to help now but not have to deal with future outreach or follow-up emails. You can usually find a way to donate directly to a group and state your data preferences (don't list me, don't add me to your mailing list, etc.), or you can avoid the credit card and payment processors (and their fees and data practices) by mailing a check. This won't work for a political contribution; your name and address must be collected. These preferences are individually determined; there's no one answer for everyone. And as you think through the privacy/publicity aspects of each of the giving choices in our fire disaster hypothetical, you'll be setting yourself up for these same questions as part of your regular giving.

After filtering the different choices through the prism of time and distance, consider your personal interests in anonymity or attention. Let's say you want to keep your involvement private. You may be able to use a pseudonym or tick the anonymous box on the crowdfunding platform; this should withhold your name from any public list of supporters. However, both the crowdfunding company and its credit card processors will have your information and can use it according to their terms of service (read the policies!). That's a very thin type of anonymity. Contributions to nonprofits can be kept anonymous, and if you avoid using a credit card you won't have payment processors to worry about. Nonprofits are motivated to honor anonymity when it's requested; it's part of the trust they hope to build with their communities. Under current law, a donation to such an organization will be kept anonymous, although certain staff at the nonprofit may know who's who, and the organization's largest donors are reported on tax forms. Actions to support a politician's work or investing in longer-term development projects are subject to political and investment rules, which generally require disclosure and discourage anonymity.

Disasters—man-made and natural—happen. As informed givers, we can plan for them. All of the choices illustrated in this chapter will exist when the next disaster strikes, and you can make better choices in the moment if you've thought about them in advance. The kind of preplanning that will benefit you when disaster strikes will leave you better prepared to respond to every kind of request.

A hypothetical disaster focuses your attention on all the givingscape choices. There's an additional, subtle lesson from thinking about disasters. The unpredictability of disasters means that at any point, any of us can be directly affected. The global pandemic made visible how each of us can be both giver and recipient. Receiving help can be profoundly influential on how you act as a giver. It will help you see why it's so important that recipients retain their dignity, expertise, and power over their lives. Experience is not the only way to learn the importance of respecting those to whom you give; it is built into ways of giving that center reciprocity and mutuality.

GIVING AND RECEIVING

In our mapping conversations in big cities and rural towns, on the coasts and in the middle of the nation, people told us how receiving help changed them. "I grew up on public assistance, [we were] often the recipient of church programs," a participant in Sturgis, South Dakota, told us. "[It] has totally shaped how I give my time, money, what I do for a career—I have seen firsthand the impact other people's generosity can have."[18] In flood-prone areas of the Great Plains, food banks, emergency shelters, and community contributions to neighbors have become part of the "normal" cycle of seasons. The regularity of the flooding reminds people in the community how they're all connected to the environment, farming, the aquifers, and each other. In her aptly titled *A Paradise Built in Hell: The Extraordinary Communities that Arise in Disaster*, Rebecca Solnit writes about experiences as disparate as hurricanes, maritime explosions, and terrorist attacks. A heightened and tangible sense of dependence between people is the shared trait of those communities that come out stronger for the experience.[19] It's pretty simple. We need each other. The more we are explicit about this in our giving, the better our chances at making meaningful change.

People receive help in different ways. For some it's hard to acknowledge their own needs. Others find it energizing; having benefitted from others, they're motivated to pay forward the opportunity. Important in all these stories is a humility that we should all strive to hold on to when we're the givers. There's a destructive tendency for givers to think they have the answers, to feel that their time or money makes them experts in the lives of the others. One way to avoid this mindset when you're on the giving side is to remember how it feels to be on the receiving end. Respect the people you're giving to. Listen to them. If the goal is to make some lasting change, the best approaches build from those contributing their lived experiences, supported by those contributing time, money, or data.

In September 2019, a small group of men and women, White and Latinx, met in a recreation center in Lincoln, Nebraska. They ranged in age from twenty-three to sixty-three. They noted the political differences within their group and in the community, discussed the importance of shopping locally, and talked about how personal priorities change at different stages in one's life. As they stood to leave, one participant noted, "Individuals can feel powerless until you organize together to do something." They all nodded.

As I reread the notes from our mapping conversations, I remembered that every group included a mix of activities that crossed "traditional" lines of politics, charity, civics, and shopping. The mapping conversations are designed to get people thinking about what they do as individuals and then reflecting on how those acts add up in a community. In every single conversation, the richness of the discussion centered on two topics. The first is the breadth of activities and what did or did not count as giving. People disagreed heartily, with pride and curiosity, as they talked about doing things "they were raised to do" or that "are just how we do things (in a particular place/tradition)." Legal distinctions didn't matter as much in these mapping conversations as personal meaning. Some actions are optional, some behaviors may be expected, and others are obligatory. At a personal level, these distinctions seemed very ingrained in people. They knew for themselves what was a choice and what was an obligation. The richness of the group conversations comes from this collective reflection on all the different actions and a genuine curiosity about how their individual acts added up.

This richness may stem from another theme common to the mapping conversations. It's unusual to talk about giving. We heard the same thing in Annapolis, Maryland; Athens, Georgia; Albuquerque, New Mexico; and Arlington, Virginia: "We don't talk about this here." Perhaps this is because most of the places that might hold such a conversation—whether it be a church, a school, a community group—have vested interests in the *to whom* part of the issue because they all need contributions.

Family behavior, modeling after one's parents or grandparents even if that modeling means doing something other than what the elders do, was the most frequently mentioned source of learning about giving. The people we talked with noted that this learning happened by doing, not talking. In Lakeside, California, one participant noted (translated from Spanish): "My mom made tortillas and sold them to the neighbors. That was our only source of money, and we never made enough to eat well. She would still give tortillas to the people who were facing hard times. I live my life as she did. No matter how poor I am, we give."[20] Three thousand miles away, in Washington, DC, a participant noted, "My mother taught me to use what is around and reuse everything. That is where my environmental interest comes in."[21] And people raised in Christian, Muslim, and Jewish traditions noted that their parents' religious traditions shaped their own understanding of giving and responsibility. This was true even for people who no longer saw themselves as part of their childhood religious traditions. They noted that they still strove to tithe, give zakat, or make tzedakah as they were taught, albeit to many different causes and institutions.[22]

Somewhat unexpectedly, talking about *how* we give allows us to broach a lot of challenging topics—from religious or political beliefs to issues of wealth, from life stages to our dependence on the internet. It's critical to focus these conversations on the how and not the how much or to whom/what issues. The first question, how, actually works to open up the discussion, allowing people to share all kinds of choices and for others to reflect on their own behavior. This question allows people who disagree on politics or who are unfamiliar with others' cultural or linguistic traditions to still talk about actions that mean a great deal to them. It lowers the judgmental heat between people: while causes and preferred outcomes may vary, the tactics or hows of getting there can overlap or inspire. Perhaps it will even open up receptivity to ideas just beyond the White philanthropic mainstream, such as solidarity or mutual aid.

We can start by looking at our current behavior. At the start of this chapter I asked you to stop reading and go gather your financial records. Now's a chance to do that again. (Or perhaps you've opened a Giving Side account. If so, open it up.) This time, think beyond the money and reflect on how you've given your time or your data, how you've made choices as a shopper or investor, how you've helped your neighbors or strangers in harm's way.

To get to that next step, changing your actions, consider talking to someone about it. Join a giving circle, a mutual aid network, or a local political group. Instead of focusing on the money, focus on the opportunity to make decisions together. Or start with a conversation about how you give with family members or friends. From there, you can reach further in terms of who participates in the conversation, who becomes part of your circles, or what your conversation touches on in terms of what counts as giving.

In considering all of our voluntary choices about money, time, data, shopping, or investing, we need to keep in mind the roles that public policy plays. Whether we're talking about climate change or health care, hunger or education, art or criminal justice, the choices we make about voluntary contributions are shaped by public policy. In turn, the aggregation of our voluntary choices can also shape those policies. In the best situations, we aggregate our individual voices and our collective preferences become public policy. In the case of crowdfunding, we need to search for both the crowd and the collective message. If everyone who sought funds on a crowdfunding platform also took political action—from protesting to running for office themselves—we could educate and care for everyone, not just the few.[23]

CONCLUSION: WHOSE PROBLEM IS IT, ANYWAY?

The events of 2020 revealed many truths about the United States. In visceral ways—both painful and hope-giving—people and communities stepped up to help each other, to provide life-saving care and protection from a new virus, endemic racism, reprehensible inequality, and intensifying climate catastrophes. People improvised ways to teach children when schools closed, became experts at sewing and selling homemade masks, and delivered medicine to sheltering elders and groceries to the suddenly unemployed. Illness and death were concentrated in communities that have long borne the brunt of environmental racism, redlining, xenophobia, and discriminatory health care, education, and employment. There was amazing, creative, and ongoing community action. And this all revealed just how much we need functioning, equitable public services.

The lines between what communities can do for themselves, what philanthropy and voluntarism can do writ large, and what we must come together to build for our society as a whole became visible in ways that we cannot ignore. No matter how much we try, we cannot educate our children without public schools. No matter how much we give, we cannot crowdfund medicine, health insurance, or medical care in an equitable or just way. Creating safe communities requires both neighbors and public systems that value human life first. As people working together, we can make a lot of things happen. But much of what we need we can only provide by making sure our public systems—our biggest collective acts—work for everyone.

Whose problems are failing schools, inaccessible healthcare, environmental destruction, unlivable wages and housing, and fragile and inaccessible infrastructure? All of ours. Whose problem is it when our cities can't provide clean water and our tax dollars fund human rights violations at the border and mass incarceration systems across the country? All of ours.

There is a lot that we can do as givers, especially when we join with others. But all that we do in this voluntary capacity is shaped by the choices we make, the decisions we stand for, the people we elect to represent us, and the laws that we pass and demand to be enforced. The biggest, most powerful giving we can do is to give ourselves to the democratic project of building and running public systems that serve all of us. Only then can we exercise our options to volunteer, give money and data, and build complementary, alternative, expressive communities that reflect who we are and what we aspire to.

There are two levels at which we should be thinking and acting. Chapter 8 synthesized how the choices we make as individuals can be deeply linked to how we see ourselves connected to other people and the world around us. This conclusion looks at the policy choices—the rules, regulations, incentives, and institutions that we put in place to give, receive, and work together.

The need to create rules about digital data takes us directly to the policy level. But it's not just about data. Our current regulations and public policies about giving are geared toward the wealthy and built on a history of racialized elitism. We need rules for giving that recognize all of us, not those that further exacerbate racial and wealth divides. Once you see the larger political questions about giving, I hope you'll also see that the two levels are connected: what you do individually reflects on the broader political structures. Individually, we can make more informed choices. Together, we can change how the whole system works.

One Friday evening, about two years ago, I climbed to the top of the stairs in the building where my synagogue regularly holds services. I could now see the people I'd been hearing even as I'd entered the door from outside. Their voices and laughter were louder and more animated than usual. After all, Shabbat services were about to begin. There is always a group of people gathered at the upstairs entrance to the sanctuary, but the volume alone indicated this wasn't just the regulars gathered at the door. Sure enough, there were at least a dozen people standing outside the doors, half of them with what appeared to be toothbrushes sticking out of their mouths.

I looked from the faces in the crowd to the table around which they were standing. It was covered with stickers, small cardboard packages, and bright orange plastic rings, which I recognized immediately as those ubiquitous charity bracelets. All my Spidey sense alerts went off. A charity fundraiser on Shabbat? This wasn't normal. Charity bracelets and stickers? What could we possibly be promoting here? And why did everyone have toothbrushes in their mouths?

I approached the table. A young woman I'd only seen from across the sanctuary said hello. "Do you know Sharon?" she asked. "She needs a bone marrow transplant. Ashkenazi Jews are likely matches. Can you help?" Ah, I realized, those aren't toothbrushes, they're cheek swabs, for gathering DNA. I didn't know Sharon, but I did remember the email I'd received earlier that week, mentioning the family with a chronically ill daughter for whom a transplant was the last medical hope.

I'd read that email and done some quick homework. I'd looked into the organization that collects and analyzes the DNA swabs. It's a nonprofit organization, managing an enormous database of DNA samples. Accredited doctors and hospitals around the world can search for potential bone marrow donors for their patients. I'd read the privacy policies and data security practices. I had been relieved by what I learned, but not moved to act. The organization was taking all the right precautions with very sensitive DNA data, even as they beseeched people to contribute. When I'd been at my desk reading the email, the rational, cautious, digitally skeptical side of my brain took over. I'd gotten my questions answered, but I hadn't been moved to act. I'd been so unmoved I'd completely forgotten the email saying that this collection would happen at Friday night services.

I don't know Sharon. But here was a someone I did know, looking me in the eye, asking me to help. The people swabbing their cheeks had clearly decided to help. So had the few others sitting to the side, filling out paperwork or sealing shut cardboard envelopes with their used swabs tucked inside.

They weren't asking for money. They were asking for a very few minutes of my time. Cheek swabs don't hurt and don't leave you feeling anything—no pain, no fatigue. Your body doesn't miss the few cells you're scraping off. The possibility I was a match for Sharon was infinitesimal. But if I were, I could save a life.

And what of my concerns about genetic privacy? Was putting the digitized data of my DNA in the hands of a nonprofit a risk worth taking? I knew from my earlier research that the group only used this information to inform marrow transplant programs, that it didn't sell the data, that it took data security very seriously and protected the samples, the data, and my identity as best as possible. I also knew that none of those promises or preventive measures were guarantees. Organizations can change policies. They can be acquired by other organizations, who would then control the data and might have different policies. Data breaches happen. Putting my DNA into such a database was my decision, but doing so would implicate all of my blood relatives.

I could save a life. I remembered my conversations with Vanessa Barone of Sage Bionetworks. Remembered what I know about health disparities, and how racism has both violently excluded people from care and actively harmed them. How our historical practices redound to a present-day knowledgebase that is woefully incomplete in terms of gender and race.[1] I thought of the work Vanessa does every day to make medical research inclusive and relevant. That work requires respecting the legacies of harm as well as honestly grappling with the trade-offs of public benefit, personal privacy, and potential forms of manipulation or misuse.

I stood there, on the threshold of Shabbat services. Many traditions teach that if you "save one life, you save humanity." I thought about people who lacked access to care. The power of science. The unreliability of our digital systems and the many ways digitized data get misused. I started to reach for a swab and an envelope. Just then, the doors to the sanctuary opened.

The choices we make about giving are moral choices, as well as questions of expediency, identity, and responsibility. That the preceding scenario took place in a place of worship reminds us that religion's long tendrils continue to shape giving today, even as fewer people in the United States identify as members of any faith tradition. That the scenario involves DNA, databases, and global networks of hospitals and transplant centers draws our attention to the future we already inhabit—in which digitized data can both save a life and open doors to harm and discrimination.

It may seem a big leap from making a choice about a cheek swab to public policy about data donations. But we shouldn't do the former without having the latter in place. The privacy and data use policies that the nonprofit DNA group maintain need the force of law behind them if they're going to protect me in any way. Consciously or not, we rely on public policy and regulations when we donate money, time, and data. We want to know what organizations we can trust and on what basis. We want assurances that our contributions are being used for the purpose for which we've donated them, and not in ways we don't understand or to line someone else's pockets. And we want recourse, some means of remedy, if things go wrong.

Giving digital data is the new version of all of this. We're in the process of crafting institutions, rules, and practices for this type of giving. Doing so is also an opportunity to improve our existing practices, institutions, and rules, because our twenty-first-century giving options don't all fit into our nineteenth- and twentieth-century assumptions. While we have laws about charitable donations to nonprofit organizations and financial contributions to political activities, we're just getting started on setting the laws about donating data. All the news stories you've read about regulating data use, protecting your rights to your data, and hacks or data breaches factor in here. A starting question is whether we should even be the ones who can donate our data. Should we be the ones making this decision, or should it be up to others, such as social media or telecommunication companies, to decide how the data get used? Do we want a set of rules about what nonprofits can and can't do with our data? Maybe we need new types of organizations that are designed to earn and protect our trust (and our data) and that will help us dedicate it to the causes we care about. There are experiments and policy proposals and contentious fights happening right now on each of these possibilities. And just as we as a society answered similar questions regarding time and money one hundred years ago when we wrote the first rules for nonprofits and philanthropy, it's now time we address them for digital data.

The choices we make about giving are also political choices. The choices we make between certain products, the structural incentives for certain activities to be done by volunteers instead of paid workers, the tax incentives or data protections we do or do not receive are all shaped by policy and politics. Giving is often talked about in the context of generosity. This bigger political frame shows that it's also a matter of justice.

The lines that separate politics from charity are slippery. They're man-made—informed by tradition and negotiated in the course of public policy making. Your sense of how well they fit our times may depend on whether or not you think the system is working. Two things are true about every issue or cause: changing the situation will always require political, economic, and charitable action; and the impact that each of us can make on any large social issue depends on the actions of others. I can make a charitable donation to a social service organization, give my time to a food bank, allow my shopping data (aggregated through loyalty cards) to be mined by researchers for insights about food availability in my community, and vote for candidates committed to providing meaningful access to nutritional benefits—and there will still be hungry people in my city (unless we shift to an entirely different economic system). I need my actions to complement and compound the actions of others. Real change requires more of us to take action, and among the most important action we can take is to get others involved. Darren Walker, president of the Ford Foundation, published *From Generosity to Justice: A New Gospel of Wealth* in 2019, in which he collects interviews with a wide variety of people. Walker argues that we can think about our giving along a spectrum, from generosity to justice.[2] The consistent element in every story about pursuing justice is collective action.

PUBLIC, PRIVATE, AND EVERYTHING IN BETWEEN

Tiffani Ashley Bell responded to the fiscal bankruptcy of a major US city by building the Human Utility. Paying off a few water bills may seem small in comparison to the city's overall fiscal woes, but Tiffani sees the failure to provide water as more than just a fiscal issue. Addressing the city's utility failings is also about calling out its responsibilities to residents. In 2020, as residents pushed for a Detroit Bill of Rights, access to clean water was included, as was protection from digital surveillance. Providing a reliable source of clean water is perhaps the most basic function of a municipality—one that more and more cities in the United States are failing to meet.

The Human Utility depends on the reach of the internet to identify families that need help and donors to get them over the debt and back on their feet. It's also working to turn individual generosity into political action, seeking policy solutions that can prevent this cascade of problems in the first place. Tiffani and the Human Utility are working with residents and municipal officials to redesign water policy and revenue systems so that everyone has access to clean water. In a variety of ways, this is what NDN Collective, Ioby, Color Of Change, the Latino Community Foundation, Giving Side, Safe Passage, and iNaturalist are all doing: providing ways for people to connect to others.

The power of these collectives is more than the sum of their parts. It's more than a process of aggregation. There is an entwining and a reciprocity between Cat Chang and the iNaturalist community, between Yancy Villa and the city of Memphis, between JaLil Turner and his neighbors in the TL. The collective is made up of individuals, yes. Over time, each participating individual also absorbs some the power of the collective. They grow together.

Every collective holds political potential, but that potential only manifests through deliberate intent and action. When Masha and Amber talk about using Latinx giving circles to create philanthropists, they want to change the meaning of *philanthropist* to be both more inclusive and a step toward building power. Their structure emphasizes collective responsibility between donor and recipient, supports activism and political engagement, and makes sure people feel like they bring their whole selves, their whole identity to the group. They help people gain power on boards of nonprofits, in corporate settings, in big foundations, and in public policy. Ioby invests specifically in helping community activists engage with their local governments. Helping people find and build their own crowds is a first step toward building the power of those crowds.

The political math behind the Human Utility, Ioby, and the Latino Community Foundation's Giving Circle Network is deceptively simple. Every person who gives and every person who gets help is also a voter. Crowds are important not only because of the money they generate but because a crowd of givers can become a crowd of voters. Research on giving circles shows this kind of change is by no means automatic for giving circle participants.[3] If it is to happen, it needs to be deliberately built into the work of the circle; it needs to be organized. Simply giving with others benefits the givers but doesn't necessarily lead to big changes in the community. If the goal is to use giving circles or other collectives as a way of changing communities, there needs to be deliberate attention to making this happen.

Big-money political donors have outsize influence because they have one vote and many dollars. Crowds are made up of many people, each with a vote. People who give on crowdfunding platforms and in giving circles are well-suited to take more action. The same concerns that motivate people to give can also motivate them to vote. Today's givingscape offers fertile soil for new giving behaviors.

GIVING BY THE REST OF US

Crowdfunding is a good place to shift our perspective from our actions to the public policies and regulations that shape giving. It's one area where change is already underway and new rules and regulations are being proposed. As Anna Landre says (chapter 8), relying on individual donations for services, programs, or supports that everyone needs is no way to change the system. If you want to change the system, change the system. And a good place to start is with the rules. The ideas that follow are relevant to individual people, as well as to the public policy agendas of nonprofits, foundations, and other types of associations. These rules matter: they determine who can come together to make change, how we can do it, how and where we can express ourselves, and what choices we can make without pressure or observation from outsiders. Put another way, they are about our rights to assembly, association, expression, and privacy.

GETTING POLITICAL: ON ANONYMITY, DISCLOSURE, AND ACTION

We can contribute time, money, and data to both political and charitable causes. It's not always clear when something becomes political and when it's charitable, and we know that real change requires both kinds of actions. In daily practice, these lines may not matter. But when it comes to giving money, the difference between visibility into political funding and anonymous charitable funding matters immensely. Governing ourselves in a democratic fashion depends on knowing who is doing what, including who is providing the money that powers our electoral candidates and systems. Our political system has many flaws, and money in politics is surely one of them. We'll never be able to fix this problem if we can't see it. We need to know who is paying for what with regard to candidates, campaigns, and elections. At the same time, people should have the option to contribute to community and charitable causes as they choose, including doing so anonymously.

The only way to maintain both these opportunities—named political contributions and anonymous charitable ones—is to draw lines between the two kinds of activities and organizations and to enforce them. The lines may never seem exactly right, but we shouldn't give up on them. In fact, getting involved as an advocate in the political discussions about where these lines should be drawn, what the rules for engagement are, and how to differentiate charitable behavior from political action is another domain ripe for participation. Because these rules shape how each of us can participate in our democracy, they shouldn't be written by the few.

TAX POLICY AND BEYOND

We give in many more ways than public policy recognizes. The rules that differentiate charitable giving from political donations and the rules that provide incentives for giving money should reflect the desires of the many, not the few. Neither is true now. Our tax incentives for charitable giving privilege the wealthy and White. There are options for changing these laws that would provide economic incentives to many more of us—namely, shifting the regulatory incentive from a tax break to a tax credit.[4] We, and the foundations and nonprofits that focus on policy change, should demand inclusive tax benefits that will reward everyone for participating and not those that exacerbate inequality.

As is important as changing tax policy is thinking beyond it. Tax policy is not the only domain that might encourage more people to give. Many of our activities happen on digital platforms and revolve around the exchange of digital data. It's time to consider how the rules that shape our digital environments influence our ability to speak out, to come together, and to take action together or individually. There are laws that govern broadband access, for example, that make it more expensive and more difficult for people in rural areas (and redlined parts of big cities) to get online. The regulations that would make it easier and safer for you to donate your digital data for research purposes have mostly been written with an eye toward allowing corporations to profit from your data. The time to influence these policy decisions is now—and the implications go beyond privacy protection. They have to do with protecting your right to make decisions about information about you.

Public policy that has incentivized giving money to nonprofits should be reexamined in light of the many different actions people now take. Tax law now limits the benefits of charitable deductions to fewer Americans than ever before. In response, there are numerous proposals seeking to expand the tax benefits to more people, including a one-time $300 tax deduction put forward in 2020 to encourage giving during the pandemic. But the big public policy opportunity is to think beyond taxes, starting from a real picture of how we give, and create incentives that encourage and benefit the many and not the few.

THE RULES THAT WILL MATTER

Digital networks and data undergird our lives. They are not only the means by which we communicate and connect; they power all of the institutions with which we interact. Your bank depends on digital systems, the energy grid depends on them, schools and hospitals, transportation networks and entertainment, government services, employment opportunities, and, yes, civic participation, community engagement, and giving. Yet we have not designed our policy incentives or protections to align with these broader issues. The time is now.

You can get involved in creating these systems and rules, as an advocate, an organizer, or a designer, or by speaking on behalf of the interests of your community. Creating the legal and technological systems that serve all of us will take collective participation. The first step is to question the proposals you hear about data ownership. Digital data can't be owned the way physical goods can. "Owning" your data, and selling it for pennies, won't work the way owning a car or pair of shoes does. These proposals may well reduce your choices for sharing your data for public purposes. They are likely designed to benefit those who have enough money to "buy" everyone else's data, leaving us effectively broke in the digital economy. These ownership-based proposals don't account for the relational or representative nature of digital data. This is one of those moments when it will pay to not be a first mover. A good rule of thumb is to not sign away your rights (don't sell what you're being told you own) before you've considered all the options. And because those options are just now being created, it's best to not lock yourself in (or out) of future possibilities.

MEMBERSHIP, CITIZENSHIP, AND DEMOCRACY

Essayist Annie Dillard wrote that how we spend our days is how we spend our lives.[5] Similarly, how you give is how you participate. In politically fraught times, a lot of energy is spent making others of some people or fighting about inclusion and exclusion. Democracies are defined by who they exclude (even as their leaders rhetorically focus on who is included). But political membership need not be defined only by those who have the vote, especially when we remind ourselves of the fights that African Americans, immigrants, and women have had to undertake to earn—and still struggle to protect—the vote. Every step—from fighting for emancipation to repealing exclusionary immigration laws to passage of the Nineteenth Amendment to protecting the franchise today—depends on both political and collective action.

The majority of people in the United States have had to fight to obtain the right to vote, a fight that continues today. We've had to organize outside the system to get the right to participate in that system. The collective action that ultimately earned African Americans and women the right to the vote is a form of democratic participation in its own right (and one that scholars such as Sarah Song argue should be sufficient for political membership in democracies).[6]

Giving is one type of participation. By itself, it can be deeply rewarding. But to make it a participatory act that drives community change, redresses our historical and structural inequities, and contributes to building a more just society, it needs to be done with others and be informed by a clear set of moral and political values.[7] The many different stories in this book, from Color Of Change to the NDN Collective, from Latinx giving circles to the rules about donating DNA, demonstrate that steps taken to address a community issue *can* be steps into the political process. It isn't automatic; it has to be intentional. It happens by directly addressing the political context in which giving happens, by building crowds to build power, and by helping each of us see our role in something bigger than ourselves.

Participation matters now more than ever. In giving time, money, or data (or all three), you have a means of shaping the society you want. Democracies depend on participation, inside, outside, in favor of, and in opposition to those in governing positions.

We are our democracy. We are the ones who make our communities strong. Participation is the outcome that matters for this book. By mapping the ways we give, highlighting the industries of giving products and the way they work, and introducing you to the possibilities of digital data as a giving resource, I've tried to show the many ways you can participate. I do hope you will.

Acknowledgments

This book would not exist without the people who told me their stories. You met forty of them in the preceding pages, but I interviewed dozens more and listened to more than 330 others from around the country in 2019. These are their stories. I hope I've told them truthfully. I am grateful to the team that coordinated, led, and analyzed dozens of mapping conversations: Nichelle Hall, Sebastian John Martinez Hickey, Matilda Nickel, Brigitte Pawliw-Fry, Jeff Rodriguez, Heather Robinson, and Laura Seaman. My work at the Digital Civil Society Lab is only possible because of the intellectual and professional guidance Rob Reich has provided over the last decade. The leadership, staff, and community of Stanford's Center on Philanthropy and Civil Society have helped me with big ideas and small favors, small ideas and big favors. Thank you.

I've had the great good fortune to learn about giving from many people over many years; to list all of them would be impossible. Those whose ideas and actions directly influence this book include Shena Ashley, Samir Doshi, Caitriona Fay, Isoke Femi, Emilia Fernandez-Villela, Ellen Friedman, Angela Gallegos-Castillo, Allen Gunn, R. Noa Kushner, Robin Larsen, R. Michael Lezak, Lance Linares, Jasmine McNealy, Mutale Nkonde, Jonathan Palash-Mizner, Tawana Petty, Robin Robinson, Nadia Roumani, Del Seymour, Reverend Cecil Williams, my parents, Maria's Regalitos of the Mission Education Center, and the late Peter Hero and Maria X. Martinez. Thank you for introducing me to your ways of being, seeing, and giving.

A grant from the Generosity Commission covered the costs of the mapping conversations and provided opportunities to discuss the meaning of people's stories in light of national quantitative research. Victoria Vrana has challenged my thinking and made perspective-changing introductions; thank you for those opportunities. Twenty-eight amazing days of writing in Bellagio, Italy, courtesy of the Rockefeller Foundation, produced a draft manuscript, some of which appears in the preceding pages. That experience, and the friends made while there, including Julie Ries, Ken Miller, Leah Warshawski, Todd Soliday, Joan Berzoff, and Lew Cohen, helped me imagine something better.

I am grateful to Noah Friedlander for graphing assistance and for the professional guidance from Caroline Lester, Alison MacKeen, and Katie Morris. Special thanks to Jenny Stephens and Gita Devi Manaktala.

Appendix A: Methods and Mapping Conversations

"How do you give?"

I've asked this question of hundreds of people over the years, and we spent eight months in 2019 in mapping conversations across the country centered on this question. From San Diego, California, to Birmingham, Alabama, and Grand Rapids, Michigan, and in community centers, living rooms, public libraries, and pubs, we facilitated groups ranging in size from five to twenty-five talking about how they give. These mapping conversations focused on *how*: Do you volunteer your time through a faith institution, canvas neighborhoods for a political cause, or serve food at a nonprofit pantry? Do you shop for products that donate to causes or buy shoes from a company that promises to give a pair to a needy person? Do you donate money to a nonprofit, ride a bus instead of drive to work, or shovel your elderly neighbor's stoop in the winter months? The people we spoke with do all of these things and many more.

Here's how the mapping conversations work. With the help of local partners (ranging from church leaders to youth organizations, political activists to pub owners), we gather a group of people, anywhere from a few to a few dozen, and give each person a stack of sticky notes and a marker. We prompt them with the instruction: "List all the things you do to make the world a better place." Everyone takes a few minutes to write down their ideas, one idea per sticky note. When everyone has a good-sized stack (usually after five minutes), the group goes up to a whiteboard or blank wall and sticks their notes on it. Then everyone works together to cluster the sticky notes into meaningful categories. It gets a little chaotic, but that's part of the fun. After ten minutes or so, the group invariably comes up with clusters or categories that capture most (if not all) of the notes. Typical categories include donating money to charity, volunteering with nonprofits, caring for extended kin, helping on a political campaign, raising money for a cause, helping neighbors, buying food directly from farmers, screening certain things out of their investments, taking a leadership role in a civic or religious community, or making environmentally friendly purchases. Chances are the group will debate about whether or not voting counts, or subscribing to the local newspaper, or riding a bike instead of driving. These disagreements are very much part of the process; the goal is discussion, not consensus.

Once the notes are clustered, the group sits down and talks about what they see. Invariably, people will think of activities they do once someone else mentions them. "I also choose to take the bus, for environmental reasons," or "I brought food to folks in the neighborhood after the storm wiped out electricity for a few days," or "I drive my elderly neighbors to their doctors' appointments."[1]

In holding these conversations, I didn't gather people's names or ages or their racial, religious, or gender identities. I (and my research team) worked hard to make sure the groups were diverse because we were interested in the range of products and actions people used.[2] We weren't looking to correlate behaviors to different groups of people. To model the possibilities of respectful data, we didn't collect information we weren't going to use.

There's great potential in these mapping conversations, and from what we heard, great interest in having more of them. If you're interested in hosting such a discussion, you can find the Do-It-Yourself Guide for hosts (along with notes and maps from those we led over the summer of 2019) as appendix A of the report available here: https://pacscenter.stanford.edu /publication/how-we-give-now-conversations-across-the-united-states/.

Appendix B: Glossary and Buzzwords

I've tried to avoid as much philanthropy jargon as I possibly could in writing this book, but there is still some terminology specific to giving that is helpful to understand. There are also a lot of buzzwords—concepts, new ideas, and fancy language that comes and goes, in and out of fashion—as in any industry. I've been tracking the buzzwords on my blog at https://philanthropy.blogspot.com/ for twenty years. The highlights for each year are captured in my annual forecast, the Blueprint series. Each year's report becomes available for free every December at www.lucybernholz.com and https://pacscenter.stanford.edu/resources/blueprints/. Use those resources to stay up to date on the latest in giving buzz. Key terms from the book are defined ahead.

Algorithm   A set of instructions that are written into software to conduct specified analyses.

Algorithmic bias   Human and social biases that get recreated in software and in the datasets that are used to train algorithms. Unchecked, software and digital systems amplify and exacerbate human biases.

Artivists   Take art and mix it with activists and you get artivists! Whether it's graffiti on garbage trucks or the murals that acknowledge the heritage of our neighborhoods, artivists use their media to provoke and motivate action.

Benefit corporations   These are a type of for-profit company in the United States that include positive social, environmental, and labor impacts as part of their legally defined goals.

Biometrics   Biometrics refers to digital data that is collected from your body and used to provide access to or verification in a system, including fingerprints, iris scans, and facial-recognition software. The use of biometric data is exploding and raises important questions about consent and privacy.

Blockchain   A type of software that can be designed and governed to provide a permanent, unchangeable record of transactions.

Cause marketing   Product or commercial company–based promises to support or donate money to named causes.

Charity washing (also good washing, green washing, impact washing)   Rather than alter its business practices, a company that simply adds a nonprofit cause to its marketing efforts is said to be charity washing. Others take the easy way out and claim impact by cloaking themselves in the language of social good without really doing anything.

Citizen science/community science   Citizen science, also called community science, is a mix of amateurs and professionals coming together to collect, share, and analyze data to address scientific questions.

Civic tech   Technologies and the community groups that create them that are explicitly aimed at improving interactions between governments and residents.

Collective impact   The idea of government, nonprofits, the public, and commercial businesses working together in an explicit framework toward shared goals.

Commons   A form of collective governance, usually over natural resources (pastures, fishing areas), which dates backs to before the age of corporations and intellectual property in Western culture. Commons governance is still found in many places. Since the rise of the internet, there has been renewed interest in bringing commons governance to digital or knowledge resource.

Community credit unions   Credit unions with nonprofit and community-based boards of directors that aim to serve specific communities.

Community foundations   Community foundations are public charities that both raise and distribute grant funds for usually geographically defined communities. Community foundations also exist to serve specific demographic groups.

Constituent feedback   Now that almost everyone on the planet has a mobile phone, the cost of speaking directly to constituents is within reach for almost any organization. Getting feedback from beneficiaries has never been less expensive, though it's still not simple. Using the information one gathers is also hard.

Crowdfunding   Originally, crowdfunding referred to giving campaigns that ask givers to contribute small amounts that don't come due until pledges for the entire campaign have been reached; this requirement is now sometimes ignored. Common crowdfunding platforms include Kickstarter, Indiegogo, Patreon, DonorsChoose, and Ioby.

Dark money   Money used to fund political candidates or campaigns that has been routed in certain ways to make it difficult to identify its source(s).

Data philanthropy   Companies providing access to their datasets for "social good" purposes. Popularized by the United Nations, the term is misleading in that there really isn't any kind of donation happening and, more importantly, it doesn't involve asking individuals about their data.

Data trusts   Data trusts are a new organizational form that focuses on governing the agreements between data providers and data users. Some refer directly to trust law; others are just using the term. Civic data trusts aim to put the communities represented in the data in charge of the trust.

Deep fakes   A video that mixes together images and audio, making it look like people are doing and saying things that they didn't really do or say. This is video photoshopping on steroids as the connection to algorithmic systems means the videos can be constantly updated with the latest rumors and targeted at those most susceptible.

Direct donations   Gifts from one person to another, without an organization in the middle.

Donor-advised funds (DAFs)   Giving products that allow a donor to set up an account from which she can direct financial donations to nonprofit organizations over time.

Effective altruism   An approach to giving based in utilitarian philosophy that emphasizes the use of evidence and rational decision-making in pursuit of doing the most good.

Encryption   Encryption refers to data that is rendered unreadable except to those with the right set of software-encoded keys. There are different levels of encryption built into different software programs and apps.

Explicability gap   This is the distance between the power of machine-learning algorithms to process data and our ability to understand them and hold them accountable. The gap becomes ever more problematic as software and algorithmic analysis becomes buried in ever more decision-making processes.

Giving circles   Groups of people who pool donations and make collective decisions about where to give the money.

Giving days   Dedicating a specific day to fundraising for a certain cause. With the spectacular success of #GivingTuesday (https://hq.givingtuesday.org), a networked, disbursed branding of the first Tuesday after the Thanksgiving holiday in the United States, giving days have reached a new pitch.

Human in the loop   Technical slang for requiring that at some point in a computational process—such as in self-driving cars, predictive algorithms, or even mobile-phone-based mapping programs—people should be directly involved and be able to take charge.

Impact investing   Actively investing in companies that aim to earn financial, social, and environmental returns.

Internet of Things   Digital connections are now linking our watches, shoes, refrigerators, thermostats, cars, and almost anything else that can hold a teeny tiny chip. Each of these devices becomes a sensor—a collector and distributor—of data about our habits, our activities, and us.

Metadata   This is data about data. Think of your online data as the contents of a written note and metadata as the address and stamped information that appears on the envelope in which your note is mailed. Metadata is increasingly understood to be both useful in organizing massive datasets and a source of information that companies and governments collect and store on each of us.

Mesh network   Noncommercial, low-cost, low-distance communications networks that offer alternatives to commercial internet service providers.

Mobile giving   Making donations from a cell phone, usually by texting. Also called fingertip giving.

Nonprofit starvation cycle   A phrase born from the persistent belief that nonprofits should spend as little as possible running their operations and from donors' resistance to paying the core costs of staff, rent, utilities, and the like. By consistently underpaying on these basics, nonprofit organizations rarely have any free working capital, every penny goes to program services, and there is nothing left to invest in improvements.

Overhead myth   The name given to an oversimplified measure that uses administrative costs as a meaningful indicator of organizational effectiveness. In the last few years, a coordinated response to debunk the attention given to administrative costs has gained significant traction. Nonprofits, foundations, donors, and charity-ranking sites all discourage close attention on overhead cost ratios even as they continue to report them. Nonprofit organizational costs are like rubbernecking; we know we shouldn't look, but we just can't help ourselves.

Pay for privacy   More software means more ways to collect data on our individual behavior, store it somewhere, and seek ways to monetize it. As long as business models depend on the monetization of large quantities of individual data, there will be an incentive for software to default to privacy invasion. One option, for those with money, is to pay for a software version that spies less. The more pervasive this kind of software is, the more our privacy inequality will come to mirror income inequality.

Pay to play   The direct blending of political tactics into philanthropy. Pay to play (in the context of philanthropy) involves using charitable donations to buy access to important political decision-makers.

Peer-to-peer services   Peer-to-peer is another name for the sharing economy. There is a deepening divide among enterprises that help people share cars, bikes, and couches. Some of them are still rooted in a resource-saving, sharing mentality, while others, particularly those funded by venture capital, have taken on the growth expectations and business practices of big-ticket commercial enterprises.

Point-of-sale donations   Contributions made as part of a purchase, specifically as an add-on at the cash register.

Public interest technology   Technology and the training to build it that incorporates engineering and public policy and which is meant to serve noncommercial purposes. Modeled on the movement that created public interest law several decades ago, the public interest technology movement is just getting started.

Ransomware   Software that encrypts all the files on a computer system, allowing the data kidnapper to hold it hostage until a ransom is paid. Ransomware attacks became almost common in 2016, and many of the victims were not-for-profit hospital systems and community clinics.

Sector agnostic   Funders who make both social investments and grants and who work with both commercial and nonprofit partners describe themselves as sector agnostic. They are interested in solutions, not the tax statuses of their organizational partners.

Sharing economy   Along with the rise in ecoshopping and conscientious consumerism, businesses that let people share cars, bikes, tools, clothing, and office space are booming. The sharing economy describes the entirety of these car-share types of businesses. These businesses are popular because they help customers both save money and see their savings as good for society.

Social impact bond   A financing scheme in which foundations or social investors pay the first money for new prevention programs and partner with local governments to monitor their progress toward predetermined benchmarks. If the programs are successful, the early funders get paid back with dollars saved and the government carries on the programs.

Notes

INTRODUCTION

1. Eric Klinenberg, *Palaces for the People: How Social Infrastructure Can Help Fight Inequality, Polarization, and the Decline of Civic Life* (New York: Crown Books, 2019).

1 PHILANTHROPY BY THE REST OF US

1. The resources from the mapping conversations also include a do-it-yourself guide to leading conversations like this. See https://pacscenter.stanford.edu/publication/how-we -give-now-conversations-across-the-united-states.

2. Lucy Bernholz and Brigitte Pawliw-Fry, *How We Give Now: Conversations across the United States*, Stanford Center on Philanthropy and Civil Society, Stanford University, November 2019, https://pacscenter.stanford.edu/publication/how-we-give-now-conversations -across-the-united-states/.

3. Bernholz and Pawliw-Fry, *How We Give Now*. In addition to donations of money and volunteering time, these categories include sharing kindness, donating material goods (in-kind), leadership roles, environmental choices, civic engagement, mentoring, family support, educating others, purchasing choices, religious practices, career choices, promoting philanthropy, advocacy, connecting others, learning, cooking, social media promotion, creating art, donating bodily resources, and caring for self.

4. Urban Institute, "On Track to Greater Giving," infographic, 2018, https://www.urban.org /sites/default/files/ui-ontracktogreatergiving-poster2.pdf.

5. Giving USA, "Giving USA 2020: Charitable Giving Showed Solid Growth, Climbing to $449.64 Billion in 2019, One of the Highest Years for Giving on Record," Giving USA, June 16, 2020, https://givingusa.org/giving-usa-2020-charitable-giving-showed-solid-growth -climbing-to-449-64-billion-in-2019-one-of-the-highest-years-for-giving-on-record/.

6. Kaitlin Ahmad, Nathan Dietz, and Robert T. Grimm Jr., "Philanthropy's Future in Flux as Volunteering and Giving Rates Waver," Independent Sector, January 10, 2020,

https://independentsector.org/news-post/philanthropys-future-in-flux-as-volunteering
-and-giving-rates-waver/.

7. Ahmad, Dietz, and Grimm, "Philanthropy's Future."

8. Corporation for National and Community Service, Volunteering in America Report, 2018, https://www.nationalservice.gov/serve/via.

9. Data from OpenSecrets.org, Center for Responsive Politics, "2020 Election to Cost $14 Billion, Blowing Away Spending Records," accessed December 5, 2020, https://www.opensecrets.org/news/2020/10/cost-of-2020-election-14billion-update/.

10. Global Impact Investing Network, The Annual Impact Investor Survey 2020, (New York: Global Impact Investing Network, June 11, 2020), https://thegiin.org/research/publication/impinv-survey-2020.

11. Studies were commissioned or conducted by a range of organizations, including the Urban Institute, Independent Sector, and the American Enterprise Institute. Predictions ranged because of the use of different economic models and different variables. These studies are available online. See Urban Institute, "On Track to Greater Giving," 2018, accessed June 10, 2019, https://www.urban.org/sites/default/files/ui-ontracktogreatergiving-poster2.pdf; Indiana University Lilly Family School of Philanthropy, Charitable Giving and Tax Incentives: Estimating Changes in Charitable Dollars and Number of Donors Resulting from Five Policy Proposals (Indianapolis: Indiana University, 2019), https://independentsector.org/wp-content/uploads/2019/06/Charitable-Giving-and-Tax-Incentives-Report-June2019.pdf, (commissioned by Independent Sector); Alex Bill and Derrick Choe, Charitable Giving and the Tax Cuts and Jobs Act (Washington, DC: American Enterprise Institute, June 2018), https://www.aei.org/wp-content/uploads/2018/06/Charitable-Giving-and-the-Tax-Cuts-and-Jobs-Act.pdf.

12. Tax Policy Center, Racial Disparities and the Income Tax System (Washington, DC: Tax Policy Center, January 30, 2020), https://apps.urban.org/features/race-and-taxes/; James Andreoni and Jon Durnford, The Effects of the 2017 Tax Reform on Itemization Status and the Charitable Deduction, July 17, 2019, https://econweb.ucsd.edu/~jandreon/AndreoniDurnford20190715a.pdf.

13. Indiana University Lilly Family School of Philanthropy, Changes to the Giving Landscape (Indianapolis: Indiana University, 2019), https://scholarworks.iupui.edu/bitstream/handle/1805/21217/vanguard-charitable191022.pdf.

14. Caroline Shenaz Hossein, "Mutual Aid and Physical Distancing are Not New for Black and Racialized Minorities within the Americas," Histphil, March 24, 2020, https://histphil.org/2020/03/24/mutual-aid-and-physical-distancing-are-not-new-for-black-and-racialized-minorities-in-the-americas/.

15. Erika Kohl-Arenas and Megan Ming Francis, "Movement Capture and the Long Arc of the Black Freedom Struggle," HistPhil, July 14, 2020, https://histphil.org/2020/07/14/movement-capture-and-the-long-arc-of-the-black-freedom-struggle/. See also Francis's

syllabus and podcast on philanthropy and movement capture at https://www.philanthro
pyandsocialmovements.com/syllabus/.

16. Shenaz Hossein, "Mutual Aid."

17. See Paul J. Dimaggio and Helmut K. Anheier, "The Sociology of Nonprofit Organizations
and Sectors," *Annual Review of Sociology* 16 (1990); Jonathan Levy, "Altruism and the Ori-
gins of Nonprofit Philanthropy," in *Philanthropy in Democratic Societies*, ed. Rob Reich,
Lucy Bernholz, and Chiara Cordelli (Chicago, University of Chicago Press, 2016); "From
Fiscal Triangle to Passing Through: Rise of the Nonprofit Corporation," in *Corporations and
American Democracy*, ed. Naomi R. Lamoreaux and William J. Novack (Cambridge, MA:
Harvard University Press, 2017).

18. Gene Takagi, "A Prediction for Nonprofits in 2018: Rise of the 501(c)(4) Organizations,"
Nonprofit Law Blog, NEO Law Group, January 25, 2018, http://www.nonprofitlawblog
.com/a-prediction-for-nonprofits-in-2018-rise-of-the-501c4-organizations/.

19. In 1958, in a case involving the NAACP and the Attorney General of Alabama, the US
Supreme Court ruled that associational membership lists can be kept private from the
government.

20. Nicholas J. Duquette, "Founders' Fortunes and Philanthropy: A History of the U.S.
Charitable-Contribution Deduction," *Business History Review* 93, no. 3 (2019), https://
doi.org/10.1017/S0007680519000710.

21. Duquette, "Founders' Fortunes and Philanthropy"; Rob Reich, *Just Giving: Why Philanthropy Is Failing Democracy and How It Can Do Better* (Princeton, NJ: Princeton University
Press, 2018).

22. James Andreoni and Jon Durnford, *The Effects of the 2017 Tax Reform on Itemization and
the Charitable Deduction*, July 17, 2019, https://econweb.ucsd.edu/~jandreon/Andreoni
Durnford20190715a.pdf; Andreoni and Durnford, "Lost Your Charitable Deduction in
2018? You Are Not Alone," July 15, 2019, cited in Roger Colinvaux and Ray D. Madoff,
"Charitable Tax Reform for the 21st Century" (September 16, 2019), *164 Tax Notes 1867*
(2019), https://ssrn.com/abstract=3462163.

23. There are twenty-nine subsections of the tax-exempt section of the tax code. The (c)
(3) and (c)(4) types are most common. See https://www.irs.gov/charities-non-profits
/exempt-organization-types.

24. Filing reports from WinRed and ActBlue are available from the Federal Election Commission website. See https://www.fec.gov/data/browse-data/?tab=filings.

25. Venmo is a phone application that allows people to send money directly from one phone to
another.

26. Scott Eastman, "How Many Taxpayers Itemize Under Current Law?," Tax Foundation,
September 12, 2019, https://taxfoundation.org/standard-deduction-itemized-deductions
-current-law-2019/.

27. Edelman Trust Barometer, January 20, 2019, https://www.edelman.com/trust-barometer.

28. Elisabeth S. Clemens, *Civic Gifts: Voluntarism and the Making of the American Nation-State* (Chicago: University of Chicago Press, 2020). Rob Reich first introduced me to the language of "philanthropy as political artifact."

29. Michael Scherer, "Mark Zuckerberg and Priscilla Chan Donate $100 Million More to Election Administrators, Despite Conservative Pushback," *Washington Post*, October 13, 2020, https://www.washingtonpost.com/politics/zuckerberg-chan-elections-facebook/2020/10/12/0e07de94-0cba-11eb-8074-0e943a91bf08_story.html.

2 THE GIVINGSCAPE

1. Author interview, Christine Liu, December 6, 2019.

2. See https://massivesci.com/about/.

3. Author interview, Cat Chang, August 23, 2019.

4. Author interview, Cat Chang, August 23, 2019.

5. Author interview, Cat Chang, August 23, 2019.

6. Jeremy Snyder, "Crowdfunding for Covid-Related Needs: Unfair and Inadequate," Hastings Center, March 30, 2020, https://www.thehastingscenter.org/crowdfunding-for-covid-related-needs-unfair-and-inadequate/; Nathaniel Popper and Taylor Lorenz, "GoFundMe Confronts Coronavirus Demand," *New York Times*, March 26, 2020, https://www.nytimes.com/2020/03/26/style/gofundme-coronavirus.html.

7. Michael Wyland, "Donor-Advised Fund Giving Reflects Larger Philanthropy Patterns—Mostly," *Nonprofit Quarterly*, February 28, 2018, https://nonprofitquarterly.org/donor-advised-fund-giving-reflects-overall-us-philanthropy-patterns-mostly/.

8. See the IRS guidance on donor-advised funds: https://www.irs.gov/charities-non-profits/charitable-organizations/donor-advised-funds.

9. The Forum for Sustainable and Responsible Investment, *2018 Trends Report*, https://www.ussif.org/trends.

10. The nature of digital surveillance is too big an issue to be taken up in this volume, but it's important to note that our technologies bring benefits and challenges to changemaking in many ways. For example, although cellphones make it easier than ever for police to track activists and protestors, they also make it possible for everyday people to document police brutality. This dualism is on full display in the Black Lives Matter movement and the street protests about racial injustice and policing that were so much a part of 2020. Important work on these issues comes from Allissa V. Richardson, *Bearing Witness while Black: African Americans, Smartphones, and the New Protest #Journalism* (Oxford: Oxford University Press, 2020); André Brock, *Distributed Blackness: African American Cybercultures* (New York: NYU Press, 2020); Sarah J. Jackson, Moya Bailey, and Brooke Foucault Welles, *#Hashtag Activism: Networks of Race and Gender Justice* (Cambridge, MA: MIT Press, 2020); Sarah

Florini, *Beyond Hashtags: Racial Politics and Black Digital Networks* (New York: NYU Press, 2019); Jen Schradie, *The Revolution that Wasn't: How Digital Activism Favors Conservatives* (Cambridge, MA: Harvard University Press, 2019).

11. See Jasmine McNealy, "An Ecological Approach to Data Governance," Databite no. 127, *Data & Society*, January 8, 2020, video, podcast, https://datasociety.net/events/databite -no-127-jasmine-mcnealy/.

12. Oxford philosopher Lucido Floridi has a short video explaining this: "On Personal Data, Forgiveness, and the Right to Be Forgotten," Markkula Center for Applied Ethics, March 10, 2015, YouTube video, https://www.youtube.com/watch?v=JVTu-0SfvzQ. Legal scholar Jasmine McNealy also discusses the limited nature of transactional value in "An Ecological Approach to Data Governance."

13. The two organizations that sponsor iNaturalist are the California Academy of Sciences and National Geographic Society.

14. Kurt Wagner, "Facebook's Grip on Data Leaves Nonprofits Leery of Donate Button," *Bloomberg News*, February 13, 2020, https://www.bloomberg.com/news/articles /2020-02-13/facebook-s-grip-on-data-leaves-nonprofits-leery-of-donate-button.

15. Summer Allen, *The Science of Generosity* (Berkeley, CA: Greater Good Science Center, May 2018), https://www.templeton.org/discoveries/the-science-of-generosity.

16. Suzanne Perry, "The Stubborn 2% Giving Rate," *Chronicle of Philanthropy*, June 17, 2013, https://www.philanthropy.com/article/The-Stubborn-2-Giving-Rate/154691.

17. Jessica Semega et al., *Income and Poverty in the United States, 2018: Current Population Reports* (Washington, DC: US Census Bureau, 2019).

18. Patrick M. Rooney, "The Growth in Total Household Giving Is Camouflaging a Decline in Giving by Small and Medium Donors: What Can We Do about It?," *Nonprofit Quarterly*, August 27, 2019, https://nonprofitquarterly.org/total-household-growth -decline-small-medium-donors/.

19. Tomio Geron, "The Business behind Change.Org's Activist Petitions," *Forbes*, November 5, 2012, https://www.forbes.com/sites/tomiogeron/2012/10/17/activism-for-profit-change -org-makes-an-impact-and-makes-money/#354d3d147ffa.

20. Cassie Mogilner, Zoe Chance, and Michael I. Norton, "Giving Time Gives You Time," *Psychological Science* 23, no. 10 (2012).

3   CROWDFUNDING AND ITS ANCIENT COUSINS

1. Jessica Bearman et al., *The Landscape of Giving Circles/Collective Giving Groups in the U.S., 2016* (Indianapolis: The Giving Circles Research Group, 2017), 5.

2. Mark Hicks, "Water a Human Right, Detroit Demonstrators Say," *Detroit News*, December 11, 2019, https://www.detroitnews.com/story/news/local/detroit-city/2019/12/11 /protesters-want-end-residential-shutoffs-claim-water-human-right/4393976002/.

3. Joel Kurth, "How to Get Help with Detroit Water Payments and Avoid Shutoffs," *Bridge Michigan*, August 19, 2019, https://www.bridgemi.com/detroit/how-get-help-detroit-water-payments-and-avoid-shutoffs.

4. "United Nations Officials Visit Detroit to Investigate Violations Human Right to Safe Drinking Water," Food & Water Watch, October 17, 2014, https://www.foodandwaterwatch.org/news/united-nations-officials-visit-detroit-investigate-violations-human-right-safe-drinking-water.

5. Author interview, Tiffani Ashley Bell, May 6, 2019.

6. Tim Cadogan, "GoFundMe Sees Spike in Campaigns for People, Small Business amid COVID-19 Pandemic," BNN Bloomberg interview, May 8, 2020, YouTube video, https://youtu.be/jVjgL1KLa3k.

7. Cadogan, "GoFundMe Sees Spike."

8. Lauren S. Berliner and Nora J. Kenworthy, "Producing a Worthy Illness: Personal Crowdfunding amidst Financial Crisis," *Social Science & Medicine* 187 (2017), https://doi.org/10.1016/j.socscimed.2017.02.008.

9. This can be said about much of big philanthropy and is a core critique of books by Anand Girardharas and Rob Reich.

10. Sites searched on August 19, 2019: Kickstarter, GoFundMe, and Indiegogo.

11. "A Brief History of Kickstarter," https://www.kickstarter.com/stories/fiveyears.

12. All data on Kickstarter is from https://www.kickstarter.com/help/stats.

13. The Kickstarter Charter: https://www.kickstarter.com/charter.

14. Gina Martinez, "GoFundMe CEO One-Third of Site's Donations are to Cover Costs," *Time*, January 30, 2019, https://time.com/5516037/gofundme-medical-bills-one-third-ceo/. Data from the GoFundMe 2020 Giving Report, https://www.gofundme.com/2020.

15. See Washington State Office of the Attorney General, "Attorney General Files Lawsuit against Company behind Asylum Playing Cards Crowdfunded Project," May 1, 2014, https://www.atg.wa.gov/news/news-releases/attorney-general-files-lawsuit-against-company-behind-asylum-playing-cards.

16. See California Association of Nonprofits, "Principles for Responsible Crowdfunding," accessed August 17, 2020, https://calnonprofits.org/publications/article-archive/708-urgent-help-ensure-fair-online-fundraising-practices. See also CalNonprofits' open letter on AB 2208, August 14, 2020, https://calnonprofits.org/33-advocacy/710-support-letter-for-assembly-bill-2208.

17. Author interview, Reverend Eleanor Williams, December 16, 2019.

18. Author interview, Yancy Villa, November 15, 2019.

19. Matt Stempeck, "A Timeline of Civic Tech Tells a Data-Driven Story of the Field," *Civic Hall*, May 28, 2019, https://civichall.org/civicist/how-civic-tech-has-evolved-over-the-last-25-years/.

20. Author interview, Yancy Villa, November 15, 2019.

21. Author interviews, September 12, 2019.

22. Jessica Bearman et al., *Landscape 2016.*

23. Bearman et al., *Landscape 2016*, 6.

24. Sara Lomelin, who helped start giving circles through the Latino Community Foundation, now runs Philanthropy Together, an incubator of giving circles with a focus on racial equity and social justice. The Community Investment Network connects and supports African American giving circles, and Amplifier is a network for Jewish circles. Author interview, Sara Lomelin, June 18, 2020.

25. Author interview, Amber Gonzalez-Vargas, August 11, 2019.

26. Author interview, Masha Chernyak, April 29, 2019.

27. Angela M. Eikenberry and Jessica Bearman, *The Impact of Giving Together: Giving Circles Influence on Members' Philanthropic and Civic Behaviors, Knowledge, and Attitudes* (Omaha: Forum of Regional Associations of Grantmakers, Center on Philanthropy at Indiana University, and University of Nebraska at Omaha, May 2009), https://www.academia .edu/12175637/The_Impact_of_Giving_Together_Full_Report; Angela M. Eikenberry, "Giving Circles: Self-Help/Mutual Aid, Community Philanthropy, or Both?," *International Journal of Self Help and Self Care* 5, no. 3 (2007).

4 GIVING IS POLITICAL

1. Cited in Sarah Hansen, "Here's What the Racial Wealth Gap in America Looks Like Today," *Forbes*, June 5, 2020, https://www.forbes.com/sites/sarahhansen/2020/06/05/heres -what-the-racial-wealth-gap-in-america-looks-like-today/?sh=3d1bd2ea164c. See also Mortiz Kuhn, Moritz Schularick, and Ulrike I. Steins, *Income and Wealth Inequality in America, 1949–2016*, Institute Working Paper 9 (Minneapolis: Federal Reserve Bank of Minneapolis, June 14, 2018), https://doi.org/10.21034/iwp.9; Kriston McIntosh et al., "Examining the Black-White Wealth Gap," Brookings, February 27, 2020, https://www .brookings.edu/blog/up-front/2020/02/27/examining-the-black-white-wealth-gap/.

2. Reich, *Just Giving.*

3. Eitan Hersh, *Politics Is for Power: How to Move Beyond Political Hobbyism, Take Action, and Make Real Change* (New York: Simon and Schuster, 2020), 136.

4. Bureau of Labor Statistics, American Time Use Survey, 2018, https://www.bls.gov/charts /american-time-use/activity-by-sex.htm.

5. Author interview, Rashad Robinson, May 6, 2019.

6. See https://www.stophateforprofit.org/july-30-statement.

7. The distinction between safety and security shapes the work of many communities and activists—notably, Tawana Petty and the Detroit Community Technology Project. See https://alliedmedia.org/dctp.

8. Author interview, Kate Robinson, August 16, 2019.

9. Safe Passage 2018 highlights included forty-five jobs for local neighbors. See https://tlcbd .org/safe-passage-2018-old-version?rq=safe%20passage%202019.

10. See https://tlcbd.org/safe-passage-2018-old-version?rq=safe%20passage%202019.

5 INVESTING ACROSS GENERATIONS

1. Blaine Townsend, "From SRI to ESG: The Origins of Socially Responsible and Sustainable Investing," *Journal of Impact & ESG Investing* 1, no. 1 (2017): 4, https://www.bailard.com /wp-content/uploads/2017/06/Socially-Responsible-Investing-History-Bailard-White -Paper-FNL.pdf

2. Author interview, Mary Margaret Pettway, August 28, 2019.

3. See Celia Carey, "Quiltmakers of Gee's Bend," Alabama Public Broadcasting, 2005, Vimeo video, https://vimeo.com/50174695.

4. A study by In Other Words and Artnet News found that only 2.37 percent of all acquisitions and gifts and 7.6 percent of all exhibitions at thirty American museums were by African American artists in the decade between 2008 and 2018. Julia Halperin and Charlotte Berns, "The Long Road for African American Artists," Artnet News, September 20, 2018, https://news.artnet.com/market/african-american-research-museums -1350362.

5. Hugh Eakin, "For Better or Worse, Our Greatest Museums are Built on the Backs of Billionaires," *Washington Post*, March 29, 2019, https://www.washingtonpost.com/opinions /2019/03/29/better-or-worse-our-greatest-museums-are-built-backs-billionaires/.

6. David Bank, "Souls Grown Deep Foundation to Invest $1 Million in Artists' Hometowns in the U.S. South," ImpactAlpha, June 25, 2019, https://impactalpha.com /souls-grown-deep-foundation-to-invest-1-million-in-artists-hometown-in-the-u-s-south/.

7. Author interview, Mary Margaret Pettway, August 28, 2019.

8. Nick Estes, *Our History is the Future: Standing Rock versus the Dakota Access Pipeline, and the Long Tradition of Indigenous Resistance* (London: Verso Books, 2019).

9. Data retrieved August 28, 2020 from https://gofossilfree.org/divestment/commitments.

10. Author interview, Marilyn Waite, June 10, 2019.

11. Author interview, Marilyn Waite, June 10, 2019.

12. See https://www.inclusiv.org/about-us/.

13. Clean Energy Federal Credit Union, "About Us," accessed June 11, 2019, https:// www.cleanenergycu.org/home/about-us/our-story.

14. Federal Reserve Bank of the United States, *Report on the Economic Well-Being of U.S. Households, 2018* (Washington, DC: Board of Governors of the Federal Reserve System,

2019), 25–26, https://www.federalreserve.gov/consumerscommunities/files/2018-report-economic-well-being-us-households-201905.pdf.

15. See https://www.calvertimpactcapital.org/invest.

16. The Kapor Center; see https://www.kaporcenter.org/.

17. National Philanthropic Trust, *The 2019 DAF Report* (Jenkintown, PA: National Philanthropic Trust, 2019), https://www.nptrust.org/reports/daf-report/.

18. It's important to note that there are many skeptics about impact investing. Definitions are inconsistent, and debates rage over costs and lower returns of designated "impact investments."

6 THE GOOD, BAD, AND UNKNOWN OF GIVING DATA

1. *How We Give Now* mapping conversations, summer 2019, compiled data.

2. Author interview, Leo Salas and David Leland, July 18, 2019.

3. Information from Point Blue Volunteer website, https://www.pointblue.org/engage-with-us/volunteer/.

4. Cameron Norris, "Soundscapes to Landscapes," *HackSpace*, September 2019, https://hackspace.raspberrypi.org/articles/soundscapes-to-landscapes.

5. Good discussions of citizen science, community science, and civic science—and the tensions they entail—can be found in Aya H. Kimura and Abby Kinchy, *Science by the People: Participation, Power, and the Politics of Environmental Knowledge* (New Brunswick, NJ: Rutgers University Press, 2019); Ruha Benjamin, *People's Science: Bodies and Rights on the Stem Cell Frontier* (Stanford, CA: Stanford University Press, 2013); Alondra Nelson, *Body and Soul: The Black Panther Party and the Fight against Medical Discrimination* (Minneapolis, MN: University of Minnesota Press, 2013); Mary Ellen Hannibal, *Citizen Scientist: Searching for Heroes and Hope in an Age of Extinction* (New York: Experiment Press, 2016); Elizabeth Good Christopherson, Dietram A. Scheufele, and Brooke Smith, "The Civic Science Imperative," *Stanford Social Innovation Review* 16, no. 2 (Spring 2018).

6. Mary Ellen Hannibal presents a useful look at iNaturalist in *Citizen Scientist*.

7. Author interview, Mira Bowin, July 25, 2019.

8. Author interview, Mira Bowin, July 25, 2019.

9. Author interview, Mira Bowin, July 25, 2019.

10. iNaturalist, "Year in Review 2019," https://www.inaturalist.org/stats/2019.

11. Author interview, Tony Iwane, July 10, 2019.

12. Author interview, Tony Iwane, July 10, 2019.

13. Mad Price Ball, "Introducing Myself as Executive Director," *Mad Price Ball* (blog), June 1, 2017, https://www.madpriceball.net/introducing-myself-as-executive-director/.

14. See https://www.openhumans.org/about/.

15. Author interview, Mad Price Ball, September 9, 2019.

16. Lucy Bernholz, "Purpose Built Associations," in *Digital Technologies and Democracy Theory*, ed. Lucy Bernholz, Hélène Landemore, and Rob Reich (Chicago: University of Chicago Press, 2020).

17. Author interview, John Wilbanks, April 30, 2019.

18. Brian M. Bot et al., "The mPower Study, Parkinson Disease Mobile Data Collected Using ResearchKit," *Scientific Data* 3 (March 2016), https://doi.org/10.1038/sdata.2016.11

19. Author interview, Vanessa Barone, July 9, 2019.

20. Author interview, Vanessa Barone, July 9, 2019.

21. Author interview, Vanessa Barone, July 9, 2019.

22. Antonio Regalado, "More than 26 Million People Have Taken an At-home Ancestry Test," *MIT Technology Review*, February 11, 2019, https://www.technologyreview.com/s/612880/more-than-26-million-people-have-taken-an-at-home-ancestry-test/.

23. Dani Shapiro, *Inheritance: A Memoir of Genealogy, Paternity, and Love* (New York: Knopf, 2019).

24. See, for example, Alondra Nelson, *The Social Life of DNA: Race, Reparations, and Reconciliation after the Genome* (Boston: Beacon Press, 2016); Dorothy Roberts, *Fatal Invention: How Science, Politics, and Big Business Re-create Race in the Twenty-First Century* (New York: New Press, 2011).

25. Kim Tallbear, *Native American DNA: Tribal Belonging and the False Promise of Genetic Testing* (Minneapolis: University of Minnesota Press, 2013).

26. Author interview, Brady Rogers, July 26, 2019.

27. Author interview, Brady Rogers, July 26, 2019.

28. Author interview, Brady Rogers, July 26, 2019.

29. Author interview, Brady Rogers, July 26, 2019.

30. See McNealy, "An Ecological Approach."

31. See, for example, H. F. Nissenbaum, *Privacy in Context: Technology, Policy, and the Integrity of Social Life* (Stanford, CA: Stanford Law Books, 2010); Alice E. Marwick and danah boyd, "Networked Privacy: How Teenagers Negotiate Context in Social Media," *New Media and Society* 16, no. 7 (2014): 1051–1067, https://doi.org/10.1177/1461444814543995.

32. It's important to note here the contributions of Black women to this work. From Ida B. Wells's work documenting lynching to data justice work done today by scholars and activists such as Ruha Benjamin, Joy Boulamwini, Harlo Holmes, Safiya Noble, Tawana Petty, and Latanya Sweeney, Black women have been at the forefront.

33. More about Creative Commons can be found at https://creativecommons.org/faq/.

34. Chris Jensen, "6 Myths about 'Ethical' Open Source Licenses," Hacker Noon, April 17, 2018, https://hackernoon.com/6-myths-about-ethical-open-source-licenses-3bfbd042b1dc. See also Matthew Bietz, Kevin Patrick, and Cinnamon Bloss, "Data Donation as a Model for Citizen Science Health Research," *Citizen Science: Theory and Practice* 4, no. 1 (2019): 6, https://doi.org/10.5334/cstp.178.

7 RETAIL THERAPY

1. John Mazzone and Samie Rahman, *The Household Diary Study: Mail Use and Attitudes in FY 2017* (Washington, DC: United States Postal Service, 2018), 38. This study found that US households received 11.6 million pieces of nonprofit marketing mail out of a total of 118.4 million pieces of mail. See https://www.prc.gov/docs/105/105134/USPS_HDS _FY17_Final%20Annual%20Report.pdf.

2. While my version of the game is strictly observational, it's in line with a panel study conducted by a consumer insights company and a research panel company. The study found that donors received an average of 17.7 donation requests per week, every week, by mail and email. See Greymatter Research, *The Donor Mindset Study VII: Cutting through the Noise: How much mail and e-mail donors receive, and how much are they reading?*, June 28, 2018, https://greymatterresearch.com/communication/.

3. The 2018 Blackbaud Index tracked 17 percent of all giving to the month of December. See Blackbaud, Inc., "Blackbaud Institute Releases 2018 Charitable Giving Report," Blackbaud, February 20, 2019, https://www.blackbaud.co.uk/newsroom/article/2019/02/20 /blackbaud-institute-releases-2018-charitable-giving-report.

4. Jocelyn Daw, *Cause Marketing for Nonprofits* (New York: John Wiley & Sons, 2006).

5. Arthur H. De Long and Allen P. De Long, self-sealing envelop, US Patent 667,426, filed April 6, 1900, and issued February 5, 1901. See https://pdfpiw.uspto.gov/.piw?PageNum =0&docid=00667426&IDKey=81C6607B9BD8&HomeUrl=http%3A%2F%2Fpatft.uspto .gov%2Fnetahtml%2FPTO%2Fpatimg.htm.

6. I have even seen this at cashiers' stations at the California Department of Motor Vehicles.

7. Engage for Good, *2017 America's Charity Checkout Champions*, accessed July 12, 2019, https://engageforgood.com/new-survey-americas-charity-checkout-champions-2017/.

8. Engage for Good, *2017 Checkout Champions*, 3–4.

9. Aradhna Krishna, "Can Supporting a Cause Decrease Both Donations and Happiness? The Cause Marketing Paradox," *Journal of Consumer Psychology* 21, no. 3 (July 2011), https:// doi.org/10.1016/j.jcps.2011.02.001.

10. See, for example, Xiaoli Nan and Kwangjun Heo, "Consumer Responses to Corporate Social Responsibility (CSR) Initiatives: Examining the Role of Brand-Cause Fit in Cause-Related Marketing," *Journal of Advertising* 36, no. 2 (2007), https://doi.org/10.2753 /JOA0091-3367360204.

11. See annual reports on community social responsibility from different corporations: Walgreens, https://www.walgreensbootsalliance.com/corporate-social-responsibility; Costco, https://www.costco.com/sustainability-introduction.html; Walmart, https://corporate.walmart.com/global-responsibility/community.

12. Patricia Mooney Nickel and Angela M. Eikenberry, "A Critique of the Discourse of Marketized Philanthropy," *American Behavioral Scientist* 52, no. 5 (2009).

13. Krishna, "Cause Marketing Paradox."

14. Krishna, "Cause Marketing Paradox," 343.

15. Nina Mazar and Chen-Bo Zhong, "Do Green Products Make Us Better People?," *Psychological Science* 21, no. 4 (2010).

16. Chun-Tuan Chang and Xing-Yu Chu, "The Give and Take of Cause-Related Marketing," *Journal of the Academy of Marketing Science* 48, no. 2 (2019).

17. Workshop report, Washington, DC, August 13, 2019.

18. Workshop report, Rapid City, South Dakota, September 18, 2019.

19. Author interview, Caroline Kangas, July 30, 2019.

20. The expenditure approach to GDP is calculated by adding personal consumption to business investment, government spending, and net exports in a certain time period: GDP = (C + I + G + NX) In this equation C= private consumption; G = government expenditures; I = sum of country's investments; and NX = net exports.

21. Thorstein Veblen, *The Theory of the Leisure Class* (New York: Macmillan, 1899).

22. The role of labor unions in American collective life is well-studied, although participation through unions and voluntarism/giving are usually discussed as separate spheres. See Margaret Levi, "The Devasted House of Labor," in *Antidemocracy in America: Truth, Power, and the Republic at Risk*, ed. Eric Klinenberg, Caitlin Zaloom, and Sharon Marcus (New York: Columbia University Press, 2019). The changing nature of work is an important phenomenon that touches on much of what this book describes. For more, see Mary L. Gray and Suri Siddharth, *Ghost Work: How to Stop Silicon Valley from Building a New Global Underclass* (New York: Houghton-Mifflin, 2019).

23. Stephen J. Dubner and Greg Rosalsky, "Do Boycotts Work?" Freakonomics Radio, January 21, 2016, https://freakonomics.com/podcast/do-boycotts-work-a-new-freakonomics-radio-podcast/.

24. Author interview, Eric Shih, August 2, 2019.

8 NAVIGATING THE GIVINGSCAPE

1. Author interview, Jamie Bennett, April 24, Providence, Rhode Island.

2. Author interview, Mario Lugay, August 8, 2019.

3. Author interview, Mario Lugay, August 8, 2019.

4. Author interview, Mario Lugay, August 8, 2019.

5. Legal restrictions on voting, and our ongoing political fights over guaranteed access to the franchise, are important policy frameworks here, but people in the mapping conversations were talking about their own views of the importance of voting as an act of civic participation.

6. Doing it yourself saves you from having to share your digital data with yet another third party.

7. Sarah Holder, "Minimum Wage Still Can't Pay for a Two-Bedroom Apartment Anywhere," *CityLab*, June 19, 2019, https://www.citylab.com/equity/2019/06/affordable-housing-minimum-wage-rent-apartment-house-rental/592024/.

8. Bernholz and Pawliw-Fry, *How We Give Now* workshop conversation, September 18, 2019, Rapid City, South Dakota.

9. Theresa Vargas, "'The American Healthcare System Has Just, Quite Literally, Ruined My Future,' a Disabled Georgetown Student Tweeted. Then She Got a Reprieve," *Washington Post*, June 15, 2019, https://www.washingtonpost.com/local/the-american-healthcare-system-has-just-quite-literally-ruined-my-future-a-disabled-georgetown-student-tweeted-then-she-got-a-reprieve/2019/06/14/f53bc1ee-8eef-11e9-b08e-cfd89bd36d4e_story.html.

10. Author interview, Cat Chang, August 23, 2019.

11. iNaturalist, "Year in Review 2019," https://www.inaturalist.org/stats/2019.

12. iNaturalist, "Year in Review 2019"; James Maughn's profile page, https://www.inaturalist.org/people/jmaughn.

13. Tess Srebro, "VolunteerMatch Celebrates 20 Years of Connecting Good People with Good Causes," *VolunteerMatch Blog*, April 25, 2018, https://www.3blmedia.com/News/VolunteerMatch-Celebrates-20-Years-Connecting-Good-People-Good-Causes.

14. Bernholz and Pawliw-Fry, *How We Give Now: Conversations across the United States*, compiled data, 2019.

15. Bernholz and Pawliw-Fry, *How We Give Now*, compiled data, 2019.

16. See "Guidelines for Giving" from the Center for International Disaster Response, https://www.cidi.org/how-to-help/toolkit/.

17. Adam Minter's book *Secondhand: Travels in the New Global Garage Sale* (New York: Bloomsbury Publishing, 2019) tracks how donated goods are processed through a supply chain of stores, Goodwill locations, and manufacturers. There are many good reasons to donate old clothes, but disaster response is not one.

18. Bernholz and Pawliw-Fry, *How We Give Now* workshop conversation, September 16, 2019, public library, Sturgis, South Dakota.

19. Rebecca Solnit, *A Paradise Built in Hell: The Extraordinary Communities that Arise in Disaster* (New York: Viking, 2009).

20. Bernholz and Pawliw-Fry, *How We Give Now* workshop conversation, August 25, 2019, Lakeside, California.

21. Bernholz and Pawliw-Fry, *How We Give Now* workshop conversation, August 13, 2019, Washington, DC.

22. Bernholz and Pawliw-Fry, *How We Give Now* workshop conversations, thirty-three sessions compiled.

23. A 2020 report from Grantmakers for Education used data from DonorsChoose, which helps classroom teachers raise funds for their classrooms. The report found that crowdfunding for basic supplies is becoming standard practice and that schools in high-poverty areas have less success than schools in low-poverty areas. In other words, the poor get poorer. See Grantmakers for Education, *A View from the Classroom: What Teachers Can Tell Philanthropy About the Needs of Schools* (Portland, OR: Grantmakers for Education, February 2020), https://www.edfunders.org/ViewFromTheClassroom.

CONCLUSION

1. See Alondra Nelson, *The Social Life of DNA*.

2. This phrasing, *from generosity to justice*, is also found in Anand Giridharadas's 2018 bestseller, *Winners Take All: The Elite Charade of Changing the World* (New York: Random House, 2018).

3. Eikenberry, "Giving Circles."

4. The Urban Institute maintains an online library of research on charitable tax credits, which can be accessed at https://www.urban.org/search?search_api_views_fulltext=charitable%20 tax%20credit. See also Indiana University Lilly School of Philanthropy, *Charitable Giving and Tax Incentives: Examining Changes in Charitable Giving and Numbers of Donors from Five Policy Proposals* (Indianapolis: Indiana University, 2019), https://independentsector.org /wp-content/uploads/2019/06/Charitable-Giving-and-Tax-Incentives-Report-June2019 .pdf.

5. Annie Dillard, *The Writing Life* (New York: Harper Perennial, 2013).

6. Sarah Song, *Immigration and Democracy* (Oxford: Oxford University Press, 2018).

7. There is a great deal of scholarship on this question, ranging across disciplines. Key resources include Theda Skocpol, *Diminished Democracy: From Membership to Management in American Civic Life* (Norman: Oklahoma University Press, 2003); Angela Eikenberry (2007); Eikenberry and Bearman, *Impact of Giving Together*; Edgar Villanueva, *Decolonizing Wealth: Indigenous Wisdom to Heal Divides and Restore Balance* (San Francisco, CA: Berrett-Koehler Publishers, 2013).

APPENDIX A

1. A report on these conversations, pictures of the map, and the data are available online. See https://pacscenter.stanford.edu/how-we-give-now-philanthropy-by-the-rest-of-us/. The report and DIY guide are available at https://pacscenter.stanford.edu/publication/how-we-give-now-conversations-across-the-united-states/.

2. The research team included Nichelle Hall, Sebastian John Martinez Hickey, Matilda Nickell, Brigitte Pawliw-Fry, Heather Robinson, Jeffrey Rodriguez, and Laura Seaman.

Bibliography

Ahmad, Kaitlin, Nathan Dietz, and Robert T. Grimm Jr. "Philanthropy's Future in Flux as Volunteering and Giving Rates Waver." Independent Sector, January 10, 2020. https:// independentsector.org/news-post/philanthropys-future-in-flux-as-volunteering-and-giving-rates -waver/.

Allen, Summer. *The Science of Generosity*. Berkeley, CA: Greater Good Science Center, May 2018. https://www.templeton.org/wp-content/uploads/2018/05/GGSC-JTF-White-Paper -Generosity-FINAL.pdf.

Andreoni, James, and Jon Durnford. *The Effects of the 2017 Tax Reform on Itemization Status and the Charitable Deduction*. July 17, 2019. https://econweb.ucsd.edu/~jandreon/Andreoni Durnford20190715a.pdf.

Ball, Mad Price. "Introducing Myself as Executive Director." *Mad Price Ball* (blog), June 1, 2017. https://www.madpriceball.net/introducing-myself-as-executive-director/.

Bank, David. "Souls Grown Deep Foundation to Invest $1 Million in Artists' Hometowns in the U.S. South." ImpactAlpha, June 25, 2019. https://impactalpha.com/souls-grown-deep -foundation-to-invest-1-million-in-artists-hometown-in-the-u-s-south/.

Bearman, Jessica, Julia Carboni, Angela Eikenberry, and Jason Franklin. *The Landscape of Giving Circles/Collective Giving Groups in the U.S., 2016*. Indianapolis: The Giving Circles Research Group, 2017.

Berliner, Lauren S., and Nora J. Kenworthy. "Producing a Worthy Illness: Personal Crowd-funding amidst Financial Crisis." *Social Science & Medicine* 187 (2017): 233–242. https:// doi.org/10.1016/j.socscimed.2017.02.008.

Benjamin, Ruha. *People's Science: Bodies and Rights on the Stem Cell Frontier*. Stanford, CA: Stanford University Press, 2013.

Bernholz, Lucy. "Purpose Built Associations." In *Digital Technologies and Democracy Theory*, edited by Lucy Bernholz, Hélène Landemore, and Rob Reich, 88-110. Chicago: University of Chicago Press, 2019.

Bernholz, Lucy, and Brigitte Pawliw-Fry. *How We Give Now: Conversations across the United States.* Stanford Center on Philanthropy and Civil Society. Stanford University. November 2019. https://pacscenter.stanford.edu/publication/how-we-give-now-conversations-across-the-united-states/.

Bietz, Matthew, Kevin Patrick, and Cinnamon Bloss. "Data Donation as a Model for Citizen Science Health Research." *Citizen Science: Theory and Practice* 4, no. 1 (2019): 1–11. https://doi.org/10.5334/cstp.178.

Blackbaud, Inc. "Blackbaud Institute Releases 2018 Charitable Giving Report." Blackbaud, February 20, 2019. https://www.blackbaud.co.uk/newsroom/article/2019/02/20/blackbaud-institute-releases-2018-charitable-giving-report.

Bot, Brian M., Christine Suver, Elias Chaibub Neto, Michael Kellen, Arno Klein, Christopher Bare, Megan Doerr, Abhishek Pratap, John Wilbanks, E. Ray Dorsey, Stephen H. Friend, and Andrew D. Trister. "The mPower Study, Parkinson Disease Mobile Data Collected Using ResearchKit." *Scientific Data* 3 (March 2016): 160011. https://doi.org/10.1038/sdata.2016.11.

Brill, Alex, and Derrick Choe. *Charitable Giving and the Tax Cuts and Jobs Act.* Washington, DC: American Enterprise Institute, June 2018.

Brock, André. *Distributed Blackness: African American Cybercultures.* New York: NYU Press, 2020.

Cadogan, Tim. "GoFundMe Sees Spike in Campaigns for People, Small Businesses amid COVID-19 Pandemic." BNN Bloomberg interview, May 8, 2020. YouTube video. https://youtu.be/jVjgL1KLa3k.

California Association of Nonprofits. "Principles for Responsible Crowdfunding." Accessed August 17, 2020. https://calnonprofits.org/publications/article-archive/708-urgent-help-ensure-fair-online-fundraising-practices.

California Association of Nonprofits. CalNonprofits. Open letter on AB 2208. CalNonprofits, August 14, 2020. https://calnonprofits.org/33-advocacy/710-support-letter-for-assembly-bill-2208.

Carey, Celia. "Quiltmakers of Gee's Bend." Alabama Public Broadcasting, 2005. Vimeo video, 56:45. https://vimeo.com/50174695.

Chang, Chun-Tuan, and Xing-Yu Chu. "The Give and Take of Cause-Related Marketing." *Journal of the Academy of Marketing Science* 48, no. 2 (2019): 203–221.

Christopherson, Elizabeth Good, Dietram A. Scheufele, and Brooke Smith. "The Civic Science Imperative." *Stanford Social Innovation Review* 16, no. 2 (Spring 2018): 46–52.

Clemens, Elisabeth S. *Civic Gifts: Voluntarism and the Making of the American Nation-State.* Chicago: University of Chicago Press, 2020.

Colinvaux, Roger, and Ray D. Madoff. "Charitable Tax Reform for the 21st Century." *164 Tax Notes 1867* (2019). September 16, 2019. https://ssrn.com/abstract=3462163.

Daw, Jocelyn. *Cause Marketing for Nonprofits.* New York: John Wiley & Sons, 2006.

Dillard, Annie. *The Writing Life.* New York: Harper Perennial, 2013.

Dimaggio, Paul J., and Helmut K. Anheier. "The Sociology of Nonprofit Organizations and Sectors." *Annual Review of Sociology* 16 (1990): 137–159.

Dubner, Stephen J., and Greg Rosalsky. "Do Boycotts Work?" Freakonomics Radio, January 21, 2016. https://freakonomics.com/podcast/do-boycotts-work-a-new-freakonomics-radio-podcast/.

Duquette, Nicholas J. "Founders' Fortunes and Philanthropy: A History of the U.S. Charitable-Contribution Deduction." *Business History Review* 93, no. 3 (2019): 1–32. https://doi.org/10.1017/S0007680519000710.

Eakin, Hugh. "For Better or Worse, Our Greatest Museums Are Built on the Backs of Billionaires." *Washington Post*, March 29, 2019. https://www.washingtonpost.com/opinions/2019/03/29/better-or-worse-our-greatest-museums-are-built-backs-billionaires/.

Eastman, Scott. "How Many Taxpayers Itemize under Current Law?" Tax Foundation, September 12, 2019. https://taxfoundation.org/standard-deduction-itemized-deductions-current-law-2019/.

Eikenberry, Angela M. "Giving Circles: Self-Help/Mutual Aid, Community Philanthropy, or Both?" *International Journal of Self Help and Self Care* 5, no. 3 (2007): 249–278.

Eikenberry, Angela M., and Jessica Bearman. *The Impact of Giving Together: Giving Circles Influence on Members' Philanthropic and Civic Behaviors, Knowledge, and Attitudes.* Omaha: Forum of Regional Associations of Grantmakers, Center on Philanthropy at Indiana University, and University of Nebraska at Omaha, May 2009. https://www.academia.edu/12175637/The_Impact_of_Giving_Together_Full_Report.

Engage for Good. *2017 America's Charity Checkout Champions.* Accessed July 12, 2019. https://engageforgood.com/new-survey-americas-charity-checkout-champions-2017/.

Estes, Nick. *Our History Is the Future: Standing Rock versus the Dakota Access Pipeline, and the Long Tradition of Indigenous Resistance.* London: Verso Books, 2019.

Federal Reserve Bank of the United States. *Report on the Economic Well-Being of U.S. Households, 2018.* Washington, DC: Board of Governors of the Federal Reserve System, 2019. https://www.federalreserve.gov/consumerscommunities/files/2018-report-economic-well-being-us-households-201905.pdf.

Floridi, Lucido. "On Personal Data, Forgiveness, and the Right to Be Forgotten." Markkula Center for Applied Ethics, March 10, 2015. YouTube video. https://www.youtube.com/watch?v=JVTu-0SfvzQ.

Florini, Sarah. *Beyond Hashtags: Racial Politics and Black Digital Networks.* New York: NYU Press, 2019.

Fuller, Jacqueline, and Joe Huston. "A Proactive Approach to Disaster Relief." *The Keyword* (blog), Google.org, August 14, 2019. https://blog.google/outreach-initiatives/google-org/proactive-approach-disaster-relief/.

Geron, Tomio. "The Business behind Change.org's Activist Petitions." *Forbes*, November 5, 2012. https://www.forbes.com/sites/tomiogeron/2012/10/17/activism-for-profit-change-org-makes-an-impact-and-makes-money/?sh=50efb20c7ffa.

Giridharadas, Anand. *Winners Take All: The Elite Charade of Changing the World.* New York: Random House, 2018.

Giving USA. "Giving USA 2020: Charitable Giving Showed Solid Growth, Climbing to $449.64 Billion in 2019, One of the Highest Years for Giving on Record." Giving USA, June 16, 2020. https://givingusa.org/giving-usa-2020-charitable-giving-showed-solid-growth-climbing-to-449 -64-billion-in-2019-one-of-the-highest-years-for-giving-on-record/.

Global Impact Investing Network. *The Annual Impact Investor Survey 2020.* (New York: Global Impact Investing Network, June 11, 2020). https://thegiin.org/research/publication /impinv-survey-2020.

GoFundMe 2020 Giving Report. Accessed December 15, 2020. https://www.gofundme .com/2020.

Grantmakers for Education. *A View from the Classroom: What Teachers Can Tell Philanthropy about the Needs of Schools.* Portland, OR: Grantmakers for Education, February 2020. https:// www.edfunders.org/ViewFromTheClassroom.

Gray, Mary L., and Suri Siddharth. *Ghost Work: How to Stop Silicon Valley from Building a New Global Underclass.* New York: Houghton-Mifflin, 2019.

Greymatter Research. *The Donor Mindset Study VII: Cutting through the Noise: How Much Mail and E-mail Donors Receive, and How Much Are They Reading?*, June 28, 2018. https:// greymatterresearch.com/communication/.

Grimm, Robert T., and Nathan Dietz. *Shifting Milestones, Fewer Donors and Volunteers.* College Park: University of Maryland, School of Public Policy, October 16, 2019. https://dogood.umd .edu/research-impact/publications/shifting-milestones-fewer-donors-and-volunteers.

Halperin, Julia, and Charlotte Burns, "The Long Road for African American Artists," Artnet News, September 20, 2018, https://news.artnet.com/the-long-road-for-african-american-artists /african-american-research-museums-1350362.

Hannibal, Mary Ellen. *Citizen Scientist: Searching for Heroes and Hope in an Age of Extinction.* New York: Experiment Press, 2016.

Hansen, Sarah. "Here's What the Racial Wealth Gap in America Looks Like Today." *Forbes*, June 5, 2020. https://www.forbes.com/sites/sarahhansen/2020/06/05/heres-what-the-racial-wealth -gap-in-america-looks-like-today.

Hersh, Eitan. *Politics Is for Power: How to Move Beyond Political Hobbyism, Take Action, and Make Real Change.* New York: Simon and Schuster, 2020.

Hicks, Mark. "Water a Human Right, Detroit Demonstrators Say." *Detroit News*, December 11, 2019. https://www.detroitnews.com/story/news/local/detroit-city/2019/12/11/protesters -want-end-residential-shutoffs-claim-water-human-right/4393976002/.

Holder, Sarah. "Minimum Wage Still Can't Pay for a Two-Bedroom Apartment Anywhere." *CityLab*, June 19, 2019. https://www.citylab.com/equity/2019/06/affordable-housing-minimum -wage-rent-apartment-house-rental/592024/.

Hossein, Caroline Shenaz. "Mutual Aid and Physical Distancing are Not New for Black and Racialized Minorities within the Americas." *Histphil*, March 24, 2020. https://histphil .org/2020/03/24/mutual-aid-and-physical-distancing-are-not-new-for-black-and-racialized -minorities-in-the-americas/.

Hossein, Caroline Shenaz, ed. *The Black Social Economy in the Americas: Exploring Diverse Community-Based Markets*. New York: Palgrave Macmillan, 2018.

Indiana University Lilly Family School of Philanthropy. *Changes to the Giving Landscape*. Indianapolis: Indiana University, 2019. https://scholarworks.iupui.edu/bitstream/handle/1805 /21217/vanguard-charitable191022.pdf.

Indiana University Lilly Family School of Philanthropy. *Charitable Giving and Tax Incentives: Estimating Changes in Charitable Dollars and Number of Donors Resulting from Five Policy Proposals*. Indianapolis: Indiana University, 2019. https://independentsector.org/wp-content/uploads /2019/06/Charitable-Giving-and-Tax-Incentives-Report-June2019.pdf.

Jackson, Sarah, Moya Bailey, and Brooke Foucault Welles. *#Hashtag Activism: Networks of Race and Gender Justice*. Cambridge, MA: MIT Press, 2020.

Jensen, Chris. "6 Myths about 'Ethical' Open Source Licenses." Hacker Noon, April 17, 2018. https://hackernoon.com/6-myths-about-ethical-open-source-licenses-3bfbd042b1dc.

Kimura, Aya H., and Abby Kinchy. *Science by the People: Participation, Power, and the Politics of Environmental Knowledge*. New Brunswick, NJ: Rutgers University Press, 2019.

Klinenberg, Eric. *Palaces for the People: How Social Infrastructure Can Help Fight Inequality, Polarization, and the Decline of Civic Life*. New York: Crown Books, 2019.

Kohl-Arenas, Erica. *The Self-Help Myth: How Philanthropy Fails to Alleviate Poverty*. Berkeley: University of California Press, 2016.

Kohl-Arenas, Erika, and Megan Ming Francis. "Movement Capture and the Long Arc of the Black Freedom Struggle." *HistPhil*, July 14, 2020. https://histphil.org/2020/07/14 /movement-capture-and-the-long-arc-of-the-black-freedom-struggle/.

Krishna, Aradhna. "Can Supporting a Cause Decrease Both Donations and Happiness? The Cause Marketing Paradox." *Journal of Consumer Psychology* 21, no. 3 (July 2011): 338–345. https://doi.org/10.1016/j.jcps.2011.02.001.

Kuhn, Mortiz, Moritz Schularick, and Ulrike I. Steins. *Income and Wealth Inequality in America, 1949–2016*. Institute Working Paper 9. Minneapolis: Federal Reserve Bank of Minneapolis, June 14, 2018. https://doi.org/10.21034/iwp.9.

Kurth, Joel. "How to Get Help with Detroit Water Payments and Avoid Shutoffs." *Bridge Michigan*, August 19, 2019. https://www.bridgemi.com/detroit/how-get-help-detroit-water -payments-and-avoid-shutoffs.

Levi, Margaret. "The Devasted House of Labor." In *Antidemocracy in America: Truth, Power, and the Republic at Risk*, edited by Eric Klinenberg, Caitlin Zaloom, and Sharon Marcus, 111–118. New York: Columbia University Press, 2019.

Levy, Jonathan. "Altruism and the Origins of Nonprofit Philanthropy." In *Philanthropy in Democratic Societies*, edited by Rob Reich, Lucy Bernholz, and Chiara Cordelli, 19–43. Chicago: University of Chicago Press, 2016.

Levy, Jonathan. "From Fiscal Triangle to Passing Through: Rise of the Nonprofit Corporation." In *Corporations and American Democracy*, edited by Naomi R. Lamoreaux and William J. Novak, 213–244. Cambridge, MA: Harvard University Press, 2017.

Marwick, Alice E., and danah boyd. "Networked Privacy: How Teenagers Negotiate Context in Social Media." *New Media & Society* 16, no. 7 (2014): 1051–1067. https://doi.org/10.1177/1461444814543995.

Martinez, Gina. "GoFundMe CEO One-Third of Site's Donations are to Cover Costs." *Time*. January 30, 2019. https://time.com/5516037/gofundme-medical-bills-one-third-ceo/.

Mazar, Nina, and Chen-Bo Zhong. "Do Green Products Make Us Better People?" *Psychological Science* 21, no. 4 (2010): 494–498.

Mazzone, John, and Samie Rahman. *The Household Diary Study: Mail Use and Attitudes in FY 2017*. Washington, DC: United States Postal Service, 2018. https://www.prc.gov/docs/105/105134/USPS_HDS_FY17_Final%20Annual%20Report.pdf.

McIntosh, Kriston, Emily Moss, Ryan Nunn, and Jay Shambaugh. "Examining the Black-White Wealth Gap." Brookings, February 27, 2020. https://www.brookings.edu/blog/up-front/2020/02/27/examining-the-black-white-wealth-gap/.

McMillan Cottom, Tressie. *LowerEd: The Troubling Rise of For-Profit Colleges in the New Economy*. New York: New Press, 2018.

McNealy, Jasmine. "An Ecological Approach to Data Governance." Databite no. 127. *Data & Society*, January 8, 2020. Video, podcast. https://datasociety.net/library/an-ecological-approach-to-data-governance/.

Miner, Luke. "For a Longer, Healthier Life, Share Your Data." *New York Times*, May 22, 2019. https://www.nytimes.com/2019/05/22/opinion/health-care-privacy-hipaa.html.

Ming Francis, Megan. *Civil Rights and the Making of the Modern American State*. Cambridge: Cambridge University Press, 2014.

Ming Francis, Megan. "The Price of Civil Rights: Black Politics, White Money, and Movement Capture." *Law and Society Review* 53, no. 1 (March 2019): 275-309.

Minter, Adam. *Secondhand: Travels in the New Global Garage Sale*. New York: Bloomsbury Publishing, 2019.

Miree, Kathryn, and Winton Smith. "The Unraveling of Donor Intent: Lawsuits and Lessons." *Journal of Practical Estate Planning* 11, no. 5 (October 2009): 13–49.

Mogilner, Cassie, Zoe Chance, and Michael I. Norton. "Giving Time Gives You Time." *Psychological Science* 23, no. 10 (2012): 1233–1238.

Mooney Nickel, Patricia, and Angela M. Eikenberry. "A Critique of the Discourse of Marketized Philanthropy." *American Behavioral Scientist* 52, no. 5 (2009): 974–989.

Mudaliar, Abhilash, and Hannah Dithrich. *Sizing the Impact Investing Market*. New York: Global Impact Investing Network, April 1, 2019. https://thegiin.org/research/publication /impinv-market-size.

Nan, Xiaoli, and Kwangjun Heo. "Consumer Responses to Corporate Social Responsibility (CSR) Initiatives: Examining the Role of Brand-Cause Fit in Cause-Related Marketing." *Journal of Advertising* 36, no. 2 (2007): 63–74, https://doi.org/10.2753/JOA0091-3367360204.

National Philanthropic Trust. *The 2019 DAF Report*. Jenkintown, PA: National Philanthropic Trust, 2019. https://www.nptrust.org/reports/daf-report/.

Nelson, Alondra. *Body and Soul: The Black Panther Party and the Fight against Medical Discrimination*. Minneapolis: University of Minnesota Press, 2013.

Nelson, Alondra. *The Social Life of DNA: Race, Reparations, and Reconciliation after the Genome*. Boston: Beacon Press, 2016.

Nissenbaum, H. F. *Privacy in Context: Technology, Policy, and the Integrity of Social Life*. Stanford, CA: Stanford Law Books, 2010.

Norris, Cameron. "Soundscapes to Landscapes." *HackSpace*, September 2019. https://hackspace .raspberrypi.org/articles/soundscapes-to-landscapes.

Open Secrets. "2020 Election to Cost $14 Billion, Blowing Away Spending Records." Open Secrets.org. Center for Responsive Politics, October 28, 2020. https://www.opensecrets.org /news/2020/10/cost-of-2020-election-14billion-update/.

Perry, Suzanne. "The Stubborn 2% Giving Rate." *Chronicle of Philanthropy*, June 17, 2013. https://www.philanthropy.com/article/The-Stubborn-2-Giving-Rate/154691.

Popper, Nathaniel, and Taylor Lorenz. "GoFundMe Confronts Coronavirus Demand." *New York Times*, March 26, 2020. https://www.nytimes.com/2020/03/26/style/gofundme-coronavirus .html.

Reckhow, Sarah. *Follow the Money: How Foundation Dollars Change Public School Politics*. New York: Oxford University Press, 2012.

Regalado, Antonio. "More than 26 Million People Have Taken an At-home Ancestry Test." *MIT Technology Review*, February 11, 2019. https://www.technologyreview.com/s/612880 /more-than-26-million-people-have-taken-an-at-home-ancestry-test/.

Reich, Rob. *Just Giving: Why Philanthropy Is Failing Democracy and How It Can Do Better*. Princeton, NJ: Princeton University Press, 2018.

Richardson, Allissa V. *Bearing Witness while Black: African Americans, Smartphones, and the New Protest #Journalism*. Oxford: Oxford University Press, 2020.

Roberts, Dorothy. *Fatal Invention: How Science, Politics, and Big Business Re-create Race in the Twenty-First Century*. New York: New Press, 2011.

Rooks, Noliwe. *Cutting School: Privatization, Segregation, and the End of Public Education*. New York: New Press. 2017.

Rooney, Patrick M. "The Growth in Total Household Giving Is Camouflaging a Decline in Giving by Small and Medium Donors: What Can We Do about It?" *Nonprofit Quarterly*, August 27, 2019. https://nonprofitquarterly.org/total-household-growth-decline-small-medium-donors/.

Schradie, Jen. *The Revolution that Wasn't: How Digital Activism Favors Conservatives.* Cambridge, MA: Harvard University Press, 2019.

Skocpol, Theda. *Diminished Democracy: From Membership to Management in American Civic Life.* Norman: Oklahoma University Press, 2003.

Semega, Jessica, Melissa Kollar, John Creamer, and Abinash Mohanty. *Income and Poverty in the United States, 2018: Current Population Reports.* Washington, DC: US Census Bureau, 2019.

Shapiro, Dani. *Inheritance: A Memoir of Genealogy, Paternity, and Love.* New York: Knopf, 2019.

Shain, Susan, and Sumina Sengupta. "One Thing You Can Do: Make Your Donations Count." *New York Times*, August 14, 2019. https://www.nytimes.com/2019/08/14/climate/nyt-climate-newsletter-greta.html.

Scherer, Michael. "Mark Zuckerberg and Priscilla Chan Donate $100 Million More to Election Administrators, Despite Conservative Pushback." *Washington Post*, October 13, 2020. https://www.washingtonpost.com/politics/zuckerberg-chan-elections-facebook/2020/10/12/0e07de94-0cba-11eb-8074-0e943a91bf08_story.html.

Snyder, Jeremy. "Crowdfunding for Covid-Related Needs: Unfair and Inadequate." Hastings Center, March 30, 2020. https://www.thehastingscenter.org/crowdfunding-for-covid-related-needs-unfair-and-inadequate/.

Solnit, Rebecca. *A Paradise Built in Hell: The Extraordinary Communities that Arise in Disaster.* New York: Viking, 2009.

Song, Sarah. *Immigration and Democracy.* Oxford: Oxford University Press, 2018.

Stackpole, Thomas. "How Dorothy's Ruby Slippers Came to the Smithsonian." *Smithsonian Magazine*, November 2016. https://www.smithsonianmag.com/smithsonian-institution/how-dorothys-ruby-slippers-came-to-the-smithsonian-180960760/.

Stempeck, Matt. "A Timeline of Civic Tech Tells a Data-Driven Story of the Field." *Civic Hall*, May 28, 2019. https://civichall.org/civicist/how-civic-tech-has-evolved-over-the-last-25-years/.

Srebro, Tess. "VolunteerMatch Celebrates 20 Years of Connecting Good People with Good Causes." *VolunteerMatch Blog*, April 25, 2018. https://www.3blmedia.com/News/VolunteerMatch-Celebrates-20-Years-Connecting-Good-People-Good-Causes.

Takagi, Gene. "A Prediction for Nonprofits in 2018: Rise of the 501(c)(4) Organizations." *Nonprofit Law Blog*, NEO Law Group, January 25, 2018. http://nonprofitlawblog.com/a-prediction-for-nonprofits-in-2018-rise-of-the-501c4-organizations/.

Tallbear, Kim. *Native American DNA: Tribal Belonging and the False Promise of Genetic Testing.* Minneapolis: University of Minnesota Press, 2013.

Tax Policy Center. *Racial Disparities and the Income Tax System.* Washington, DC: Tax Policy Center, January 30, 2020.

Tompkins-Strange, Megan. *Policy Patrons: Philanthropy, Education Reform, and the Politics of Influence*. Cambridge, MA: Harvard Education Press, 2016.

Townsend, Blaine. "From SRI to ESG: The Origins of Socially Responsible and Sustainable Investing." *Journal of Impact & ESG Investing* 1, no. 1 (2017): 1–16. https://www.bailard.com /wp-content/uploads/2017/06/Socially-Responsible-Investing-History-Bailard-White-Paper -FNL.pdf.

"United Nations Officials Visit Detroit to Investigate Violations Human Right to Safe Drinking Water." Food & Water Watch, October 17, 2014. https://www.foodandwaterwatch.org/news /united-nations-officials-visit-detroit-investigate-violations-human-right-safe-drinking-water.

Vargas, Theresa. "'The American Healthcare System Has Just, Quite Literally, Ruined My Future,' a Disabled Georgetown Student Tweeted. Then She Got a Reprieve." *Washington Post*, June 15, 2019. https://www.washingtonpost.com/local/the-american-healthcare-system-has-just -quite-literally-ruined-my-future-a-disabled-georgetown-student-tweeted-then-she-got-a-reprieve /2019/06/14/f53bc1ee-8eef-11e9-b08e-cfd89bd36d4e_story.html.

Villanueva, Edgar. *Decolonizing Wealth: Indigenous Wisdom to Heal Divides and Restore Balance*. San Francisco: Berrett-Koehler Publishers, 2013.

Veblen, Thorstein. *The Theory of the Leisure Class*. New York: Macmillan, 1899.

Vox, Ford, Kelly McBride Folkers, and Arthur Caplan. "Medical Crowdfunding's Dark Side." *Health Affairs* (blog), October 23, 2018. https://www.healthaffairs.org/do/10.1377/hblog 20181019.834615/full/.

Wagner, Kurt. "Facebook's Grip on Data Leaves Nonprofits Leery of Donate Button." *Bloomberg News*, February 13, 2020. https://www.bloomberg.com/news/articles/2020-02-13 /facebook-s-grip-on-data-leaves-nonprofits-leery-of-donate-button.

Walker, Darren. *From Generosity to Justice: A New Gospel of Wealth*. New York: Ford Foundation/ Disruption Books, 2019.

Washington State Office of the Attorney General. "Attorney General Files Lawsuit against Company behind Asylum Playing Cards Crowdfunded Project." May 1, 2014. https://www.atg .wa.gov/news/news-releases/attorney-general-files-lawsuit-against-company-behind-asylum -playing-cards.

Wong, Alice, ed. *Disability Visibility: First-Person Stories the Twenty-First Century*. New York: Vantage Books, 2020.

Wood, Molly. "The Ethics of Hiding Your Data from the Machines." *Wired*, August 22, 2019. https://www.wired.com/story/ethics-hiding-your-data-from-machines/.

Wyland, Michael. "Donor-Advised Fund Giving Reflects Larger Philanthropy Patterns— Mostly." *Nonprofit Quarterly*, February 28, 2018. https://nonprofitquarterly.org/donor-advised -fund-giving-reflects-overall-us-philanthropy-patterns-mostly/.

Index

GitHub, 118
GiveDirectly, 43, 49
Giving, 2, 9, 19, 37, 151, 181, 205n3, 206n22
  anonymity of, 29–30
  changes in, 22
  choices, making of, 57
  citizen science, 115
  as collective, 8
  commodification of, 7–8, 106, 109
  connections, building of, 162
  democratizing of, 7, 10
  digital data, 12
  digital underpinnings of, 33
  digitized data, 112
  encouraging, ways of, 23–24
  family behavior, 168
  forms of, 7
  and generosity, 176
  givers and recipients, 7–8
  as good, 24
  how many asks, 133–135
  and humility, 167
  hybridization of, 40
  by individuals, 4–5
  intangible factors of, 56
  and justice, 176
  mechanisms for, 161
  middleman, eliminating of, 162–163
  "missing middle," 57
  as moral choices, 175
  online, 33–34
  as participation, 182
  as political choices, 176
  productization of, 106
  and proximity, 148
  public policies, 172, 178–179
  racialized elitism, 172
  rules about, 3–4
  and shopping, 135, 140, 142, 145, 147
  as social act, 6, 67
  tax systems, 6, 20–21, 30–31

  of time, 13–14, 16, 33, 43, 49, 52, 56–59, 81, 158–160, 182
  by wealthy, privileging of, 30
  White culture, venerating of, 22
Giving circles, 8, 51, 61, 75, 77, 169, 178, 182
  as collective decision-making, 62
  and intentionality, 76
  and philanthropy, 177
  technology, role in, 62
Giving Institute, 17
Givingscape, 7, 22, 43–44, 58, 84, 109, 149, 152, 166, 178
  and crowdfunding, 65–66, 156
  digitized data, 8
  donor-advised funds (DAFs), 46–47, 107
  money, contributing of, 46
  as product market, 45–48, 50
  products of, as tools, 59
Giving Side, 150–152, 169, 177
Giving Tuesday, 65, 134
Giving USA, 17, 20
GLAAD, 83
Global Biodiversity Information Facility, 117
GlobalGiving, 69
Global Impact Investing Network, 18
GoFundMe, 32–33, 46, 50, 65–67, 152, 156–157
  donor protection guarantee, 70
Gonzalez-Vargas, Amber, 76–77
Good giving, 142
Goodwill, 40, 207n17
Grantmakers for Education, 208n23
GuideStar, 17

Health care, 23, 35
Health research
  diagnostic purposes, used for, 126–127
  mobile health studies, 124–125
  personal data, 119–123, 128
Hersh, Eitan, 81–82
High Museum of Art, 96

Memphis (Tennessee), 72–73, 177
Michigan, 65
Mina, Margaret, 88
Minter, Adam, 207n17
Mobile health studies, 122, 124–125
Montgomery bus boycott, 145
Mount Rushmore, 102
MoveOn, 83
Mutual aid, 3, 8, 11, 24–25, 48–49, 107,
    109, 169.
Mutual funds, 106–7
Mutuality, 166

National Association of Attorneys General, 70
National Center for Charitable Statistics, 14
National Federation of Community
    Development Credit Unions, 104–105.
    See also Inclusiv
National Geographic Society, 199n13
National Portrait Gallery, 96
National Rifle Association (NRA), 28
National Rifle Association for Legislative
    Action, 28
Native Americans, 100–103, 123–24
Navajo nation, 111
NDN Collective, 102–103, 107, 148, 177,
    182
Netherlands, 35
Networked privacy, 128–29
New Orleans (Louisiana), 83
New York, 73
Nineteenth Amendment, 182
Noble, Safiya, 204n32
Nonprofits, 2–3, 6, 12, 22, 25, 35, 70, 134,
    153–154, 160–61, 165, 176, 178–180
    501(c)(3)s and 501(c)(4)s, 27–29, 31, 49,
    64
    charitable gifts, 11, 21, 50
    corporate code, 27
    giving landscape, as standard part of, 26
    marketing mail, 205n1
    overhead costs, 45

public programs, 5
railroad barons, 26
robber barons, 27
social welfare, 28
tax-deductible gifts to, 16–17, 19, 34
tax status of, 34
tax system, 19
trust, associated with, 34, 120
volunteering for, 17–18
North America, 103
North Dakota, 103

Oakland (California), 41, 106
Oakland Food Policy Council, 41
Obama, Michelle, 96
Oglala Lakota Nation, 101
Oklahoma City (Oklahoma), 127
Open Collective, 59
Open Humans, 120
Open source software, ethical licenses for,
    130–131
Osmond, Marie, 137

Pandemics, 5, 18, 36, 134, 156, 180. *See also*
    COVID-19
Patreon, 67
Personal data, 119, 153
    awareness about, 129
    as civil rights issue, 129
    individual rights and corporate property,
    129
Personal Genome Project (PGP), 120
Petaluma (California), 113
Pettway, Lucy, 96
Pettway, Mark, 96
Pettway, Mary Margaret, 96–97, 99–100, 158
Petty, Tawana, 89, 201n7, 204n32
Philanthropy, 3, 6, 11, 13, 17, 27, 77, 79,
    125, 171, 176
    circular economy, 98
    civil society, 80
    giving circles, 177